Alan Lacer's
Woodturning Projects
& Techniques

POPULAR WOODWORKING BOOKS
CINCINNATI, OHIO
popularwoodworking.com

Contents

Foreword

This book is a collection of my writings over a fifteen-year period for *American Woodworker Magazine.* That work was unusual for me in the sense that the audience generally were not hardcore woodturners, but woodworkers who did furniture, carving, cabinetry and various other aspects of working wood. Certainly there were readers with lathes (actually a large number of them if the surveys were correct) and some were already addicted to this love of mine. However, I always had to keep the readership majority in mind. Projects and techniques I wrote about needed to keep all of this in perspective, but my secret objective was always to tempt the non-turners to try woodturning.

I set out to make specific projects for a range of interests and skill-levels (not only fundamental ones), and I always incorporated a few challenges. Of course, there is the eternal challenge of good design: most of the projects did not require simply duplicating what I made (unlike most furniture projects) but encouraged the reader to make their own interpretation. Funny, because it's the natural way of turning that if you tried to do the same form, it is doubtful it would be the same anyway!

Here you'll find projects for the furniture maker (legs, a stool, duplication), for the sports person (game calls, fishing lures, bocce ball, baseball bat), around the kitchen (bowls, plates, pepper mills, ice cream scoop handle, butter knife, toothpick holder), for the shop (awl, lathe stand, tool handles, screwdriver handles, shopmade chucks) and more.

And the techniques presented here cover topics for those who have little or no turning experience and even occasionally topics that seasoned turners struggle with such as using a detail gouge, sharpening, skew chisels and so forth. Most of the core tools have specific sections devoted to edge shaping, edge creation and use (bowl gouges, spindle roughing gouge, detail/spindle gouges, skew chisels). There is even a taste of hollow turning (Christmas ornaments and Lowrider boxes) and working larger scale projects (lamp, baseball bat, table legs). Finishing is covered within most projects, but there is also coverage of specific techniques for finishing almost any turned object (oils, shellac, oil/varnish blend and even marbling).

Personally, I benefitted immensely from writing these articles. They were opportunities for me to stay sharp (there are some very critical readers out there who helped keep me honest!), continue to learn, keep developing topics and ideas, strengthen my writing skills and aid me immensely in my teaching pursuits (something that now consumes much of my time as a woodturner).

I encourage you to read this collection of articles and challenge yourself to try some things you have never attempted; you might be pleasantly surprised to find a fresh direction to your turning.

Alan Lacer

TOOLS &
TECHNIQUES

CHAPTER ONE

Bowl Gouges

All you need to turn a gorgeous bowl is one fine tool

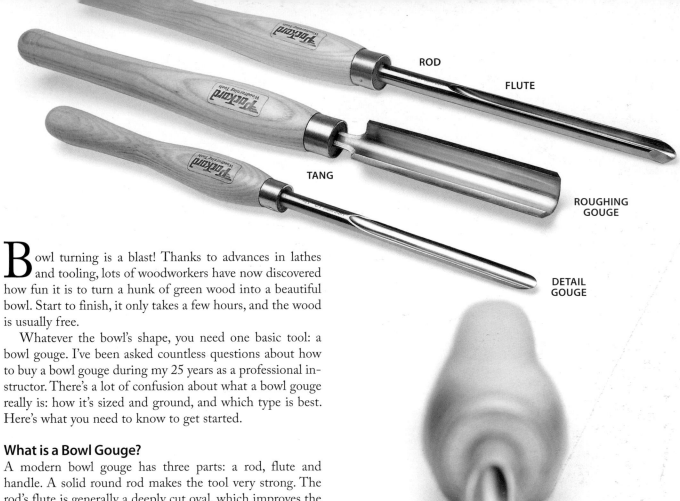

ROD

FLUTE

TANG

ROUGHING GOUGE

DETAIL GOUGE

STRAIGHT FLUTE

B owl turning is a blast! Thanks to advances in lathes and tooling, lots of woodworkers have now discovered how fun it is to turn a hunk of green wood into a beautiful bowl. Start to finish, it only takes a few hours, and the wood is usually free.

Whatever the bowl's shape, you need one basic tool: a bowl gouge. I've been asked countless questions about how to buy a bowl gouge during my 25 years as a professional instructor. There's a lot of confusion about what a bowl gouge really is: how it's sized and ground, and which type is best. Here's what you need to know to get started.

What is a Bowl Gouge?

A modern bowl gouge has three parts: a rod, flute and handle. A solid round rod makes the tool very strong. The rod's flute is generally a deeply cut oval, which improves the tool's chip-cutting action. A bowl gouge usually has a large handle, about 16" long, for increased leverage. A bowl gouge is often confused with a roughing gouge. A roughing gouge is used in spindle work, such as turning a table leg, to remove a blank's square corners or to cut a cylinder or taper. It should not be used for faceplate work, such as turning a bowl. A roughing gouge has a tang, which isn't designed to take as much downward pressure as a rod. The tang could bend or break under the larger force involved in turning a bowl. Bowl gouges are also often confused with detail gouges, which are also called spindle, fingernail or shallow gouges. A detail gouge has a shallower flute than a bowl gouge. A detail gouge is designed for shaping small elements, particularly in spindle work, although it is used in bowl turning for shaping rims, bases and feet.

Flute Shapes

The flute is the inner, milled portion of a bowl gouge's rod. The flute's shape varies among manufacturers. It's deep oval may have round or straight sides. Both types are easy to learn how to handle, so it doesn't really matter which one you get. Individual turners have their favorites, but no single design is a runaway winner.

Bowl Gouge Sizing Systems

Manufacturers use two different, competing systems to size bowl gouges, which can be confusing. In the commonly used English system, a gouge's size is approximately the width of its flute. In the less commonly used North American system, the gouge's size is exactly the diameter of the rod (which I think makes a lot more sense). As a result, the same gouge is usually labeled ⅛" smaller in the English system than in the North American system. For example, a ½" gouge in the English system is the same size tool as a ⅝" gouge in the North American system. It's important to note which system a dealer uses before you order.

NORTH AMERICAN SIZE

ENGLISH SIZE

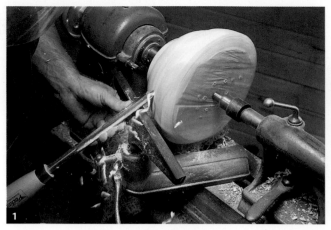

A 1/2" bowl gouge is a nicely balanced size for most bowl turning on a standard-size lathe (see Sources, page 9). With this workhorse tool, you can turn 5" to 24" diameter bowls.

A 3/8" bowl gouge is a better choice if you own a mini-lathe. This gouge is large enough to turn a bowl as big as the machine can handle, but it's not so aggressive that it will bog down a mini-lathe's smaller motor.

A 1/4" bowl gouge was traditionally used for finishing the inside or outside of a bowl. I prefer to make a light finishing cut with a 1/2" gouge that has a finger-nail profile (see "Edge Profiles," page 9).

A 5/8" or 3/4" bowl gouge is useful for making heavy, aggressive cuts on bowls larger than 14" in diameter. Turning a monster bowl usually requires a heavy-duty, large-capacity lathe with a 2-hp or larger motor.

Bowl Gouge Sizes

Bowl gouges are available in a wide range of sizes. You don't need a whole set. If you own a standard-size lathe with a 12" to 14" swing, buy a ½" gouge, English system (⅝" North American). All the gouges shown here are sized by the English system.

Bowl Gouge Steel

Look for a bowl gouge made from high-speed steel (HSS), rather than high-carbon steel. A HSS gouge resists wear much longer and can't normally be softened by overheating on the grinder. There are three general grades of HSS to choose from (see Chart, right); all can be made equally sharp to begin with, but higher grades hold their edge longer. Most HSS gouges are made from M2 steel, which is an excellent alloy. I recommend that you buy an M2 gouge first, before you become an expert sharpener, because the extra steel you'll remove while learning how to sharpen is less expensive!

Type of HSS Steel	Average Price of ½" Gouge	Approximate Wear Factor*
M2	$50	5
M4 and 2030	$70	15
A11 and 2060	$100	22

*Average ability to resist wear compared to high-carbon steel, according to manufacturers

Edge Profiles

Bowl gouges come with many different edge profiles. This shape is also called the tool's grind, because it's created and altered on the grinding wheel. Each profile has its pros and cons. You don't have to worry too much about which profile a new tool has, because you can reshape it. Whatever its profile, or price, a new tool often needs reshaping or more sharpening. For more information on grinding and sharpening a bowl gouge, see Sources, below.

Traditional Grind

Many bowl gouges come with a traditional profile. This shape is easy to sharpen but has limitations. For some bowl shapes, it's difficult to rub the bevel on either the inside or even the outside of the bowl.

Fingernail Grind

I call this profile the fingernail grind. It's more versatile than the traditional profile, so I recommend it for beginners. Few gouges come with this profile, though; usually, you must grind it yourself.

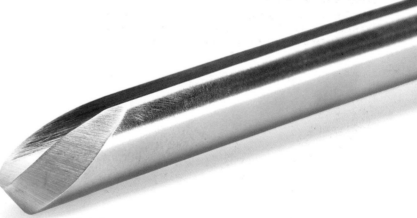

Irish Grind

This swept-back profile has been called many names, including Irish, Celtic, side grind, and Ellsworth. This is the most versatile profile, allowing you to rough, scrape and finish a bowl with a single tool. It is a bit more difficult to sharpen and use than other profiles.

SOURCES Packard Woodworks, (800) 683-8876, www.packardwoodworks.com: 112" M2 HSS bowl gouge, #100122, $64.95.

CHAPTER TWO

Bowl Gouge Sharpening

Do it by hand, just like you turn

STRAIGHT SECTION

Top View
The end of a traditional profile is straight across.

VERTICAL EDGE

Side View
The cutting edge is approximately vertical.

1

Shaping and sharpening the traditional profile is very easy. Simply start at one side and rotate the tool on the grinder's tool rest. Stop grinding when sparks flow evenly over the cutting edge. These sparks indicate the edge is sharp.

2

Use a protractor to check the angle of your profile (see Sources, page 14). There is no perfect angle for all situations. To start, 45° to 60° is fine. With experience, you'll see how different angles affect a tool's performance.

How do you make a velvety smooth bowl with evenly thick walls and crisp details? Well, it's not done by sanding the heck out of it. The secret is to use a bowl gouge that is properly shaped and very sharp.

Most bowl gouges aren't ready to do this kind of fine work right out of the package. They must be shaped, sharpened and honed. Shaping a bowl gouge means altering its profile, also called its grind. Sharpening maintains the profile and renews a dull edge. Honing further sharpens the edge. I'll cover how to do all three operations freehand style.

I prefer sharpening freehand, as opposed to using a jig, because it's similar to turning a bowl. When you sharpen, the tool sits on a rest and meets a round object—in this case, the grinding wheel. You rub the bevel on the round object and manipulate the edge. That's what turning is all about, too. Once you've learned to sharpen freehand, you're all set to make a fantastic bowl.

How to Sharpen 3 Profiles

Woodturners shape their bowl gouges into three basic groups of profiles: traditional, fingernail and swept-back. Any gouge can be modified on the grinder to match these profiles. Your choice of profile depends on your skill level and preference.

I use a coarse wheel for shaping a bowl gouge and a finer one for sharpening (see "Equipment," page 14). The basic procedures for shaping and sharpening are the same. After you shape the profile, you grind a bevel to follow the shape.

Most bowl gouges are made from high-speed steel (HSS). If your HSS gouge turns blue as you grind, don't

worry. This change won't soften the steel. If the tool becomes too hot to hold, don't quench it in water. Let it cool in the air or lay it on a metal surface to dissipate the heat.

When you're sharpening a gouge, it's important to grind the entire bevel, rather than just the edge. To find the correct position, contact the heel of the bevel first, and then raise the tool's handle until the entire bevel contacts the grinding wheel.

Traditional Profile

The traditional profile is the easiest to sharpen. It's created by rotating the tool. To begin, set the tool rest to create a 45°–60° bevel. Lay the tool on the rest, positioned to start at one side (**Photo 1**). Slowly push the gouge toward the wheel. When you contact the wheel, rotate the gouge until you reach the other side, and then reverse direction. As you grind, hold the gouge firmly on the rest and keep its end square to the wheel.

The traditional profile works well in general but has some limitations. It's good for shaping the outside of a bowl that's mounted with its opening facing the headstock. But if the bowl is mounted the other way, facing the tailstock, this profile doesn't work as well. The traditional profile is good for opening up most of a bowl's interior, but not too good at the transition from the sides to the bottom unless the tool is ground with a very steep angle. This profile doesn't have drawn-back sides, so it's more difficult to make the fine finishing cuts that are possible with the fingernail and swept-back profiles.

OVAL END

Top View
The end of a fingernail profile should be oval, but not too pointy.

CONVEX EDGE

Side View
The line from the point to the top should be straight or slightly convex, never concave.

Fingernail Profile

Grinding the fingernail profile requires more dexterity than making the traditional profile, but it's not difficult. In fact, the operation is very similar to a few cuts in bowl turning itself.

To begin, set the tool rest about 120° to the wheel (**Photo 3**). The front edge of the tool rest must be very close—⅛" or less—to the wheel, so you can't pinch your fingers in the gap. Rest the gouge on top of two fingers and push it slowly toward the wheel. Contact the middle section of the bevel first. Then raise the gouge's handle until the full bevel touches the wheel. Begin a slow upward twist, continuing until the tool is heeled over on its side (**Photos 4** and **5**). Repeat this process on one side of the gouge until sparks come over the edge and travel down inside the flute—that's the sign the edge is done. Do the same procedure on the other side of the tool and then work on the middle of the gouge to make a uniform, continuous bevel.

The fingernail profile is the best shape for a beginning bowl turner. It's more versatile than the traditional profile. It works well whether the bowl is mounted toward the headstock or tailstock and is useful for detailing work on a rim or foot. The sides can be used for shear cutting and shear scraping finishing cuts.

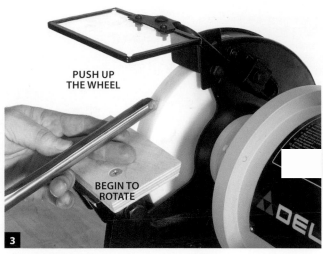

PUSH UP THE WHEEL

BEGIN TO ROTATE

3

Sharpen the fingernail profile in a fluid motion, one side of the bevel at a time. Begin at the center. You'll rotate the tool and push it up the grinding wheel, all in one shot, using your fingers for support.

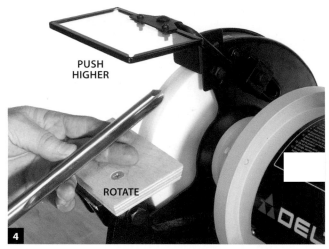

PUSH HIGHER

ROTATE

4

Twist the gouge and push it higher on the grinding wheel.

PUSH HIGHER YET

ROTATE MORE

5

Stop twisting and pushing when the tool is fully on its side, at a 90° rotation. Make light passes in this manner, on each side, until sparks just begin to come over the cutting edge.

OVAL END

Top View
The swept-back end is oval or elliptical, but not too pointy.

SWEPT-BACK PROFILE

Side View
The sides are ground back much farther than a fingernail profile. The line from the point to the top should be straight or slightly convex, never concave.

Swept-Back Profile

The swept-back profile is the most difficult profile to create, but it doesn't take a lot of practice to master. If you have trouble, remember that you can't ruin a turning tool by grinding; you only shorten it.

To begin, set the tool rest in the same manner as for a fingernail profile. The procedure is very similar to making a fingernail profile, but here you work on the long sides of the tool first (**Photo 6**). When both sides are done, grind the front (**Photo 7**). Then blend the front into the sides (**Photo 8**). Aim for a uniform bevel, but the transition doesn't have to be completely smooth. The front and sides are used in two different turning operations, so the area in between isn't critical.

The swept-back profile is also called an Irish, Celtic or Ellsworth grind. It's the most versatile profile. Your bowl gouge can be used as a roughing, scraping and fine finishing tool. It's easy to level any surface, inside or out, when using the gouge in a shear cutting or shear scraping action. The swept-back profile is not for beginners, however. It can be too aggressive for inexperienced hands. A gouge with a swept-back profile also requires considerable power from the lathe to remove large amounts of material. Some small lathes don't have enough horsepower to handle it.

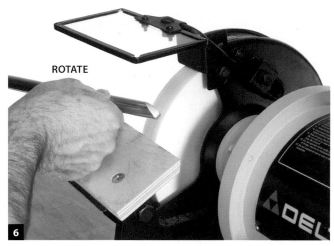

ROTATE

6

Begin making a swept-back profile by grinding the sides. Hold the gouge on its side and slightly rotate it to create the sweep.

ROTATE

7

Grind the gouge's front. Begin with the center; then slightly rotate with a small upward push.

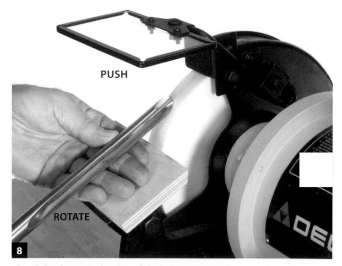

PUSH

ROTATE

8

Blend the front and sides of the gouge by pushing and twisting the gouge up the wheel. This technique is similar to that used to create the fingernail profile.

Final Step: Honing

I hone all my bowl gouges after sharpening and routinely touch them up at the first hint of dullness during turning. Honing isn't absolutely necessary, but it has many benefits. A honed gouge produces a cleaner cut, makes crisper details and reduces the time I spend sanding. The more often you hone, the less time you'll spend going back to the grinder for sharpening.

HSS gouges are very tough steel. Most slipstones don't work well on HSS because they cut too slow, or not at all. I use a special diamond slipstone that cuts much faster and fits the radius of every bowl-turning gouge (see Sources, below).

I hone the bevel first (**Photo 9**). The trick is to hold the stone flat on a bevel. Straight from the grinder, this bevel should be slightly concave. The stone should always contact the ground bevel at two points: the back or heel, and the area below the cutting edge, called the toe. I start honing by only contacting the heel and then angle the stone to touch both surfaces. Honing the flute is much easier (**Photo 10**).

Equipment

Most turners use a bench grinder to reshape and sharpen their tools. Just about any equipment will do, but here's what I suggest (see Sources, below):

- 8" grinder. I prefer a slow-speed model that runs about 1,725 rpm. I haven't tried them all, but I really like the heavy-duty Delta 23-275, $175. It has lots of power and feels very stable.
- Rock-solid tool rests. This is the greatest weakness of most grinders, but not the Delta. Look for supports that have no flex. They should be easy to angle and move in and out. I added wood platforms to the Delta's tool rests to make larger support areas.
- Friable grinding wheels. They come in white, pink, blue or orange. I prefer a #60 or #80-grit for sharpening and a #46 or coarser grit for shaping. Look for a J- or K-level hardness for turning tools.
- Diamond wheel dresser. Dressing a wheel is critical for good sharpening. A dresser cleans, flattens and sharpens the wheel by exposing fresh grit. I prefer this T-handle dresser ($35, see **Photo 11**) because it works extremely fast.
- Movable lamp. It should be able to illuminate either side of both wheels.
- A face shield or safety glasses and a dust mask. Be sure to use these because the grinding dust is a health hazard. Dressing a wheel creates lots of dust.

9

10

Using a diamond slipstone to hone a gouge really improves its performance. Hone the ground bevel first by bracing the gouge and moving the stone up and down.

Hone the inside of the gouge using the slipstone's rounded edges. Brace the gouge against your side, place the stone flat on the gouge's flute and slide the stone back and forth.

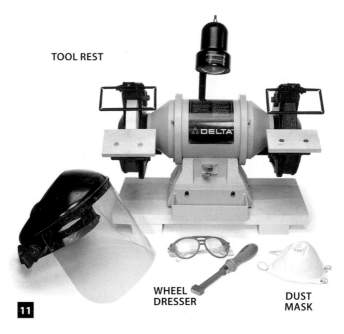

TOOL REST

11

WHEEL DRESSER

DUST MASK

SOURCES Craft Supplies (800) 551 8876 www.woodturnerscatalog.com Jet 8" Slow Speed Grinder #105097, $329.99. ☺ MSC, (800) 645-7270, www.mscdirect.com 8" dia., #60-grit wheel, #86758562, $65.86. Bushing set, #00390955, $4.65. 8"-dia., #46-grit wheel, 05867163, $24. Bushing set #00390989, $1. Steel protractor, #06475172, $13.75. ☺ Packard Woodworks, (800) 683-8876, www.packardwoodworks.com Diamond Jim grinding wheel dresser, #141504, $39.95. ☺ Alan Lacer, Worker of Wood, (715) 426-9451, www.alanlacer.com Diamond Slipper slipstone, $88. ☞

CHAPTER THREE

The Spindle Roughing Gouge

Master this basic turning tool

When I introduce someone to woodturning, I choose the spindle roughing gouge. When I work with kids, it's the first tool I place in their hands. Why? Because, used correctly, the spindle roughing gouge is the safest, most user-friendly turning tool of them all. And don't be fooled by its name. The spindle roughing gouge can leave a very clean surface. Master this tool, and you'll learn basic techniques that apply to using virtually all cutting type turning tools. However, the spindle roughing gouge must be shaped and sharpened correctly and used in the appropriate applications—or its friendliness can quickly disappear.

Designed for spindle work A spindle roughing gouge is designed to quickly shape square wooden blanks that are mounted on the lathe so the grain runs parallel to the bed.

Borrowed from, and primarily made in England, this tool is deeply fluted (curved), and its cutting edge is straight (**Photo 1**). In the U.S., most turning sets come with a completely different roughing tool, a large, shallow gouge with a domed or fingernail shape. This tool looks a bit like a spindle detail gouge on steroids. Users of "American" style roughing gouges are usually instructed not to attempt removing a blank's square corners on the lathe; instead, they're directed to saw off the corners before mounting the blank.

Spindle roughing gouges are available in several sizes. My advice is to buy the largest size, as it simplifies a leveling cutting action (**Photo 2**). The spindle roughing gouge is not the best choice for detail work or for making quick turns. And don't even think of using it to rough out a bowl or vessel blank (**Photo 3**). Its large surface area makes it awkward to maneuver in a confined space, its long straight edges leave exposed sides and corners that will easily catch, and its tang is not strong enough to engage the cutting edge far beyond the tool rest. Using a spindle roughing gouge for bowl turning is dangerous; use a bowl gouge instead.

Strengths

The spindle roughing gouge is a great choice for creating cylinders of any size (**Photo 4**). And it's the best tool for removing the corners on any square stock measuring up to 5" x 5" (much faster than tilting the table saw blade and running the stock through numerous times; it's safer, too).

TURNING GOUGES 101

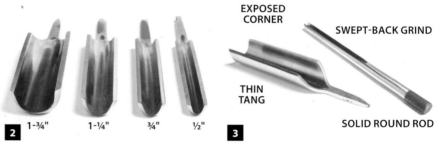

AMERICAN STYLE (OR CONTINENTAL)

TANG

SPINDLE ROUGHING

BOWL GOUGE **SPINDLE DETAIL GOUGE**

1 The spindle roughing gouge is one of four gouges commonly used for turning. It is instantly recognizable by its deeply fluted semi-circular shape, vertically ground edge and tang-style end.

1-¾" 1-¼" ¾" ½"

2 Spindle roughing gouges come in several different sizes. Widths are measured across the inside of the flute. You don't need them all; just buy the largest size you can find.

EXPOSED CORNER **SWEPT-BACK GRIND**

THIN TANG

SOLID ROUND ROD

3 Never use a spindle roughing gouge—a tang-type tool—for bowl turning. A bowl gouge is machined from solid rod, so it can extend far beyond the tool rest, to reach deep inside a bowl.

The spindle roughing gouge handles straight tapers with ease, and it can also produce tapers that are slightly convex or concave. Don't ask this tool to turn quickly or detail—is simply does not perform these tasks with a lot of control.

Using the Spindle Roughing Gouge

The spindle roughing gouge is a cutting tool (some turning tools are designed for scraping), so the edge requires support from the bevel during use. Start with the flute on the tool rest and the handle held low (**Photo 5**). Point the flute in the direction of travel. Move the tool forward so its bevel contacts the wood (no wood chips or dust should fly when the bevel touches). Raise the handle slightly, to engage the wood—make sure the cutting occurs on the leading half of the flute. Then move the tool in the intended direction. When you change directions, the tool's orientation reverses, so the opposite half of the flute does the cutting.

It's safe to cut anywhere along the leading half of the flute. If the tool's leading corner touches the wood, it won't catch; only a lifting of wood fibers will occur.

If you raise the handle too far, the tool will stop cutting and begin to scrape. Scraping dulls the tool, tears the wood

USING THE SPINDLE ROUGHING GOUGE

Use the spindle roughing gouge on any surface that is cylindrical or gently tapered. The stock's size doesn't matter: A large tool will always do a better job of leveling the surface than a small one.

To use the spindle roughing gouge, hold the handle low and point the flute in the direction of travel. Engage the wood and move in the intended direction.

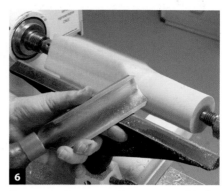

To remove the corners from a square blank, start in the middle and move toward the end. Reverse directions to finish the job.

The spindle roughing gouge can create long tapers and shallow concave or convex shapes. Always work curved shapes from large to small diameters—the concave portion of this leg must be worked from both directions.

Virtually all of the shapes on this handle can be completed with the spindle roughing gouge. Rolling the ends and cutting the flat area for the ferrule are the exceptions.

Although it's called a "roughing" gouge, this tool can leave a very clean surface if you make light cuts. The surface on the left resulted from a heavy cut.

surface and takes more energy to make the cut—this usually results in some loss of control.

To rough a square blank (remove the corners, that is), start in the middle (**Photo 6**). When working difficult woods that are quite hard or "chippy," it's best to nibble off the corners in several light passes rather than with a few heavy cuts.

For concave and convex shapes, work from larger to smaller diameters (**Photos 7** and **8**). To make smooth finishing cuts, angle the tool about 45° to the axis of the lathe and make light cuts (**Photo 9**).

Shaping and Sharpening

Preparing any turning tool for use includes these three steps: Shaping the profile, putting an edge on that shape by grinding, and completing the edge by honing. When viewed from above, the spindle roughing gouge's edge should run straight across (**Photo 10**). From the side, the edge should

appear vertical or canted back at the top, no more than 5° (**Photo 11**). If your gouge does not have this profile, regrind it so it does. To shape the profile, set your grinder's tool rest so it is perpendicular to the face of the wheel. Once you've shaped the profile, set your grinder's tool rest to create the 45° bevel angle that will sharpen the profile's edge. Hold the tool flat on the rest, with the tool's edge parallel with the grinding wheel. Start at one corner and slowly roll the tool to the other corner (**Photo 12**). Grind with control, slowly and deliberately. Be sure the grinding wheel's first contacts are at the bevel's back edge—never just below the cutting edge. Stop grinding when the sparks are gently coming over the top of the tool and appear evenly along the edge.

Here's a bench test for sharpness: If the edge appears black under a light, the tool is sharp. If you see white along the edge, it isn't. (The edge of a sharp tool is ground to a point. Flat—non sharp—areas appear white, because they reflect the light.)

USING THE SPINDLE ROUGHING GOUGE

TOOL REST AT 45°

10 The edge of this spindle roughing gouge is properly shaped. When viewed from above, the edge runs straight across.

11 When viewed from the side, the edge appears vertical. It can also cant slightly back. The edge should never extend forward at the top.

12 To sharpen the tool, grind a 45° bevel behind the edge. Hold the tool parallel with the wheel's edge and flat on the tool rest. Then roll it slowly from corner to corner. Stop grinding when the sparks appear evenly along the edge.

SLIPSTONE

13 Hone the edge. With the slipstone touching only the back of the bevel, start an up and down motion on the outside edge. Then, without coming off of the back, touch the area just below the cutting edge. Maintain this two-point contact to hone effectively.

14 Use the slipstone's rounded edge to hone the inside. Hold the slipstone flat in the flute and move in an out, following the flute's curve, without tipping forward over the edge.

To achieve (and maintain) a fine edge, you must hone the tool, using a slipstone (a hone with a rounded edge). For the best results with today's woodturning tool steels, plan to use diamond plated honing materials. Hone the outside of the edge first (**Photo 13**). As you hone, be sure to maintain two points of contact on the bevel. The hone can bridge the bevel because the bevel is slightly concave, thanks to the radius of the grinding wheel. If you lift off the back of the bevel while honing, you will get a rolled (also called dubbed) edge—this will actually have a dulling effect.

To hone the inside edge, hold the slipstone flat in the tool's flute and follow the curve (**Photo 14**). If you tip over the outside of the edge you will dull it.

While using the tool, hone it at the first signs of dullness (more pressure required to cut, torn fibers, short chips or dust, a flat or dull sound when cutting). Return to the grinder if honing requires removing too much steel (because the concave area of the bevel has disappeared, or because you let the tool get too dull for honing), or if the edge was somehow damaged.

CHAPTER FOUR

Detail/Spindle Gouge

Perhaps woodturners should sell naming rights. The field has never standardized the names of its tools (or measurements of their widths or how to describe their angles), so they're often called different things. One tool stands out in this regard: Whether it's called a detail gouge, spindle gouge, shallow-fluted gouge, fingernail gouge, contour gouge, forming gouge, long-and-strong gouge or just plain "gouge," no other woodturning tool has as many names.

To avoid confusion in my classes, I call this essential tool a "detail/spindle gouge," because those are its two most commonly used names. A detail gouge is said by some to be thicker under the flute than a spindle gouge, but essentially they're the same tool.

This little gouge is used primarily for long-grain turning—when the stock is mounted so the grain runs parallel to the lathe's bed. For this application, it's hands-down the best choice for cutting coves (concave shapes). It's also excellent for rolling beads (convex shapes) and shaping ogee curves, which combine concave and convex cuts.

The features that make a detail/spindle gouge perfect for these cuts, however, also make it a poor choice for roughing, shaping cylinders or making other straight-line cuts, such as tapers. In essence, this little gouge is great for cutting details in all types of turning—even on a face-grain bowl (when the blank is mounted with its face grain against the lathe's faceplate). For this application, it's a fine choice for working the bowl's rims and the underside of its base—especially its feet.

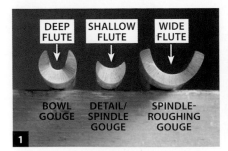

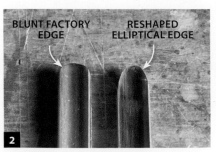

A shallow flute distinguishes a detail/spindle gouge from bowl and spindle-roughing gouges, the other two types of gouges that woodturners commonly use.

Reshape the factory edge. An elliptical profile increases the cutting surface and allows cutting on both sides, which is much better for creating details with concave and convex shapes.

Grind the edge to an elliptical shape by swinging the gouge through an arc. Set the tool rest set at 90°.

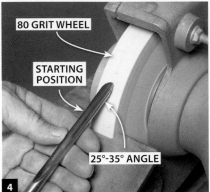

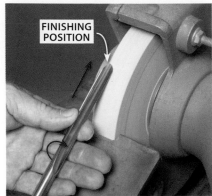

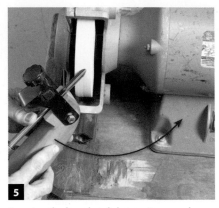

Form the bevel and sharpen the elliptical edge one side at a time, using a push-and-twist motion. Rotate the gouge to follow the edge as you move it up the wheel; reverse the action as you move it back down.

Forming the bevel and sharpening an edge with a grinding jig is easy because it automatically sets the angle and makes a wide sweeping motion that follows the elliptical shape.

A Distinctive Shape

The detail/spindle gouge is distinctively different than the other two types of gouges that turners typically use, because it has a shallow flute (**Photo 1**). Although the flute's radius and the metal's thickness below it can vary, the overall design of this gouge remains shallow when compared to the other two types. Detail/spindle gouges typically range from ¼" to 1" in width. For the scale in which I most commonly work, I prefer the ⅜" and ½" sizes (see Sources, page 22).

The bowl gouge is a heavy tool with a heavy round tang and a deep flute; it's sometimes called a "deep-fluted gouge." This gouge is the norm for turning bowls and vessels. It's great for roughing out, shaping and finishing operations in such turnings.

The spindle-roughing gouge has a flat tang and a wide flute; it's sometimes called a "half-circle gouge." This gouge is used in long-grain turning to remove the corners from blanks and create cylinders, tapers and shallow concave and slightly domed convex shapes. It isn't a detailing tool and it shouldn't be used for turning bowls because its flat tang is weak and can break or bend.

In addition to a shallow flute, the other basic design element of the detail/spindle gouge is an elliptical cutting edge. As the tool's factory edge is more likely to be straight, slightly domed or pointed like a spear, a new detail/spindle gouge typically requires reshaping (**Photo 2**).

An elliptical profile allows cutting with both sides of the tool, which is especially useful because it allows shaping coves and rolling beads in both directions. On each side of the ellipse, the more sharply-curved portion neatly cuts concave shapes, while the more broadly-curved portion easily cuts convex shapes. An elliptical profile also provides more cutting surface to work with and helps to reduce mishaps such as run-backs and dig-ins, because the edge trails away, rather than ending abruptly.

Sharpening

Sharpening consists of three separate operations: shaping, producing a sharp edge, and honing. Shaping includes two grinding actions: one to shape the elliptical edge (**Photo 3**) and another to create the bevel that supports the edge. If considerable material must be removed during these roughing operations, use a #46- or #60-grit wheel. Make sure there's virtually no gap between the tool rest and the wheel and always wear eye protection and a dust mask when grinding.

How far back you grind the elliptical shape is a question of creating access for side-cutting operations. For the gouge shown here, bringing the sides back between ⅜" and ½" is usually more than adequate. For tight places, a longer, narrower ellipse might be better.

The bevel angle is usually between 25° and 35°. This is considerably lower than the bevel angles typically found on bowl

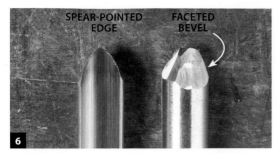

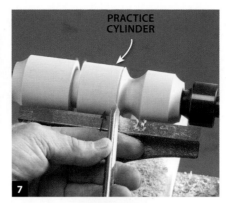

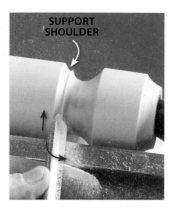

6 Avoid creating a spear-pointed edge, caused by over-grinding the sides of the tool's elliptical edge. Also avoid a faceted bevel, caused by changing the angle as you rotate the tool.

Create a cove by cutting mirror-image concave profiles. First, cut a groove to establish the depth at the center. Then make a shallow knife cut at one edge (left), just deep enough to create a shoulder that supports the tool. Push in the gouge (center) while riding its bevel against the shoulder and gradually turning it face-up (right). Complete the shape by cutting a series of incrementally deeper and wider concave profiles on both sides of the groove.

gouges and spindle-roughing gouges—the edges on these tools require much more support. Producing a bevel with a sharp edge that follows the elliptical shape you've created is difficult. Most of these tools tend to be thick at the center, but very thin at the sides. This makes it easy to over-grind the sides and lose the shape. Creating a smooth bevel is another challenge. A bevel with multiple facets leaves an inconsistent edge that will be impossible to hone.

To form a sharp edge on almost any woodturning tool you usually have two choices: Do it freehand or use a grinding jig. To sharpen the edge freehand (**Photo 4**), slightly elevate the tool rest to make it comfortable to hold the tool at the bevel angle you choose. Visually divide the tool into three sections: the center, the left half and the right half, and plan to grind one side at a time. Begin by lightly resting the tool on the wheel (the home position). Then simultaneously push and turn the tool up and onto its side while holding it against the wheel at the same angle. Reverse the action to return to the home position. Then repeat the process on the other side. Repeat the process on both sides until the bevel is fully formed. Finish with one or two large sweeps that connect all three sections. When grinding a detail/spindle gouge, slow down and watch closely when the bevel is nearly complete. As soon as sparks start to consistently come over the top of the edge along its full length, it's time to stop: The edge is sharp.

If sharpening freehand seems too daunting, use a grinding jig (**Photo 5**); (see Sources). Many are available and they all work well. With either method, be careful not to ruin the elliptical shape by over-grinding (**Photo 6**).

Honing

The process of refining and maintaining a sharp edge requires a flat hone for the outside bevel and a rounded hone to "slip" the inside edge. For modern high-speed steel tools, diamond or boron honing tools work best (see Sources). To hone the outside bevel, hold the gouge securely and move the hone up and down all along the cutting edge—concentrate on touching the back of the bevel to just below the edge.

To hone the inside, hold the curved hone flat in the flute and follow the edge all the way around, again with an up-and-down motion.

8 Avoid run-back. If you make the initial knife cut at less than 90°, the gouge will skate back. Instead, push the back end of the handle toward the cove until the gouge cuts in at more than 90°.

Making Concave Cuts

A detail/spindle gouge is most adept at cutting coves and other concave shapes (**Photo 7**). When cutting a cove, the goal is to cut a pair of mirror-image concave curves that meet in the center. This requires a sharp tool, good technique and close observation of the shape as it's being formed—done by watching the horizon (the top edge of the blank) as you cut.

These tools work best when they can "move into air," so practice cutting concave shapes on the ends of a cylinder or by working from both sides into a groove that you've cut with a parting tool. Always work from large to small diameters. Position the gouge at a right angle to the blank, with its flute facing the direction of the cut, and score the wood to create a small recess that will support the tool's bevel. Then begin a light and slow twisting cut with the gouge, while keeping the bevel against the wood.

Create a bead by cutting mirror-image convex profiles. Rest the gouge on the blank while holding its flute face-up (left). Lift and roll the handle so the gouge "rides the bevel" until its edge starts cutting (center). Continue the rolling action while gently advancing the gouge until it rolls completely onto its side (right). Refine the shape incrementally, by making shallow cuts on each side.

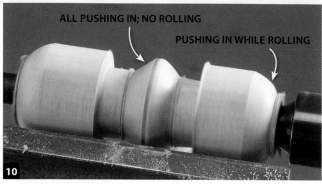

ALL PUSHING IN; NO ROLLING

PUSHING IN WHILE ROLLING

A flat "V" shape results, rather than a nicely rounded curve, if your advancing and rolling motions aren't well coordinated.

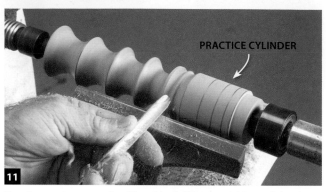

PRACTICE CYLINDER

Practice cutting coves (and beads) of different widths and depths to master the nuances of this extraordinary tool.

The greatest obstacle when cutting a cove is overcoming the tendency of the tool to skate across the wood (or "run back") when you start the cut (**Photo 8**). The underlying cause is the tool's sharp edge engaging the wood at the wrong angle, so there's no support for the bevel. This immediately pushes the tool backwards across the surface.

Cutting Convex Profiles

To create a bead, you cut a pair of mirror-image convex shapes (**Photo 9**). Here the challenge is to produce fully rounded surfaces with no flats. Begin with the flute upright, the bevel resting on the wood and the back of the handle held low. Gently lift the gouge until it begins to cut. Then, working from large to small diameters, turn the flute in the direction of the cut and gradually roll over the gouge as you continue to advance it. Aim to have the flute fully on its side at the bottom of the cut. A twisting motion that smoothly combines advancing and rolling is critical for good results (**Photo 10**).

Develop Your Skills

Mastering this tool requires practice, so use a spindle rough-ing gouge to create a bunch of 1-¾" dia. x 7" long cylinders made from softer woods such as poplar, pine or alder. Then practice cutting concave shapes that curve smoothly and continuously from top to bottom (**Photo 11**). You'll probably find that it's easier to cut smooth curves from one direction than the other. If so, devote an entire cylinder to cutting curves from the more difficult direction. As you practice, the initial knife cuts and turning/rolling moves will start to make sense.

It's a good idea to practice cutting coves of different sizes. Lay out a series of coves that gradually get smaller, (or more shallow, or both) on one or more of the cylinders. Start with a 1-¼" wide cove and reduce the width by ⅛" until you reach a cove that's only ¼" wide. Then strive to cut fully rounded, mirror-image concave shapes on every cove. You'll discover the size and shape of the gouge determines how narrow a cove can become.

To practice cutting convex shapes, prepare 10" long practice cylinders and use a parting tool to lay out beads from 1-¼" wide down to ¼" wide. Then practice as for concave shapes. Parting down to different depths dramatically changes the look of the bead. Learning how to handle the gouge accordingly is part of the exercise.

SOURCES Packard Woodworks, packardwoodworks.com, 800-683-8876, Packard 3/8" Detail Gouge, #100108, $38.50; Packard ½" Detail Gouge, #100109, $44.95; Oneway Vari-Grind 2 Attachment, #142614-2, $74.95 (requires Oneway Wolverine Grinding System, #142611, $89.95); Sharp Fast Grinding System, #140909, $99.95; Credit Card Hone, #145105, $11.95; Honing Cone, #145110, $30.95. Alan Lacer, alanlacer.com, Diamond Slipstone, $88.

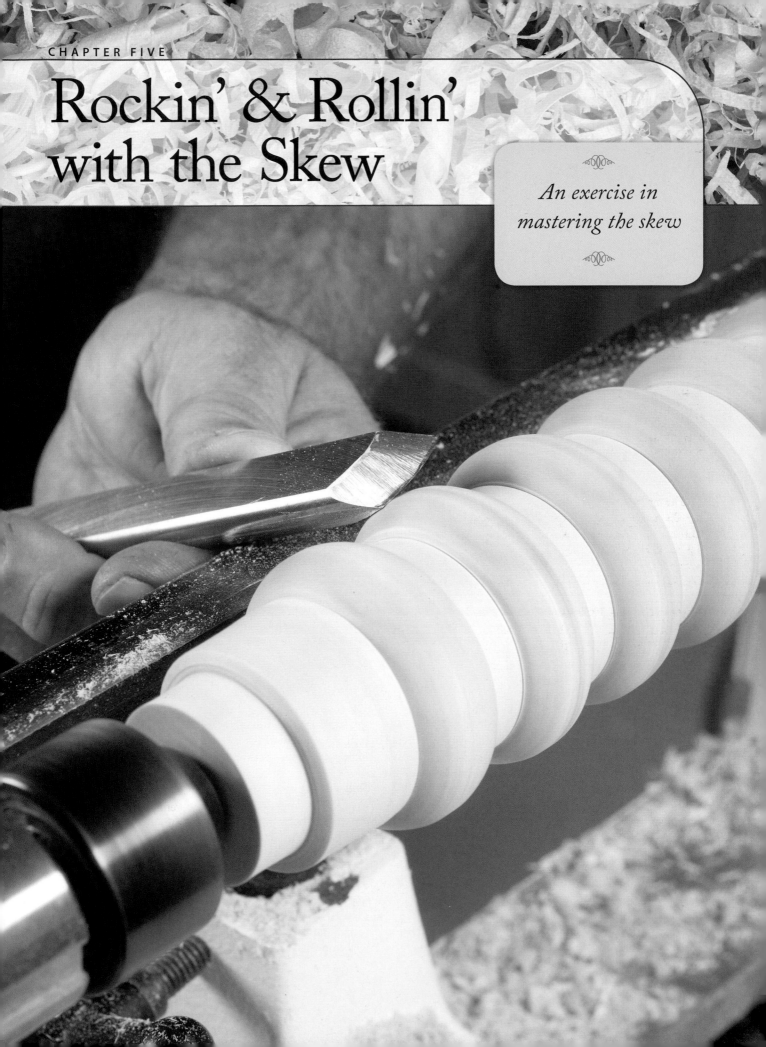

CHAPTER FIVE

Rockin' & Rollin' with the Skew

An exercise in mastering the skew

1 Posture and grip are important for a controlled approach to rolling a skew chisel. Position your left hand under the tool, touching the rest. Hold the tool handle with your right hand. Reverse hands if you are left-handed.

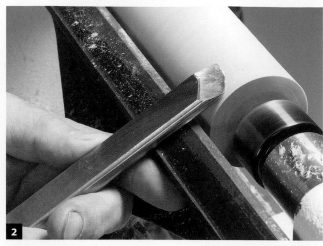

2 The best way to master the skew is on a practice blank. Start at the cylinder's end. Hold the skew's shaft at a right angle to the axis of the lathe. Rub the bevel, preparing to tilt or roll the short point of the tool into the wood.

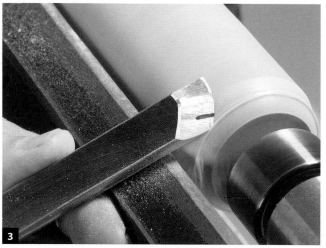

3 Lift and rotate the handle in the direction of the cut to engage the short point of the skew in the wood. Keep the bevel in constant contact with the wood. The cutting action should only take place from the red mark on the tool to the short point.

4 Make a series of rolling cuts. Continue with the lifting and rotational action and be sure to keep the bevel against the rounded surface.

Do you like a challenge? Want to develop your wood-turning skills? Can you learn from mistakes? If your answer is "yes," you're ready to tackle the rolling cut with a skew chisel. The rolling cut is most often employed to cut beads in spindle work.

Without a doubt the rolling cut can be the most difficult skew technique to learn. For that reason, I advise people to start with the planing cut. Practice makes perfect and you must practice the rolling cut to gain control over it. However, the effort is worth the time as the skew handsomely rewards all who develop skill with this cut.

Tools and Material

Start with a 1-½" to 2"-square by 6"-long piece of soft wood like poplar, alder or pine. Mount the stock between centers on the lathe. Practice the rolling cut with a ½" to ⅝"skew that's really sharp. Round the stock to a uniform cylinder. At first, limit your practice cuts on the cylinder ends only.

Roll the Skew

Practice holding the skew to the blank with the lathe off (**Photo 1**). When you're comfortable with the hand position, turn the power on and let the bevel rub on the blank without cutting any wood (**Photo 2**). Then, lift the handle as you slowly rotate the skew to hook the short point in the wood (**Photo 3**). Make this a light cut; there's no need to hog off a lot of wood. Rotate the tool as you move it slowly forward. Keep the bevel in contact with the wood at all times to maintain control. Losing bevel contact will produce the well-known slash (**Photo 11**). Repeat the cut starting at the

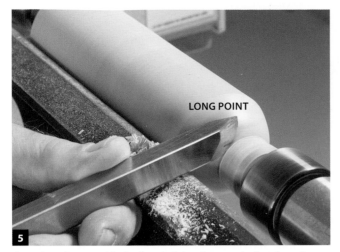

LONG POINT

5 Complete the cut with the bevel of the skew vertical to the axis of the lathe. The tool will stop cutting at this point. Pull the tool straight back to avoid catching the wood with the long point.

6 Practice on the other end of the cylinder. You find one side is easier than the other. Practice extensively on the weak side until you're comfortable with the rolling cut in either direction.

7 Time to use the rolling cut to make beads. Lay out a series of 1" to 1-¼" wide beads with the parting tool. Cut down on each side of the bead about one-third the diameter of the cylinder.

8 Draw a broad pencil line at the center of the bead. The skew should never cut in this region. When you sand the bead, the marked area will blend nicely into the rounded sides.

top of the roundover (**Photo 4**). Rotate the skew and as you lift the handle until you reach the bottom of the cut (**Photo 5**). The skew should end the cut with the bevel held vertical to the lathe's axis. The tool will stop cutting or "weathervane" at this point.

All of this involves a variety of coordinated actions. The tool must simultaneously lift, rotate and advance downhill to an ever-smaller diameter. At the same time, the tool must slide along the tool rest to accommodate the width of the curved area. Keep the bevel in contact with the side of the rounded surface with light pressure.

This mix of actions reminds me of dancing with a partner: all the steps must work together to achieve success—a fine cut with good shape and no slashes.

Work on both ends of the cylinder (**Photo 6**). Most people find the rolling cut easier either to the left or to the right. Concentrate your practice on the weak side until you feel equally comfortable in either direction. Don't get discouraged if you experience a few slashes as you practice. This is normal. Remember, the slash is always the result of the bevel loosing contact with the wood.

Once you're comfortable with the rolling cut, chuck in a fresh blank and use a parting tool to lay out some 1" or 1-¼" wide beads (**Photo 7**). Make a wide pencil line in the middle of each bead. This marks the area to stay clear of when shaping the bead (**Photo 8**). Practice on these "bead sticks" until your beads are consistent in size and shape (**Photos 9** and **10**). Keep your eye on the horizon of the curve to see how well it has developed. The perfect bead has a sweet convex curve with no flat areas. How do you achieve this? The answer is

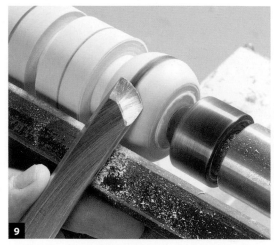

9 Make two or three light rolling cuts on each side of the bead to rough out the shape.

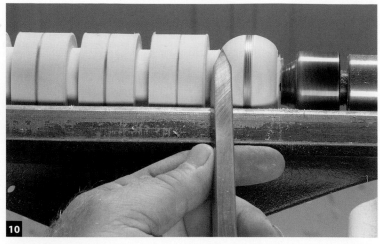

10 Make additional light rolling cuts to achieve the balanced look of a good bead. Continue making additional beads on the blank until you achieve consistently good results.

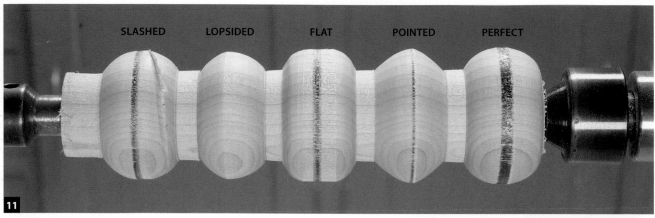

SLASHED   LOPSIDED   FLAT   POINTED   PERFECT

11 Four common beading problems: A slashed bead caused by loss of bevel contact; a lopsided bead from uneven cutting on either side; a flat bead caused by insufficient lifting and rounding; a pointed or triangular bead from pushing the tool without lifting and rolling; finally, a curved and full looking bead—the real objective.

simple; practice, practice, practice. In time you will want to practice varying the width of the beads.

The ultimate exercise to develop skew control and achieve good shape, is to turn an egg. Turning an egg is both a lot of fun and good practice. First, turn a Morse taper on one end of a 5" blank of 2 x 2 material held between centers. Be sure and leave a shouldered area to ride on top of the spindle shaft. Then, simply drive the blank directly into the headstock spindle and start rolling cuts to make an egg (**Photo 12**).

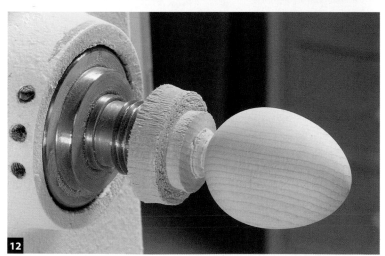

12 The ultimate skew exercise is to turn an egg. A Morse taper turned onto the end holds the egg blank in the headstock. The egg represents a challenge in tool handling and good form.

CHAPTER SIX

Reshaping the Skew Chisel

An alternate shape minimizes dig-ins

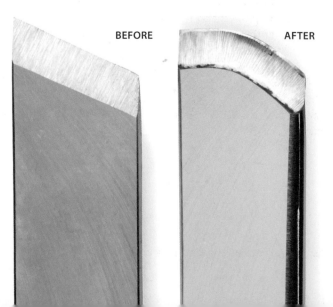

BEFORE

AFTER

Years ago, an old professional spindle turner showed me a different way to sharpen a skew. When I tried it, I was sold. This modified grind is more versatile, friendlier and more responsive than a traditional grind. Used correctly, a modified skew is difficult to catch and dig into the wood, unlike a conventional skew. In the years since, I've found that many early 20th-century turners from Maine to Indiana adopted the same alternate shape. They were all on to something good. It's easy to learn how to sharpen a modified skew. I'll show you how to take a regular skew chisel with a flat cross section and turn it into a far superior tool in an hour or so.

THE MODIFIED PROFILE

CHAMFERED EDGE   LONG POINT   STRAIGHT SECTION

70°

CURVED SECTION

ROUNDED EDGE   SHORT POINT

Begin modifying a standard skew on a belt sander. Hold the tool so the belt always travels away from you. Completely round the short point side up to the ferrule; chamfer the sharp edges of the long point side.

My skew's profile has two sections: straight and curved. The straight section begins at the skew's long point and extends one-fourth to one-third of the blade's width. The curved section continues to the skew's short point. The angle from long point to short point is about 70°, the same as on a conventional skew. I also modify my skew's body. I round over the short point side and lightly chamfer both edges of the long point side.

Shape the Sides

Begin modifying a conventional skew by reshaping its sides (**Photo 1**). I prefer to do this on a belt sander mounted in a stand and equipped with a belt designed to cut metal (see Sources, page 29). Be sure to remove all the dust from the sander and set aside its bag to avoid starting a fire. Start with a #60-grit belt; finish with a #120-grit belt. I round the short point side to glide with a smooth motion when planing and to easily rotate and pivot the tool when rolling beads.

Grind the tool's profile on a #36- or #46-grit wheel (see "The Modified Profile," above, and **Photo 2**). I use a coarse wheel because this step removes a lot of material.

Grind the straight and curved profiles. Position the tool rest about 90° to the wheel. I've mounted a wood platform on my tool rest to have a broader area of support, which is critical for modifying and resharpening a skew.

TWO TOOLS IN ONE

With both straight and curved sections, a modified skew is quite versatile.

The curved area is great for these tasks:

- Planing and rolling cuts. If you lead with the short point side and cut with the tool's curved section, you cannot dig in. Digging in is a real problem with a conventional skew and a bane to all novice turners.
- Planing chip-prone woods, such as red oak or figured maple.
- Forming the concave and convex sections of a spindle.

The straight section is great for these tasks:

- Peeling away wood, like a large parting tool.
- Slicing rounded pommels (with the long point down).
- Scraping end grain and knots.
- Working in tight areas. The curve creates a small clearance.

Begin grinding the profile's straight section. Color the old bevel with a felt-tip marker to identify where the wheel cuts.

4

Flip the tool now and then as you continue grinding. It's important to keep the bevels on both sides of the tool equally long to center the cutting edge.

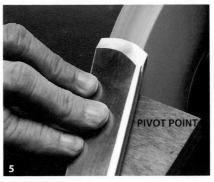

5 PIVOT POINT

Grind the curved section by using your fingers as a pivot point. Keep the spot you're grinding square to the wheel.

6

Continue grinding with a fanning motion. When you reach the short point, as shown here, reverse the direction without lifting the skew from the tool rest.

Sharpen the Edge

Switch to a #60- or #80-grit wheel. Adjust the tool rest to grind the same angle as on a conventional skew. I prefer to set this angle by measuring distances. The length of the bevel should be approximately 1-½ times the tool's thickness. The angle between both bevels will then be 35° to 40°. As you grind, you'll probably have to tweak the tool rest's angle to get it right.

Begin sharpening the straight section (**Photo 3**). Flip the tool as you go to remove the same amount of material from each side (**Photo 4**).

Now for the curved section. You'll grind and sharpen this in one long sweeping motion, using your fingers as a pivot point (**Photo 5**). Start next to the straight section, then rotate the long point off of the wheel. Continue in one fluid motion down to the short point. Stop when the area around the short point is square to the wheel (**Photo 6**). Then, without changing your hand position, rotate the tool in the opposite direction, back toward the straight section. The idea is to fan the tool back and forth without lifting it from the tool rest. Make three or four passes on one side of the tool. Then flip the tool and make an equal number of passes on the other side. Continue sharpening and flipping until the bevels meet at the cutting edge.

As with any turning tool, you'll know when to stop sharpening by watching the sparks. When they fly off evenly both above and below the bevel, the cutting edge is sharp.

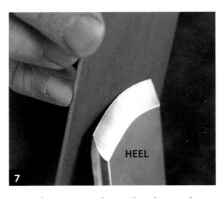

7 HEEL

Hone the cutting edge with a diamond slipstone. It's easy to find the correct angle by feel. Hold the slipstone so it contacts two points on the bevel's concave surface: the heel and the cutting edge.

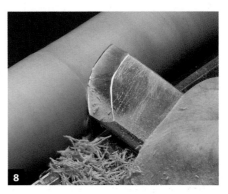

8

Check the tool's sharpness by putting it to work. Make a planing cut on a cylinder. A sharp tool will require little effort to push, produce lots of shavings and leave a very smooth surface.

To confirm that it's sharp, lift the tool and look down at the edge under a bright light. A dull area reflects light; a sharp edge disappears into a black line.

Hone and Test the Edge

I'm a big believer in honing. An extra-sharp skew is safer and performs better. I use a diamond slipstone on high-speed steel tools because it cuts fast (see Sources, below). To get the angle right, hold the slipstone so it only rubs on the bevel's heel (**Photo 7**). As you move the slipstone up and down, incline it until it touches the cutting edge as well; then maintain this two-point contact. Repeat on the other side. Hone the tool's sides near the short and long points, too. Test your tool by making a light planing cut (**Photo 8**).

SOURCES Alan Lacer, www.alanlacer.com Diamond slipstone plated on two flat sides and two round sides, $88. ☺ MSC Industrial Supply Co., (800) 645-7270, www.mscdirect.com Diamond whetstone plated on one flat side only, #01054931, $87.10. Sanding belts for metal made by Norton, 3-M and TruMaxx are available in many sizes and grits from MSC. ✐

CHAPTER SEVEN

Skew Planing

Master this tricky but useful tool

1-1½" **MODIFIED GRIND**

ROUNDED CORNERS

I prefer a large 1-½" or 1" skew for planing. The modified grind on the large skew makes the tool easier to use.

1"

1

T he skew is one of the most useful tools in the turner's arsenal. This article will get you on the right path towards mastering this tricky but useful tool. A lot of us start out trying the skew without a clue as to how it is used. The result is often a nasty dig-in that leads most people to retire their skew to a drawer someplace. There, the secrets and abilities of the skew lay dormant and undiscovered. It's not a surprising phenomenon because the skew has a steep learning curve with lots of subtlety. To add to the problem, there's just not much instruction around on how to use the skew.

I have been teaching students how to master the skew for decades. I always start with skew planing as the fundamental skew cut. Once you master this cut, you will be well on your way to confident use of the tool. I'll first show you how to practice the cut. Plan on working a number of practice pieces before tackling actual projects. Later in the book we will build on that foundation and look at other more advanced skew cuts.

Applications

The number one application for the planing cut is spindle work where the grain of the wood is parallel to the bed of the lathe. Planing cuts are used to create cylinders, tapers and shallow concave or convex cuts. After practice with planing cuts, I encourage my students to make their own tool handles using a skew (**Photo 1**). It's a great first project to hone your new skew planing skills.

The Right Skew

A wide skew is best for planing cuts (**Photo 2**). It's extremely important that the skew be very sharp. The degree of control with this tool is in direct proportion to the degree of sharpness. Be sure that the corners behind the cutting edge are softened or rounded over all the way back to the ferrule. This allows the tool to glide on those corners with a smooth motion across the tool rest.

The modified grind that I favor (curved edge for the lower two-thirds, straight across for the upper third) has one huge advantage for the planing cut: if you maintain the cut in the curved section you will almost always avoid a dig-in. Also, a curved edge cuts cleaner in woods that tend to chip.

CUP DRIVE   **SPUR DRIVE**

2

Replace your headstock's spur drive with a cup drive. A catch is inevitable when you're learning. A cup drive slips like a clutch to minimize a catch; a spur drive holds fast to the wood and aggravates a catch.

Prepare the Lathe

The next step is to prepare the lathe itself. I strongly recommend using a cup drive rather than the spur center that came with your lathe (**Photo 3**). Finally, check the tool rest and file out any nicks or dents with a mill file. Finish prepping the tool rest by rubbing on a little paraffin wax. Now your skew can glide effortlessly across the rest as it cuts.

Practice Makes Perfect

Start with a 2" x 2" x 8" square blank mounted between centers. I suggest a softer wood like yellow poplar or red alder that's straight grained and free of knots. Cut up 2 x 4's will do in a pinch. Just be sure to cut out the knots.

Always wear a full face shield. With the lathe set to a moderate speed (900 to 1400 rpm) use a spindle-roughing gouge to create a cylinder. In time you will enjoy roughing short pieces like this by planing with the skew.

Start your practice cuts with the skew at the right end of the cylinder (**Photo 4**). Slowly advance the tool to the left until you reach the edge of the wood. Turn off the lathe and admire the quality of the cut surface. Develop your skill by cutting both directions on the cylinder (**Photo 5**). Also, be sure to always cut "downhill" (larger to smaller diameters) when there is a variation in diameter.

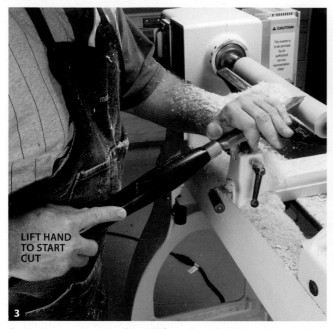

LIFT HAND TO START CUT

3

4

Start your practice cuts about 1" from the cylinder's right end. Cut with the tool's lower half, or short point, leading the cut. Rest the skew on one of its rounded corners—not flat on the tool rest. Rub the bevel on the cylinder, then gently lift the handle until the edge cuts into the wood without losing contact with the bevel. Slowly advance the tool to the left.

Practice planing in the opposite direction. Reverse your hands or shift your body around. Experiment with your front hand either below or on top of the tool.

Typical Problems with Planing Cuts

DIG-INS

This is perhaps the most feared problem as it does considerable damage to the wood and to your nerves. A dramatic dig in often causes new turners to reject the skew as having a mind of its own and a vicious one at that. As a consequence they miss out on all the skew has to offer the serious turner. To avoid dig-ins, use a large skew and stay within the lower two thirds of the edge (**Photo 6**). Even if you cut with the short point or leading edge of the skew, it won't dig-in (**Photo 7**). A dig-in always happens when the unsupported portion of the tool (the long point or trailing edge) is pulled into the wood (**Photo 8**).

RUN-BACKS

Run-back, aka screw threading or spiraling, is one of the most common problems students have when learning to plane with the skew (**Photo 9**). The cause is simple but subtle: loss of bevel support below the cutting edge. It can occur at anytime: when you first contact the wood, midway in a cut or at the conclusion of the cut. The solution is to keep the bevel in contact with the wood at all times.

CHIPPING

Just like using a hand plane or running a board over a jointer, chipping or tear-out can be a significant problem when planing with a skew. Some woods are naturally more "chippy"—such as red oak or figured woods. Borrow techniques from the hand plane user: change direction and "skew" the skew chisel by moving it from a 45° angle to the axis of the lathe to 60° or 75°. Anyone who has used a jointer knows that a slow feed rate reduces chipping. In highly figured woods I sometimes advance the tool at a crawl—but end with little or no chip out.

RIBBING

When you hear an odd humming noise and notice the wood has a corrugated or washboard appearance, you have encountered "ribbing." Slight ribbing is not considered a major flaw and can be sanded away easily. Deep ribbing is a major flaw that often happens on long narrow stock. Usually the cause can be traced to the tool bouncing in and out of the cut or the wood flexing. A dull tool contributes to both causes, so keep the skew sharp. To steady the flexing wood, many professionals use a hand on the backside of the wood (**Photo 11**). If you are not comfortable with this approach, try an overhand grip while applying downward pressure to the tool rest (**Photo 12**). Remember, practice makes perfect.

TYPICAL PROBLEMS AND HOW TO AVOID THEM

Avoid Dig-ins

DIG-IN

5

A dig-in can be dramatic, especially when using a spur drive on dry hardwood. You'll get a dig-in if the unsupported trailing edge or long point of the tool catches and is pulled down into the wood.

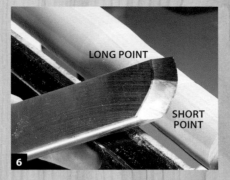

LONG POINT

SHORT POINT

6

Avoid dig-ins by using the lower 2/3 of your tool, starting just above the short point. Stay away from the red zone indicated above.

SHORT POINT

TOOL REST

7

The short point can safely enter the cut because it is supported by the tool rest. It's sometimes used to cut up to a detail although it tends to fray the fibers a bit.

Eliminate Run-Back

8

Run-backs are caused by a loss of bevel support below the cutting edge. The solution is to feel the bevel contact the wood before the cut is made. Then, maintain that feel throughout.

Minimize Chipping

9

Chips are a serious flaw that requires major sanding to fix. To avoid chipping, steepen the cutting angle for more of a shearing cut and slow the feed rate. Also, be sure to use a sharp tool.

Reduce Ribbing

10

Ribbing is a series of ridges caused by vibrating stock . To dampen vibration, support the stock with your hand. Set the tool rest close to the work and use your thumb to press down on the tool.

11

If you are uncomfortable with backing the wood with your hand, try to keep firm downward pressure on the tool. This helps to eliminate ribbing from a bouncing tool.

CHAPTER EIGHT

Woodturning Scrapers

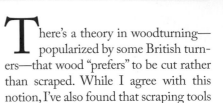

An essential part of your turning tool arsenal

There's a theory in woodturning—popularized by some British turners—that wood "prefers" to be cut rather than scraped. While I agree with this notion, I've also found that scraping tools play an essential role in woodturning.

Scraping tools are used primarily for bowl turning, vessels and end-grain hollowing. They're rarely used for spindle work, because cutting tools are better suited to the task. Scraping tools excel at roughing out shapes when the quality of the cut isn't critical, and in situations where a cutting tool can't be presented to the wood practically or safely—a situation that commonly occurs while hollow turning.

Surprisingly, a scraper can also be used as a fine finishing tool (**Photo 1**). Elevating the humble scraper to such a high level of performance may seem like creating a silk purse from a sow's ear. But as I'll show, it actually depends on how the tool is refined, how its edge is prepared and how the tool is presented to the wood.

Cutting vs. Scraping

In this story, I'll focus on the traditional notion of scrapers and scraping; that is, using only the edge, with no bevel support on the wood. Most turning tools (including gouges, skews and parting tools) are cutting tools, designed to work with support from the bevel—the tool is presented at an angle, so the bevel bears against the wood as the edge cuts. Scraping tools, on the other hand, are presented nearly straight on, so the edge receives no support from the bevel. Of course, cutting tools are sometimes used this way. And scrapers are sometimes used as cutting tools, by riding the bevel. Hence, the angle at which you present

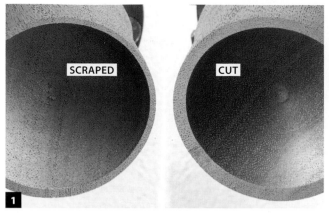

1 Used the traditional way, a scraper leaves torn and crushed fibers (left). But after refining its surface and edge and using a technique called "shear scraping," the same tool leaves a near-perfect surface (right).

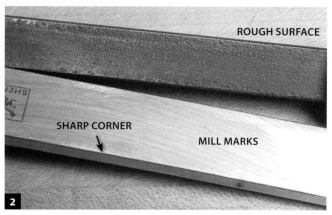

2 Two flaws commonly appear on the top surfaces of new scrapers: rough surfaces from little (or no) milling, or deep marks left from milling, along with very sharp corners.

3 Smooth the scraper's top surface by rubbing it on a large, flat diamond hone to remove the pits and coarse mill marks. Concentrate on the last inch or two.

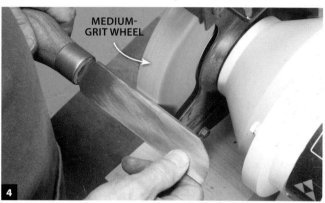

4 Soften the four long, sharp corners using a medium-grit wheel. Remove the tool rest and then freehand each corner from the leading edge to the ferrule.

the tool really determines whether you cut or scrape.

Woodturning scrapers have two basic attributes, flat steel and a bevel ground on only one side. The shape of the edge is almost endlessly variable—straight across, skewed, half-rounded, full-rounded, side-cutting with a relief behind the edge, even profiled to fit the shape you wish to create—virtually any shape the turner desires.

Refine the Tool

New scrapers often show problems right from the start. The top surface of the steel can be quite rough, or even pitted, which means it has had little or no milling. Or, it can show deep milling marks or very sharp corners along its entire length (**Photo 2**).

Smoothing the scraper's top surface gives the tool a more consistent edge. This step is especially important for fine finishing applications, because it dramatically improves the quality of the cutting burr that sharpening creates. To remove pits or mill marks, rub the top surface on a medium or fine flat diamond hone (**Photo 3** and Sources, page 37).

Softening or fully rounding the scraper's corners from be-

hind the cutting edge all the way to the ferrule makes the tool much friendlier to grip and helps it glide smoothly across the tool rest (**Photo 4**). I often follow the grinding by running the diamond hone along those edges to smooth them a bit more.

Shape the Profile

The good news about scrapers is that their profiles can be quickly and easily changed, whether for a particular application or personal preference. Install a coarse (#46-grit) wheel in your grinder and set the rest horizontal to the wheel. Then move the tool quickly and continuously to shape the edge (**Photo 5**).

The next step is to reduce the bevel angle. Unlike the bevel on a cutting tool that supports the cut, the bevel on the scraper is more for clearance (although it will also be used for support). Scrapers often come with steeply angled bevels (80° to 85°). But if the bevel inadvertently touches the wood while scraping, it can cause problems. Therefore, it's better to reduce the angle to between 60° and 70° (**Photo 6**). Change the angle on the grinder's tool rest and follow the shape of the edge as you grind. Keep the tool moving constantly, to avoid overheating.

COURSE-GRIT WHEEL

5

Shape the leading edge of the scraper, using a coarse wheel and the tool rest set in a horizontal position. You can grind the edge to almost any profile.

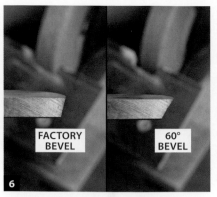

FACTORY BEVEL

60° BEVEL

6

Reduce the bevel angle to provide better clearance. The factory bevel is often too steep. Tilt the tool rest to 60° and then regrind the bevel by following the profile.

TELLTALE SPARK

60° BEVEL

7

When tiny sparks appear at the top edge, the new bevel is fully ground and a burr is being formed.

8

Test for the presence of a burr by running your thumb off the end of the top edge. This ground burr serves as the cutting edge for most scraping tasks.

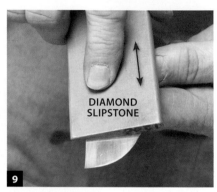

DIAMOND SLIPSTONE

9

Sharpening for finish work requires a finer edge. The first step is to remove the ground burr by polishing the scraper's top edge with a diamond hone/slipstone.

BURNISHER TILTED 5°

10

Create a new, finer burr by burnishing the edge. Tilt the burnisher about 5° toward the top of the scraper and pull it *once* across the entire edge.

Create the Edge

The final step in producing the bevel angle also produces an edge. Sparks consistently traveling over the top of the tool indicate that a heavy burr—a curl of steel along the edge—is being formed (**Photo 7**). This burr must be consistently formed across the scraper's entire profile for the tool to work properly. You can test for a consistent burr by feel (**Photo 8**). Your thumb is sensitive enough to detect even the faintest burr.

For subsequent sharpenings, you'll need to periodically regrind the edge—usually with a finer wheel, #60- or #80-grit. Simply match the rest to the bevel angle, follow the shape as you grind, and watch for the sparks.

A ground burr is a suitable cutting edge for at least 90 percent of scraping jobs, such as rough shaping and other coarse applications. However, to use a scraper for finish work, a finer, even more consistent burr is necessary. Start by removing all traces of the ground burr (**Photo 9**). A few passes with a diamond slipstone does the trick (see Sources). Then replace the ground burr with a burnished burr (**Photo 10**).

Use a burnisher to raise (or pull) the burr. Any material harder than the steel will work for burnishing, whether a carbide rod mounted in a handle or a cabinetmaker's burnisher used to sharpen card scrapers. With a single pass, pull the burnisher across the edge while holding it at a slight angle towards the top. The amount of pressure you apply dictates the size of the burr. For finishing work, the burr should be very light—almost undetectable to the touch, but certainly there.

This tiny burr wears down fairly quickly during use, but it can be easily renewed by re-burnishing. However, each time you burnish, the edge is slightly rounded. After using and pulling a burr five to 10 times, you'll need to return to the grinder to create a new "sharp edge" and then repeat the process of removing the ground burr and pulling a burnished burr. Always remove the previous burr before pulling a new one, whether ground or burnished.

TIP Renew the burr when the surface it cuts on the wood begins to degrade or when the shavings become short or turn to dust. Both results indicate the tool is dull.

11

Traditional scraping technique tips the tool's cutting edge slightly downward by raising the handle in back, while keeping the tool flat on the lathe's rest. This method leaves torn and crushed fibers, as shown in Photo 1.

12

Create a smooth surface during end-grain hollowing by shear scraping. Tilt the tool up onto its corner (45° degrees or higher) and angle it towards the work. Then move from the center to the left in order to follow the grain.

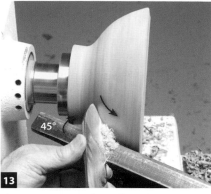

13

Shear scraping works well on the outside of a face-grain bowl because it's cutting across end grain. Lift the tool 45° in the direction of the cut and work from smaller to larger diameter.

14 RIBBONS   CURLS

The shavings tell the tale when the scraper is tilted at the correct angle for shear scraping, because they'll change from ribbons (left) to fine, twisted curls of wood (right).

TIP A bowl gouge can be used to work most of the inside of a face-grain bowl, but the scraper, held flat on the rest and close to the work, is great for blending from the lower sides to the center.

Using Scrapers

The most common scraping method is to place the tool flat on the rest and slightly tip up the handle at the back, to keep the bevel away from the wood (**Photo 11**). As the bevel doesn't ride against the wood for extra support, the tool rest must be positioned as close as possible to the work—this is a fundamental rule for using scrapers.

This method is great for rough hollowing in face-grain bowl work or for end-grain hollowing of goblets and lidded boxes. (You can use a gouge for these tasks, but using a scraper is often easier.) However, scraping often tears the grain—especially end grain—and it's harsher on softer woods than harder woods (see **Photo 1**).

Creating a smooth surface with a scraper requires a technique called "shear scraping." This method, which can produce a surface that requires very little sanding, works well on the inside of end-grain hollowed items (boxes, vessels, bowls, goblets, etc.) and on the outside of face-grain shapes.

Start by lightly burnishing the edge to create a fresh burr. Next, rather than holding the tool flat on the rest, twist it in the direction of the cut to 45° or higher. When hollowing end-grain vessels, work from the center to the edge (**Photo 12**). When shear scraping the outside of face-grain objects, work from small to large diameters (**Photo 13**). When shear scraping is executed correctly, a fine, twisted fiber of wood rolls off the edge (**Photo 14**). Slowly elevate the scraper onto its corner while making a cut. When you see the shavings change, you've reached the correct angle for shear scraping.

SOURCES Highland Woodworking, highlandwoodworking.com, 800 241 6748, Medium Diamond hone #425342 $36.99, Fine Diamond hone #425343 $44.99; Carbide Rod (to be mounted in a handle with ferrule), 3/8" dia. x 2-½", #04114310, $16.50.

CHAPTER NINE

Chucks & Chucking

Learn how to hold and keep work on the lathe

For many woodturning operations, a chuck performs the essential job of holding the work securely and safely. These operations often present unique requirements, so a dizzying array of manufactured and shop-made chucks have evolved to grasp, expand, screw, compress, trap, pull, jam, stick—and even to move the work through an eccentric pattern (see Sources, page 42). Knowing which chuck to use can be confusing, especially because most are designed for specific applications, so they all have strengths and weaknesses. Learning about chucks will expand your capabilities and make your turning safer, to boot.

Critical Concerns

Always keep three rules in mind whenever you use a chuck (see "Three Principles of Chucking," above).

Safety: Turning's first principle is to keep the work on the lathe. Using the wrong chuck or improperly mounting a blank can lead to disaster. Countless pieces have been damaged or destroyed and far too many turners seriously injured—some even fatally—by a chucking failure. Above all, remember that no chuck is 100 percent reliable. Therefore, when using a chuck, it's imperative to wear a full face shield that's ANSI-rated Z87+ (see Sources). Also, pay special attention to the speed of the lathe—excessive speed is the most common factor in lathe accidents.

Craftsmanship: A completed turning should show no trace of being affixed to the lathe. Screw holes and other mounting marks left by a chuck are evidence of mediocre work. Filling them or covering them with felt patches doesn't cut it. And never let the chuck determine key dimensions of

THREE PRINCIPLES OF CHUCKING

Make sure it's secure
Grain direction matters with many chucks. For example, face-grain mounting on a scroll chuck exposes weak short grain. The failure shown here was caused by sudden shear force due to a catch.

Leave no evidence
What chuck was used to turn these bowls? The correct answer: You can't tell. Finished turnings should show no evidence of chucking. (The real answer: All three were turned on a faceplate.)

Go for pinpoint accuracy
Inaccuracy in centering the work on the chuck can cause big problems. In the reverse-chucking setup shown here, mis-centering has caused uneven cutting, which can be very hard to repair at this stage.

your piece. (When I first started, the bases on all my bowls were 3" in diameter, because I always turned the outsides down to the 3" faceplate that I had.) Even a footed bowl on which the dimensions of the foot are based on the chuck that held it is an example of pedestrian design.

Accuracy: Failing to accurately center a piece in or on a chuck can cause problems that may be impossible to correct. Using a chuck that doesn't run true will produce similar frustrating results. Make it a practice to avoid worn or poorly made chucks.

Types of Chucks

As your turning skills increase and your projects become more adventurous, you'll keep encountering different chucks and chucking methods, most of which were devised by pioneering turners. Every chuck type has variations. And there's a turner-made version of (or one that pre-dates) virtually every commercial chuck. The chucks that follow are just the tip of the iceberg.

Chucks that Grasp

Four-jaw scrolling chucks are probably the biggest advancements in chuck technology (**Photo 1**). The better scroll chucks currently on the market have largely solved problems associated with the early versions, including issues with accuracy, wear of critical metal surfaces and a nasty tendency to loosen while turning. However, modern scroll chucks still have some quirks that are important to know about:

Grain direction matters (see "Make Sure It's Secure," above). Short-grain weakness is a critical factor when a scroll chuck is used for face-grain turning, because a catch at the wrong point can cause the wood to fracture—especially wood that's dry or brittle, or wood that naturally splits easily, such as oak.

Maximize the grip. Always use a suitably sized chuck and suitably sized jaws. (As the size and weight of the blank increases, the contact area between the wood and the chuck must also increase.) Shape the mounting point so the chuck's jaws grip as much surface area (diameter and length) as possible (**Photo 2**). Create a shoulder that rests on top of the jaws as a bearing surface. And use serrated jaws.

House the scroll mechanism. To avoid contacting the scroll mechanism's sharp spinning corners, keep the mechanisms inside the body of the chuck. This also keeps the jaws from being extended too far, so they don't fly out of the chuck.

Chucks that Expand

Often the same scroll chuck that closes on work is also designed to expand into a recess. This is most helpful when a shallow recess is the only available mount (as when turning a plate or a platter) or when chucking into a drilled or turned opening (as when turning a pepper mill). These chucks work reasonably well, as long as the outward pressure exerted while mounting doesn't split the wood. However, excessive force exerted by a catch or dig-in while turning can split the wood and break the work away from the chuck.

Chucks that Screw

No other chuck offers as wide a range of holding power as a faceplate with screws (**Photo 3**). Combined with the plate's bearing surface, screws provide remarkable chucking strength—even a chuck with a single screw in the center can offer surprising holding power. However, these chucks are only suitable for face-grain turning, when the screws mount in the blank's face grain (such as face-grain bowls, platters, stool seats and the like). Faceplates with screws should not

SCROLL CHUCKS

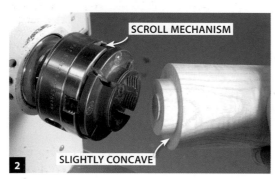

1

A scroll chuck has jaws that scroll in and out to fit turning blanks of different sizes. Most scroll chucks offer a variety of jaws and other options—including the ability to hold other types of chucks.

Labels on image 1: DEEP JAWS, SMALL JAWS, SERRATED JAW

2

To mount a blank on a scroll chuck, turn a tenon for maximum contact—as large and long as the jaws allow, with a slightly concave bearing shoulder. Keep the scroll mechanism within the chuck's body.

Labels on image 2: SCROLL MECHANISM, SLIGHTLY CONCAVE

SCREW CHUCKS

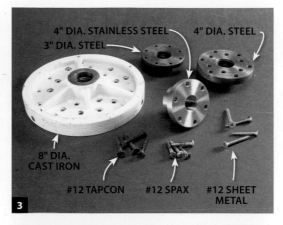

3

Labels on image 3: 4" DIA. STAINLESS STEEL, 3" DIA. STEEL, 4" DIA. STEEL, 8" DIA. CAST IRON, #12 TAPCON, #12 SPAX, #12 SHEET METAL

A faceplate with screws is an excellent choice for face-grain turning. The size of the plate, its composition, the type of screws and length of their threads combine to offer an enormous range of holding capability.

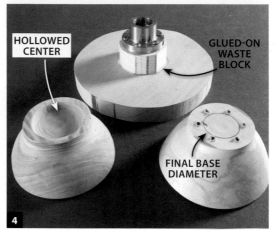

4

Labels on image 4: HOLLOWED CENTER, GLUED-ON WASTE BLOCK, FINAL BASE DIAMETER

Eliminate screw holes without losing height on the work by hollowing the area that contained the holes, turning away the holes and leaving a smaller diameter base, or gluing a waste block to the back of the blank.

---

be used if the screws will mount in the blank's end grain (including end-grain bowls, boxes and goblets, for example).

Always make sure the faceplate is flat. The mounting point on the wood must also be flat or very slightly concave—never convex or uneven, or with high spots. Here are some other key issues concerning faceplates:

Don't skimp. Buy a high-quality solid steel or hefty cast-iron faceplate. The most practical sizes are 3" and 4" dia.—choose one made of one-piece steel or stainless steel with at least four holes. Faceplates 6" in diameter and larger are usually made of cast iron. Choose one that's at least ¾" thick. In any faceplate, the more holes the better—my favorite 3" faceplate has 6 holes; sometimes I fill all 30 holes on my 8" faceplate with long #14 screws!

Use the right screws. The best choices I've found are sheet metal screws with square-drive heads, Tapcon screws (hex head, ³⁄₁₆" dia. and ¼" dia.) and SPAX (Phillips/square drive) Construction Multiple-Materials screws. Do not use wood screws, drywall screws or deck screws—they're often brittle and have too little holding power due to shallow threads and smaller diameters.

Use #10, #12 or #14 screws for most situations—always start by drilling pilot holes. Hex-head lag screws may be the best choice if the work is large and heavy and the faceplate is 10" or larger. Buy a variety of screw lengths: long for roughing (especially when screwing into what will be the opening of a bowl); shorter for finish-turning or small, light work—but always err on the long side. Even for small work, every screw must penetrate at least ½" into the wood (full threads; the lead point doesn't count). Deeper penetration and more screws are always safer paths—especially when working heavy, large diameters or work that's out of balance.

Eliminate the screw holes. Simply filling or covering them looks amateurish. Instead, learn one or more "reverse-chucking" methods. (Reverse chucking involves removing the work after completing most of the turning and mounting it in reverse, in order to finish off the base.)

Once the work has been reverse-chucked, the easiest way

COMPRESSION CHUCKS

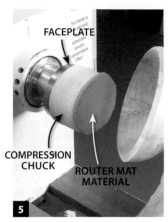

5 A compression chuck is used in conjunction with the tailstock to remount work to allow finishing its base (called "reverse chucking"). Here, the tailstock will be used to press the work against a block of wood with a padded face.

6 To center work on a compression chuck, mount it with light pressure and turn the lathe by hand to locate the high spot. Slightly loosen the tailstock, push on the mark, tighten the tailstock and mark again. Repeat until marking creates a full circle.

TRAPPING CHUCKS

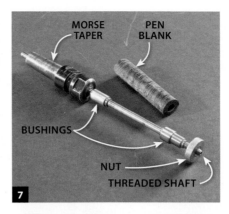

7 Mandrel chucks trap work with pre-drilled holes on a threaded shaft (between bushings in this case). One end of this pen-turning mandrel mounts in the headstock. The tailstock supports the opposite end.

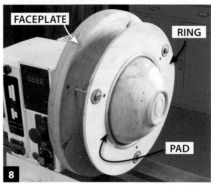

8 This trapping chuck for reverse chucking provides full access to the bottom of the work and a high level of safety. The system consists of padded rings in a variety of external and internal diameters that bolt to a dedicated base and faceplate.

to remove the holes is to turn down the base. Consider the height you lose as part of the process (and part of your design). On the other hand, if the blank is just too thin or the wood is so precious that you don't want to lose any, you have several options to choose from (**Photo 4**): Create a recess where the holes resided, plan a finished diameter inside the "screw orbit" (the ring that describes the circle of screws) or glue on a waste block (face grain to face grain) to house the screws and remove it after the turning is completed.

Scraps of hardwoods such as poplar, soft maple, ash, walnut and cherry are suitable waste-block material. Don't use weak woods such as pine, cedar and spruce, or plywood, which can separate. For dry wood, use yellow or white glue to glue on a waste block. Clamp the joint for at least 12 hours and allow at least 24 hours drying time before turning. Do not glue a piece of paper between the waste block and blank. This creates a weak joint that can separate. For wet wood, use a dry-wood waste block and medium-viscosity CA glue. Lightly clamp the joint and allow at least two hours drying time.

Chucks that Compress

A block of wood with an anti-slip pad mounted on its face (a ⅛" router mat works well) is the heart of a simple reverse-chucking setup (**Photo 5**). This type of chuck is especially useful for bowls and vessels with natural edges, thin bowls with delicate edges and for reshaping the mounting surface of

a "twice-turned" bowl for remounting into a scroll chuck. (A twice-turned bowl is roughed out of a green blank, removed and allowed to dry, and then remounted for final turning.)

Mount the block with the anti-slip material on a faceplate or in a scroll chuck. Center a nearly completed bowl or vessel on the block. Then use the tailstock center to firmly press the base of the work against the block, so that compression—and friction—holds the work while its base is shaped. Make sure to accurately center the work (**Photo 6**). This setup allows working the underside of the base, except near the tailstock center (this area must be worked after the piece comes off the lathe). This setup also allows working the sides, but only about one-quarter of the way up from the bottom.

Chucks that Trap

The most common method for mounting turning blanks with through holes—pen blanks, for example—is to trap them on a mandrel (**Photo 7**). Pepper mills, game calls, bracelets and toy wheels are frequently mounted this way.

An unusual trapping chuck for reverse chucking leaves little chance for the work to fly off the lathe (**Photo 8**). An excellent option when full access to the bottom of the work is desired, this system is especially good for full detailing of the base.

Chucks that Pull

Using vacuum pressure to hold work on the lathe is a relatively new option for reverse chucking (**Photo 9**). This system

PULL CHUCK

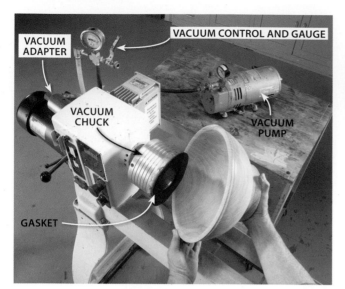

Vacuum chucking is a rapid way to mount a bowl for reverse chucking. This method provides total access to the bottom of the work, but it requires a considerable investment.

JAM CHUCKS

Jam chucking is frequently used in box-making. A tenon is turned on the base of the box to snugly fit the hollowed top. Jamming the top onto the tenon allows final shaping of the box's entire outside profile.

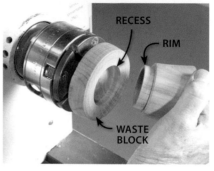

Jam chucking into a recess is another option. Here, the tenon on the box's base (now shaped and hollowed to form a rim) snugly fits into a recess turned in the waste block, so the box's bottom can be completed.

---

is great for production work or if full access to the bottom of the piece is desired, but it's not suitable for pieces that are fragile or very deep, pieces that contain voids, and woods with open pores. There are solutions for some of these issues, but choosing other chucking methods is arguably the best one.

Chucks that Jam

Jam chucks are often created for one-time use or where metal jaws might cause damage. Basically there are two approaches: Either you jam a hollowed piece over a tenon turned on a waste block (**Photo 10**) or you jam a tenon (or a rim) into a recess turned into a waste block (**Photo 11**).

If you only have a faceplate, you can use a jam chuck in lieu of a scroll chuck for end-grain hollowing (to hollow the box base shown in **Photo 11**, for example). Mount a face-grain block on a faceplate and turn a recess (a round mortise) in it. Then turn a tenon on the end of the base blank to snugly fit this recess (as shown in **Photo 2**, but with a mortised face-grain block mounted on a faceplate instead of a scroll chuck). Jam-fit the tenon into the recess or glue it. The tenon's shoulder provides additional stability by bearing against the block on the faceplate. Here's a tip: A jam fit can be tightened by adding a layer of tissue paper around the tenon or by wetting the tenon to slightly swell the wood.

Chucks that Stick

Using high-strength double-face tape (see Sources)—not carpet tape or the stuff from the local hardware store—is a great way to mount thin, face-grain, non-oily, dry-wood blanks for turning into small bowls, plates or platters. Note: This method isn't foolproof, so it's only for experienced turners; a catch may pull the piece off the lathe.

Cover a clean faceplate (lightly sanded and washed with alcohol or lacquer thinner) with the tape—don't allow the seams to overlap. Flatten one face of the blank and then clamp it against the taped faceplate for several hours. (The bond strength increases with clamp time.) For added safety, I bring up the tailstock and keep it in position while I'm turning, until the final cuts at the center. Freeing the completed work from the faceplate takes a slow, continuous pull until the tape starts to release.

Eccentric Chucks

Some chucks can move the work through preordained eccentric patterns. Such chucks have been around for centuries, but new versions can easily change the center of the work or move it through elliptical or wobble patterns.

SOURCES Oneway Manufacturing, oneway.ca, 800-565-7288, chucks and faceplates. ☯ Craft Supplies, woodturnerscatalog.com, 800-551-8876, chucks, faceplates and double-faced tape. ☯ Woodworkers Emporium, woodworkersemporium.com, 800-779-7458. a selection of chucks, especially several types of eccentric chucks. ☯ MSC, mscdirect.com, 800 645 7270, Full Face Shield with ANSI Z87+ rating: Headgear, #09797218, $28.06; Visor/Shield, #09797234, $10.06.

CHAPTER TEN

The Trapped Reverse Chuck

How to build and use this must-have bowl-turning jig

Good craftmanship requires that the bottom of a turned bowl or vessel shows no evidence of how it was mounted. (In bowl turning, the "bottom" includes the lower outside portion of the piece as well as its underside.) Learning to keep the chuck from dictating key aspects of the design, such as the bottom's shape, diameter and height, is another important skill.

This shop-made trapping chuck will dramatically improve the quality of your work in both of these important areas. It allows full access to the bottom of a bowl or vessel and frees you from limitations caused by a faceplate or any other chuck. This chuck securely holds the work, so it can't go flying across the shop—a benefit that's absent from most other such chucks, both shop-made and commercial.

Make the Chuck's Base

This chuck has two basic parts: a base on which the work is mounted and a ring to clamp the work to the base. Typically, rings of different diameters are used to clamp work of different sizes. Start by gluing together two thicknesses of ¾" Baltic birch plywood to make the chuck's base. Use yellow wood glue. Size the plywood to make a disc that's slightly less than the maximum diameter your lathe allows. Let the glue cure for a day. Then band saw the disc.

Choose a faceplate to dedicate to the chuck. I suggest at least 3" dia. for chucks up to 12", 4" dia. for chucks 14"

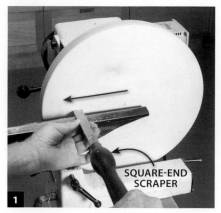

1 SQUARE-END SCRAPER

Flatten the face of a large plywood disc to create the chuck's base. Lightly scrape across the face to flatten it.

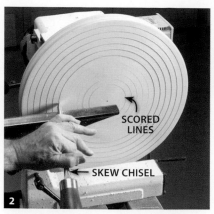

SCORED LINES

2 SKEW CHISEL

Cut shallow grooves to deepen scored lines made with dividers. Orient the skew with its long point down.

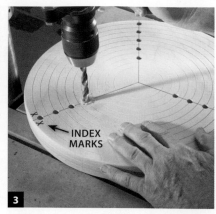

INDEX MARKS

3

Drill holes through the disc on lines that divide it into three equal segments. Mark one line of holes to index the rings.

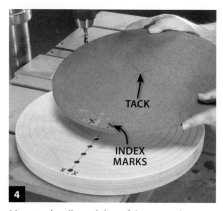

TACK

INDEX MARKS

4

Mount a hardboard disc of the same diameter on top of the base, using a tack in the center and double-sided tape near the edges. Add marks to index this disc to the base.

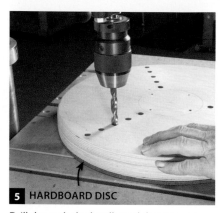

5 HARDBOARD DISC

Drill through the hardboard disc at every hole in the plywood base to create a template for drilling the chuck's rings.

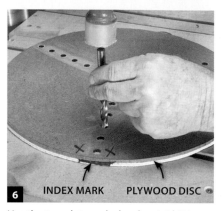

6 INDEX MARK   PLYWOOD DISC

Use the template and a brad-point bit to locate the holes on another plywood disc. Index this disc, too.

to 16", 6" dia. for 18" to 24" and bigger still for lathes with larger capacities. Larger faceplates increase the stability of this chuck, so always err on the larger side.

Center the faceplate on the disc and mount it. Then turn the disc to a cylinder, using a bowl gouge. Plywood turns poorly and dulls tools quickly, so work slowly, make light cuts and keep your gouge sharp. Finish by power-sanding, using a sanding disc mounted in a drill to make sure the rim has no sharp corners or splinters.

In order to hold the work, the disc must have a flat surface that's perpendicular to the axis of the lathe. Use a square-end scraper to true the disc (**Photo 1**). Then lightly sand the surface.

With the lathe running at slow speed (less than 400 rpm), use a pair of solid dividers (see Sources) held flat on the tool rest to mark lines every ½", starting about ½" from the rim and stopping about 4" from the center. Then deepen these lines with the long point of a skew chisel (**Photo 2**).

Remove the faceplate and place the disc on a flat surface. Then draw lines that divide the disc's face into three pie-shaped sections that are (roughly) equal in size. Permanently

mark one of these lines—this mark will be used to index the other parts when building and using the jig. Drill ⅜" dia. mounting holes along the three lines for the bolts that will hold the ring (**Photo 3**). Start at the outermost ring you cut earlier and space the holes 1" apart down to the 4" mark. Use a new or very sharp bit, make sure it's perpendicular to the drill press table and install a flat sacrificial board underneath to eliminate tearout.

Make the Rings

Attach a hardboard disc to the base to create a template for making the rings (**Photo 4**). Mark this disc to index its "key" location, as well as its outside face (when mounted on the base). Then flip over the assembly and use the holes in the base to drill through the hardboard (**Photo 5**).

Plan to cut between five and 10 rings at first. (Once you start using the chuck, you'll make many more.) Cut four rings the same diameter as the base, four two-thirds the diameter, and two half the diameter. The size of the center hole and where the drilled holes are located on the ring are the two variables, and they depend upon the piece you in-

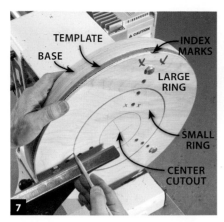

TEMPLATE
BASE
INDEX MARKS
LARGE RING
SMALL RING
CENTER CUTOUT

7

Mark the plywood disc for cutting into rings after bolting it and the template on the base and installing them on the lathe.

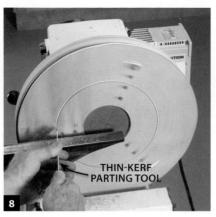

THIN-KERF PARTING TOOL

8

Cut through the disc to create the rings. Cut out the waste at the center. Then cut the small ring to create the large ring.

CLEAR PLASTIC TUBING

9

Line each plywood ring with clear plastic tubing that's been split with a utility knife.

10

To use the chuck, start by roughly centering a bowl on the appropriate groove cut in the base.

INDEX MARKS ALIGNED

11

Install the ring and use it to clamp the bowl to the plywood base using bolts, washers and wing nuts.

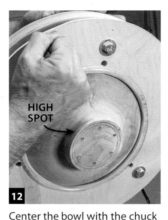

HIGH SPOT

12

Center the bowl with the chuck mounted. Mark the high spot. Gently tap it as necessary and then tighten the wing nuts.

13

Use this chuck to create a hollow base with a rim, add lines or beads, remove screw holes and chuck marks or fully round the bottom.

tend to hold. Cut the rings from ¼" or ⅜" thick Baltic birch plywood. The ¼" stock is fine for smaller chucks, but I tend to go to ⅜" or even ½" for larger rings and larger diameters.

Cut the plywood into discs the same diameter as the hardboard template. Then use the template to mark the bolt holes for drilling (**Photo 6**). For slightly more adjustability, I sometimes use a bit that's 1/64" larger than the bolts to drill these holes. As before, transfer the index marks to the plywood disc and mark its outside face.

Reinstall the faceplate on the chuck's base, making certain the base mounts flush. Lay the hardboard and one of the rings on top of the base, with all the index marks properly oriented. Then lash all three pieces together using ⅜" x 2-½" long coarse-thread bolts, washers and wing nuts.

Mark each disc for cutting into rings (**Photo 7**). Vary the center opening's size in each ring. Some discs will yield two rings. For the 14" chuck shown here, I made rings with openings from 3" to 12" in 1" increments. Rings between these sizes can be made as necessary.

Cut through the plywood disc to create each ring, using a thin-kerf parting tool (**Photo 8**). Run the lathe at 500 rpm

or slower during this process. Wear a full-face shield and engage the tailstock (when possible) to hold the cut-through disc in place.

After all the rings are cut, lightly sand all their edges and clearly mark the index points. Then line the center opening in each ring with ⅜" i.d. clear plastic tubing from the hardware store (**Photo 9**). You'll need about 20' of this tubing to line 10 rings. Note: The tubing's size will vary with the rings' thickness.

Cut the tubing about ⅛" shorter than the circumference of each hole. Observe how the hose curls. Then cut on the back of the curl, using a sharp knife or scissors. Lay the hose down and cut with the blade going away from you! Press the hose on—its natural curl will hold it in place.

Use the Chuck

Set workpiece rim-down on the chuck and center it using the circular cut marks (**Photo 10**). Then decide which ring to use by placing each likely candidate on the work with the index marks and holes in alignment (**Photo 11**). Does the center opening sufficiently grip the bowl while allowing full access to both its

MOUNT UNUSUAL SHAPES

This chuck can be used to mount work with natural edges, thin walls or delicate rims (left). Cut a groove in the face of the chuck's base to tightly house a short piece of Schedule 40 (thick-wall) PVC pipe—usually just long enough to raise the work's rim off the face. Use a scraper to lightly face off the protruding end of the pipe. Then glue on a 1/8" thick piece of textured rubber (such as a router mat) with CA glue. Position the work on the padded pipe, install a ring and you're ready to go.

You can also mount tall work by using threaded rod with washers and nuts on both ends (right). Most other reverse chucking systems don't have this capability.

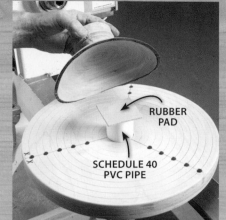

RUBBER PAD

SCHEDULE 40 PVC PIPE

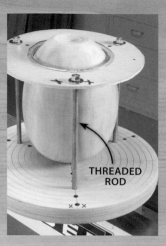

THREADED ROD

---

lower outside portion and its underside? Are the drilled holes positioned to allow the bolts to pass through without contacting the bowl?

Select the right bolts. As nearly every bowl is different, you'll need bolts of many different lengths to use with this chuck. I recommend buying sets of three ⅜" coarse-thread bolts, washers and wing nuts in ½" increments from 2" to 8". If having bolt heads whizzing past is unnerving, substitute carriage bolts.

With one washer on the ring under the bolt's head, make sure its threaded portion sufficiently protrudes through the base to install a washer and wing nut. If the bolt is slightly too long (so its unthreaded shaft appears), it's OK to use additional washers under the wing nut. Lightly tighten the wing nuts to secure the work.

Screw the chuck and mounted work onto the lathe. Then center the work to the lathe. It's helpful to have already marked the center on the underside. One method is to use a simple center finder (see Sources). Then you can simply bring up the tailstock and move the work within the chuck to align the hole on its underside with the tailstock's center.

Fortunately, it's fairly easy to center the work even if it doesn't have a center mark (**Photo 12**). Rotate the chuck by hand. Place a pencil on the tool rest and slowly move it forward to mark the high spot on the rotating work. Then nudge the work slightly away from that high spot by pushing or tapping

at the line's midpoint. Rotate the chuck and test again with the pencil. When the work is centered (or very nearly centered) the line will travel fully (or mostly) around the piece. When the work is centered (or very nearly), tighten the wing nuts and bring up the tailstock center.

Finish turning the lower outside portion of the work and finalize its base diameter (**Photo 13**). If you cut in at the base to remove mounting holes on the underside, you'll also be changing the work's height. There's no need to run the lathe very fast during these operations, as you have a lot of mass on the machine. Finish-sand the newly turned portion of the work as necessary.

Pull back the tailstock and plan the look of the work's underside. I like a bowl or vessel to sit on a rim, whether footed or not, as opposed to a fully flat surface. With this chuck you can deep-hollow a foot, add details such as beads or lines or any other surprise you may wish to give the viewer. You can also fully round the underside. Finish-sand to complete the work. Remove the chuck with the work still attached and place it on the bench. Then remove the wing nuts, bolts and ring.

Special Thanks

Eldon Rebhorn showed a version of this chuck in a book written in the 1960s. A few years later Hawaiian turner Jack Straka developed and refined this idea.

SOURCES Packard Woodworks, 800-683-8876, packardwoodworks.com, Dividers, 8", 135403, $21.95; Thin-Kerf Parting Tool #10336, $35.50; Center Finder #135510, $5.95. ◎ Oneway Manufacturing, 800-565-7288, oneway.ca, Faceplate, 3" $46.95, 4", $52.95, 6", $68.95, 8" $114.95. ◎ Grizzly Imports, 800-523-4777, grizzly.com, Router Mat, #W1320, $10.95. ℘

CHAPTER ELEVEN

The Ultimate Lathe Stand

Build a professional-quality stand that's stable, strong and heavy

A good stand is just as important as a good lathe. As a professional turner, I can't emphasize enough how important it is to have a stand that's stable, strong and heavy—particularly for bowl turning. This one meets all those requirements, and is better than many steel stands, yet it's just made from plywood.

Building your own stand has another major advantage: You can customize its height. Turning on a stand that's the right height allows you to control your tools much easier, and is less fatiguing, too. Time to do it!

Shopping List

- Sixteen ⅜" x 4" hex head bolts
- Six ¼" x 4-½" lag screws
- Sixteen ⅜" flat washers
- Sixteen ⅜" hex nuts
- Four ¼" x 1-½" hanger bolts
- Ten ¼" flat washers
- Four ¼" hex nuts
- One pair 2-½" butt hinges
- One piece of ¾" i.d. x 24" copper pipe
- Three ¾" x 5' x 5' sheets Baltic birch plywood
- Two bd. ft. hardwood

Serious beef
Double and triple thicknesses of ¾" plywood, plus 120 lbs. of sand, provide ample mass to absorb vibration.

SAND BAG
DOUBLED-UP PLYWOOD

Stable stance
The legs splay out in both directions.

Strong fastening system
The legs and rails are bolted together using copper tubes to house the nuts. These joints will never shake loose.

CUTTING LIST INCHES

REFERENCE	QUANTITY	PART	STOCK	THICKNESS	WIDTH	LENGTH	COMMENTS
TOP				2-1/8	14	34	
A	1	Interior	¾ Baltic birch plywood	2-1/8	13	33	Three layers of ¾ Baltic birch plywood
B	2	Edgebanding front & back	Oak	½	2-¼	34	Cut oversize, then trim
C	2	Edgebanding ends	Oak	½	2-¼	13	Cut oversize, then trim
BASE				33-7/8	38-7/8	18-7/8	Dimensions will vary depending on lathe's size and your height
D	2	Legs	¾ Baltic birch plywood	1-3/8	33-1/8	18-¾	Two thicknesses of ¾ Baltic birch plywood
E	2	Top rails	¾ Baltic birch plywood	1-3/8	3-½	30-¾	Two thicknesses of ¾ Baltic birch plywood
F	1	Bottom back rail	¾ Baltic birch plywood	1-3/8	3-½	35-¼	Two thicknesses of ¾ Baltic birch plywood
G	1	Bottom front rail	¾ Baltic birch plywood	1-3/8	3-½	35-¼	Two thicknesses of ¾ Baltic birch plywood, Do not angle top and bottom of front rail
H	1	Top shelf	¾ Baltic birch plywood	1-3/8	15	32-1/8	Two thicknesses of ¾ Baltic birch plywood
J	1	Bottom shelf	¾ Baltic birch plywood	1-3/8	13	34-5/8	Two thicknesses of ¾ Baltic birch plywood
K	4	Feet	Oak	¾	1-½	4	
M	1	Motor mount	¾ Baltic birch plywood	¾	12	12	
N	5	Tool dividers	Oak	½	1-¼	14-½	
P	16	Copper tubes		¾ i.d.	1-½		
Q	1	Knock-out bar holder	Oak	1	2	6	

Fig. A
Exploded View

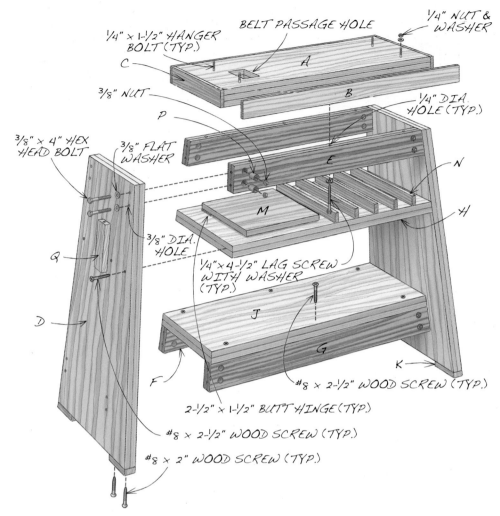

1/4" x 1-1/2" HANGER BOLT (TYP.)

BELT PASSAGE HOLE

1/4" NUT & WASHER

C

A

3/8" NUT

B

1/4" DIA. HOLE (TYP.)

3/8" x 4" HEX HEAD BOLT

3/8" FLAT WASHER

P

E

N

Q

3/8" DIA. HOLE

M

H

D

1/4" x 4-1/2" LAG SCREW WITH WASHER (TYP.)

J

G

K

#8 x 2-1/2" WOOD SCREW (TYP.)

F

2-1/2" x 1-1/2" BUTT HINGE (TYP.)

#8 x 2-1/2" WOOD SCREW (TYP.)

#8 x 2" WOOD SCREW (TYP.)

Fig. B
Leg Detail, End View

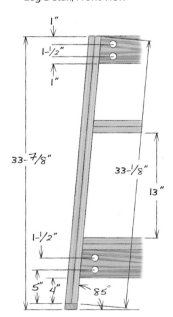

13"

33-1/8"

22"

12-7/8"   4-7/8"

18-3/4"

7-1/2"

18-7/8"

OVERALL DIMENSIONS: 36" H X 38-7/8" L X 18-7/8" D (A)

Fig. C
Leg Detail, Front View

1"

1-1/2"

1"

33-7/8"

33-1/8"

13"

1-1/2"

5"   4"   85°

Fig. D
Joint Detail

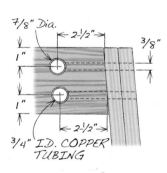

7/8" Dia.

2-1/2"

3/8"

1"

1"

2-1/2"

3/4" I.D. COPPER TUBING

See the complete plans for making the torsion beams we used to glue this plywood together (**Photo 1**) at PopularWoodworking.com/LacerBook

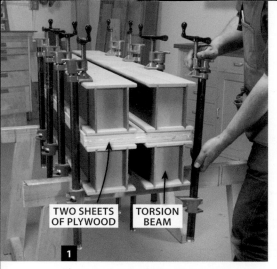

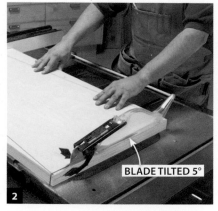

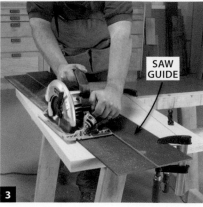

TWO SHEETS OF PLYWOOD | TORSION BEAM

BLADE TILTED 5°

SAW GUIDE

1 Glue two sheets of ¾" Baltic birch plywood face-to-face to make the legs. Use torsion beams or other large cauls to flatten the plywood and to provide even pressure.

2 Cut a 5° angle on the top and bottom of each leg. This angle creates the side-to-side splay.

3 Use a saw guide and a circular saw to taper the legs.

4 Drill holes angled at 5° for the bolts that will join the stand. Make the rails from doubled-up plywood, then cut their ends at 5°. Temporarily assemble the base with clamps.

5 Drill into the rails through the holes in the legs. Disassemble the base.

Make the Parts

First determine your stand's height and length. This stand is designed for a person about 5' 8" tall and a lathe that is 28" long with an axis 9" above its base. (I built this particular stand for a Vicmarc VL100.) Adjust the cutting list if necessary to fit your height and your lathe's dimensions.

Most of the plywood parts are made from two pieces glued together, face-to-face. Cut the pieces for these parts slightly oversize (Fig. A, Parts A, D, E, F, G, H and J). Glue them together (**Photo 1**).

Cut the top interior (A) to final size. Glue edge banding on all four sides (B and C, Fig. A). Trim the edging flush with the interior.

Double-splayed legs are the key to the base's stability (Figs. B and C). Use your tablesaw or circular saw to cut the top and bottom ends of the legs at 5° (**Photo 2**). Before you cut each leg, make sure these angles lean the same way, not in opposite directions. Lay out and cut the tapers on the long sides of the legs (**Photo 3**).

Rip the rails (E, F and G) and shelves (H and J) to final width. Trim the pieces to length, cutting their ends at 5° in opposing directions. (Leave the top shelf extra-long for now, so you can adjust its position later, if necessary.) In addition, cut the shelves' front and back edges, and the rails' top edges, at 5°. On the bottom shelf, leave the front edge square. (Note that the front bottom rail is not angled to follow the legs' taper. It is set back so you won't bump your ankles.) Make the tool dividers (N) and fasten them to the top shelf.

6 Insert the same drill bit into the rails. Using a sliding bevel, transfer the bit's angle to the rail's face. This enables you to find the exact center of the holes for the copper tubes that will hold the nuts.

7 Drill holes for the copper tubes using a 7/8" Forstner bit. Precision is important for a strong joint and easy assembly.

COPPER PIPE

8 Tap copper tubes, made from copper pipe, into the holes. Drill through the ends of the rails and through the tubes to finish the joint.

The Fastening System

To make the joints, start by laying out the bolt-holes in the legs (Fig. C and D). Tilt your drill press table to 5°, put a ⅜" bit in the chuck and drill the holes (**Photo 4**). Use a fence to ensure that all the holes are the same distance from the tapered edges of the legs. Reset the fence for the front bottom rail holes.

Temporarily clamp together the legs and all four rails. Using a hand drill and the same ⅜" bit, extend each bolt-hole into its corresponding rail (**Photo 5**). Disassemble the base. If necessary, drill these holes deeper.

Lay out the holes for the copper tubes that will hold the nuts directly from the holes you just drilled. First, draw a centerline across each hole. Insert the ⅜" bit. Adjust a sliding bevel so it's parallel to the bit (each hole may lean at a slightly different angle). Place the bevel adjacent to the hole's centerline and draw a line down the face of the rail (**Photo 6**). Mark the center of the copper-tube hole on this line (Fig.D).

Reset the drill press table to 90° and drill the copper-tube holes all the way through the rails using a ⅞" Forstner bit (**Photo 7**).

Cut 1-½" lengths of ¾" i.d. copper pipe (P) and tap them into each hole (**Photo 8**). Put the ⅜" bit back in the drill. Push the bit into each bolt hole and drill through the near side of each copper tube.

Assemble the Stand

Drill holes through the top rails for the lag screws that fasten the top. Clamp the legs and all of the rails together again. Insert a bolt through each hole. Slide a nut into the copper tube, hold it against the bolt with a flat-bladed screwdriver, and tighten the bolt.

Attach the shelves and feet (K) using countersunk wood screws. The exact position of the top shelf will depend on the length of the motor's drive belt. After determining the top shelf's proper height, cut it to length. To fasten the top shelf, mark its location, then tip the base upside down. The shelf will stay put because its ends are tapered. Run screws through the legs and into the shelf.

Attach the top. Position your lathe on the stand. (If your lathe has a separate motor, place it on the upper shelf about where it will go. Line up the lathe's pulley with the motor's pulley.) Mark the lathe's mounting holes. Mark the passage hole for the belt (Fig. A). Bolt the motor to the motor mount (M) and attach the motor mount to the top shelf using hinges.

Remove the lathe and cut out the belt-passage hole. Pre-drill holes for the hanger bolts that will fasten the lathe to the stand. Install the hanger bolts and mount the lathe. Finally, screw on the knock-out bar holder (Q) and a hanger for your wrench. Apply finish if you wish.

Special thanks to Bill Hull of Norman, OK, who helped design my original stand more than 20 years ago—it's still going strong!

CHAPTER TWELVE

Eye-Catching Finishes for Small Projects

Take a walk on the wild side of finishing

IRON & VINEGAR

CHARRED   SALT & PEPPER

MARBLED   BLEACHED

BLENDED

SALT & PEPPER FINISH

Apply India ink with a rag or brush. India ink is great for ebonizing wood.

Wipe on white gel stain to fill the pores. Continue wiping until the stain is completely removed from the surface.

Any wood that has visible pores is a candidate for a two-color finish. The basic process is to stain the wood one color and then fill the pores with another color. Using black and white on walnut is one of my favorites. Walnut blackens beautifully and whitening its pores creates delicate, graceful grain patterns. If your project is a lidded box or container, add interest by leaving the inside a natural walnut color.

The Technique

Finish-sand the workpiece to #220-grit, making sure that no sanding scratches remain. Then apply coats of India ink (**Photo 1**). India ink (available at www.dickblick.com) is an excellent material for ebonizing wood—it's easy to apply (wear gloves!), dries in less than half an hour and it won't fade. Up to three coats of ink may be required to achieve a uniform black surface. Let the ink dry completely before recoating.

Color the pores with white gel stain (**Photo 2**). Apply the gel stain with a clean white rag. Cover the piece evenly, then immediately wipe across the grain to pack the pores and completely remove the excess stain from the surface. Allow the stain to dry completely. If the pores aren't evenly filled, repeat the staining process.

Pale topcoats such as lacquer and blonde shellac help to preserve the white color in the pores. Do not use finishes that add an amber tone.

IRON & VINEGAR FINISH

Wiping a solution created by immersing steel wool in household vinegar onto woods that contain high amounts of tannic acid causes a chemical reaction that turns the wood black.

Woods that contain high amounts of tannic acid (such as white and red oak, cherry and walnut) can be ebonized by brushing on an acidic solution of iron and water. Depending on the species, the black color that results is likely to contain shades of brown, red or green. The coloring is usually uniform and consistent, without the blotching that sometimes occurs with oil-based wood stains. On oak and other woods that have large pores, the effect is particularly striking because the pores usually remain light in color.

The Technique

In a glass container, immerse a pad of steel wool (steel is mostly iron) in white vinegar from the grocery store. Screw on the lid and allow the steel wool and vinegar to react for at least a day. Shake the solution occasionally.

Finish-sand the piece you want to treat to #180-grit. The iron and vinegar solution contains lots of water, so it's a good idea to preemptively raise the grain. Dampen the sanded piece with water, let it dry and then sand lightly with #180-grit to remove the raised fibers.

Apply the solution with a cloth. There's no need to saturate the wood; a good dampening of the surface will do. On tannin-rich woods, the reaction can be instantaneous (**Photo 1**). Let the piece dry and then repeat the process. If the surface starts to feel rough, lightly sand between applications. Eventually the color will become uniformly dark; you can stop whenever you like, though. Sometimes a lighter shade of black looks great, so you may want to call it quits after one or two applications. When you're satisfied with the color, wipe down the wood with a damp cloth to remove any residue from the solution. Let the wood dry before applying a finish. Oil finishes, wiping varnishes and oil/varnish finishes enhance this coloring process.

BLEACHED FINISH

Remove the wood's natural color with two-part wood bleach. Several applications may be necessary.

Sand lightly to ghost back the walnut color. Then apply lacquer, wax or a clear water-based finish.

Bleaching often makes wood look lifeless, but I find its effect on walnut to be striking. I bleach walnut until it's nearly white and then lightly sand the surface to bring back the ghost of the original color.

The Technique

Two-part wood bleach from the paint or hardware store works the best. The two components are hydrogen peroxide and sodium hydroxide (lye), so be careful. Wear rubber gloves and eye protection and strictly follow the instructions.

Finish-sand the piece you want to bleach to #180-grit. Bleaching solutions contain lots of water, so it's a good idea to preemptively raise the grain. Dampen the sanded piece with water, let it dry and then sand lightly with #180-grit to remove the raised fibers.

Don your protective gear and follow the manufacturer's directions to apply the bleach. Some tell you to apply Part A, wait a few minutes, and then apply Part B; others tell you to mix the two parts together and apply the mixture. Wipe on a light coat of the solution (**Photo 1**). There's no need to saturate the wood; just dampen the surface. Let the piece dry. Then repeat the process—it usually takes seven or eight applications to bleach walnut white. When you're satisfied with the white color, wipe the piece with a damp cloth to remove any bleach residue. Then let it dry.

Sand lightly with #320- to #400-grit to gently ghost back the walnut color (**Photo 2**). Then apply lacquer, wax or a clear water-based finish to preserve the bleached look.

CHARRED FINISH

Ebonized wood often isn't pure black. Depending on the method used, the color usually includes shades of brown, red, purple or blue. A rich, deep, pure black is hard to achieve—unless you char the wood with a torch. This method works on any wood, although the results will look distinctly different from one species to another, depending on the character of the wood. Also, a uniform appearance is easier to achieve on face and edge grain than on end grain.

This finish is tricky because it's fairly easy to overheat the wood and cause it to crack or ignite. End grain surfaces and thin pieces (less than 3⁄8" thick) are especially vulnerable. It's a good idea to develop your charring technique by practicing on pieces that aren't "keepers."

The Technique

Finish-sand the piece you intend to char the same as for a clear finish—charring doesn't cover sanding marks or torn grain as well as you might think. Work in an area free of combustible materials. Wear a heavy protective glove to hold the piece while charring its surface, and use a propane torch with an adjustable flame so you can control the heat level.

The best approach is to char the wood to a uniform appearance in stages, stopping to brush off the burned debris between applications of heat. Start by lightly skimming the wood's surface with the flame (**Photo 1**). Make slightly overlapping passes and move the torch continuously. If the wood ignites, simply blow out the flame and let the wood cool before resuming.

After lightly charring the entire surface, let the piece cool, and then go over it with a soft metal brush to remove the ash and other completely burned debris (**Photo 2**). Brushing often accentuates the latewood, which is usually harder and more resistant to the flame than the earlywood. Torch and brush the entire surface a second time to make the charred color as uniform as possible.

The last step really brings out the rich, carbon-black color. After the piece has cooled, apply a coat of oil finish. I usually use boiled linseed oil or pure tung oil (both thinned by one-third with mineral spirits). Rags soaked with boiled linseed oil are flammable, so dispose of them properly.

BLENDED FINISH

1

Lightly scorch the wood with a torch. Move the flame continuously and quickly so the wood doesn't overheat.

2

Brush off the loose debris with a soft bristle brush. Repeat the process, if necessary, to create a consistent black color. Then apply an oil finish to intensify the black.

1

Mix equal parts pure tung oil, boiled linseed oil and gloss varnish. Premium ingredients are the key to this finish.

2

Apply an even coat of finish and then wipe the surface dry. The lustrous appearance develops as additional coats are applied.

One of my all-time favorite finishes for dark woods is a blend of high-quality oils and varnish—it's very similar to the finish espoused by master furniture maker Sam Maloof. This "hybrid" finish enriches the color of the wood, highlights the grain and gives the surface a beautiful luster without ever looking like built-up film finish. For my taste, however, its rather dark amber color adds too much yellow tone to light woods such as maple, holly and pine. This finish also dries very slowly.

The Technique

Premium ingredients are the key to this finish, which consists of equal parts 100% pure tung oil, boiled linseed oil and gloss varnish with a high resin content, such as Behlen Rockhard Table Top Varnish. This finish has a relatively short shelf life and eventually becomes unusable. So mix the three ingredients in small batches (**Photo 1**). To make this finish easier to use on large surfaces, add small amounts of mineral spirits, naphtha or turpentine to reduce its syrupy consistency.

Finish-sand the workpiece to #220-grit. Then wipe on the finish with a lint-free cloth (**Photo 2**). As soon as the piece is evenly coated, use a clean cloth to wipe the surface dry. After 30 minutes, wipe down the surface again to make absolutely sure that no residue remains. Move the piece to a dust-free area to dry. Note: The finish-soaked rags are likely to spontaneously combust, so dispose of them immediately and properly.

After two or three days, gently rub the piece with very fine abrasive wool (steel or synthetic) to remove any roughness, dust or residue from the surface. Then apply additional coats of finish, following the same procedure. The first few coats add little sheen, but eventually the finish will build and the luster will develop. The more coats you apply, the higher the sheen. Let the finish cure for several weeks before buffing to brighten the sheen, or rubbing to dull it. I usually buff my pieces with a soft towel or rub them with abrasive wool.

MARBLED FINISH

The process of floating colors on water, creating patterns and then capturing those patterns on paper or fabric probably originated somewhere in the Orient. Called "marbling," this process traveled westward through India, Persia and Turkey before arriving in Europe in the 17th century.

Marbling three-dimensional objects is less common, although it has appeared on vases, bowls, boxes and even fishing lures. Learning how to marble flat and rounded surfaces offers unique coloring opportunities for wood.

A variety of variables affects the process and its success, so it's best to learn the basics using sheets of 4" x 6" paper. Chemical contaminants, air pockets, dust, improperly mixed colors, temperature and humidity are all factors that can frustrate the marbling process.

Liquid acrylic paints, carrageenan, alum and other marbling supplies are available at art supply vendors such as www.wetpaintart.com. You'll need a blender to mix the carrageenan solution (it's food-safe, so no worries if you borrow Mom's), distilled water to thin the acrylic paints and glass jars (a pint jar for the alum solution and a gallon jar for the carrageenan solution). You'll also need a palette, a shallow tray, foam brushes, measuring spoons, rubber gloves, eyedroppers (one for each color, plus one for the distilled water), toothpicks, foam board, a bunch of 2" wide newspaper strips and practice paper (65 lb. to 75 lb. weight, and not too slick).

The Technique

Mix the carrageenan solution the day before you plan to marble (**Photo 1**). Follow directions on the bag, usually 2 tablespoons per gallon of distilled water. The solution has a two to three day shelf life, so prepare only as much as you'll need. Mix the solution in a blender for at least one minute. Then set it aside.

Finish-sand the pieces you plan to marble to #180-grit and preemptively raise the grain. Dampen the sanded pieces with water, let them dry and then sand lightly with #180-grit to remove the raised fibers.

The next day, mix the alum solution in very hot tap water, according to the package directions (usually 2 teaspoons per pint). Allow this mixture to cool before using it. In fact, make sure that everything you'll use (the solutions, the paints, the water, the pieces you plan to marble, etc.) is at the same (room) temperature.

1 Create a solution that's thick enough to float the acrylic paint used for marbling. Mix carrageenan and water in a blender. Let this solution sit overnight. Then pour it into a large shallow tray.

2 Coat the piece you plan to marble with a solution of alum to prime it for marbling. Don't touch the primed surface.

Find a dust-free area for marbling. Pour the carrageenan solution into the marbling tray to within about ¼" of the top. Use the foam brush to coat the paper (one side only) or the pieces that you plan to marble (completely) with the alum solution (**Photo 2**). The alum solution works like a paint primer to help the acrylic colors stick to the surface. It's a good idea to wear rubber gloves for this step because you should never touch the alum-treated surfaces with your bare hands—touching may affect the adhesion of the paint. Set the primed pieces aside to dry for about an hour.

Thin acrylic paint with distilled water so it will float on the surface of the carrageenan solution.

Clean the surface of the carrageenan solution just before adding the paint by skimming it with newspaper strips.

Gently squeeze drops of acrylic colors onto the carrageenan solution. The colors disperse across surface, forming rings.

Use a patterning tool to comb the layers of paint into interesting patterns. This tool is made from toothpicks and foam board.

Choose the acrylic colors you plan to use and thin them with distilled water to the consistency of whole milk so they'll float on the surface of the carrageenan solution. It's best to limit the number of colors for your first marbling attempts. One of my favorite combinations is simply black and white. An inexpensive plastic palette is great for mixing the paints (**Photo 3**). Shake the bottles to mix the paint and squeeze some of each color that you've chosen onto the palette. Then use eyedroppers to add the distilled water. Mix the thinned paint by stirring with a clean toothpick. Just before you drop the paint onto the carrageenan solution, skim its surface with a strip of newspaper (**Photo 4**). Skimming removes dust and other floating imperfections that can cause "bald spots" on the marbled surface.

Dropping the paint onto the carrageenan solution is one of the most critical—and unpredictable—steps in marbling. Using an eyedropper, gently squeeze a drop of color onto the center of the solution. Avoid creating bubbles when you squeeze. The drop should immediately disperse across the surface. If it sinks to the bottom of the tray, the paint is too thick—thin it further and try again. (Paint drops on the bottom will cause no harm, as marbling occurs on the surface.)

Using a different eyedropper, gently squeeze a drop of the next color onto the dispersed color. As each drop disperses, it creates a ring where it meets the previous drop. Alternate squeezing drops of different colors until the surface is covered with rings (**Photo 5**). You'll learn that some colors disperse more aggressively than others—experimenting with different colors is one good reason to practice on sheets of paper.

Creating patterns in the floating colors is, perhaps, the most mesmerizing step in the process. You simply pull patterning tools slowly and gently through the paint (**Photo 6**). Effective patterning tools can be made from nothing more than toothpicks and foam board. Varying the spacing between toothpicks is one simple way to modify the patterns you create.

7 Position the workpiece over a paint pattern that you like.

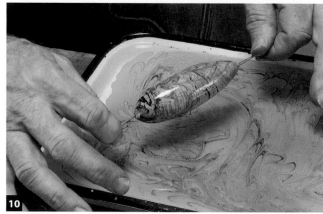

8 Gently dip the workpiece onto the paint and roll it across the pattern.

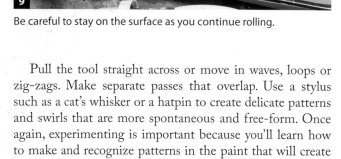

9 Be careful to stay on the surface as you continue rolling.

10 The goal is to cover the entire surface in one continuous motion.

Pull the tool straight across or move in waves, loops or zig-zags. Make separate passes that overlap. Use a stylus such as a cat's whisker or a hatpin to create delicate patterns and swirls that are more spontaneous and free-form. Once again, experimenting is important because you'll learn how to make and recognize patterns in the paint that will create interesting marbled effects on your projects.

Transferring a pattern that you like onto the workpiece is the pivotal step (**Photos 7-10**). Starting at one corner (or edge), barely dip the piece into the paint pattern. Then gently and continuously roll it across the painted surface to transfer the pattern. This sounds easy, but it's tricky, because it's easy to miss an area or submerge the piece too far. The goals are to stay on the surface and move fluidly. A two-dimensional object (paper or a flat board) is often much easier to successfully dip and roll than a three-dimensional one.

Pull the marbled piece from the tray and examine it to see what you've achieved. This is the moment of truth, when you learn if everything came together. I can say from experience that each success is thrilling—when I teach marbling wood to my friends, there's always lots of celebratory yelping at each "reveal."

Immediately dunk the marbled surface in a clean pail of water to rinse off any carrageenan and paint that didn't adhere. You can also hold the piece under a trickling faucet—just don't smack the surface with a high-pressure water stream.

What you see now is the permanent pattern. Don't touch the marbled surface at this point—it's far too tender. Set the piece aside to dry for at least an hour. If you intend to put a finish on top of the marbled surface, wait at least a week to allow the paint to cure. I've successfully used a variety of topcoats, including wax, shellac, water-based polyurethane and epoxy.

You can usually marble several items from the same batch of colors, but eventually the patterns will start to break down. When this happens, simply skim the surface three or four times with newspaper strips to remove the paint (use a fresh strip for each pass), and the carrageenan solution is ready for another round of marbling. When you're done for the day, thoroughly clean all of your equipment. I use only hot water for cleaning, as soap residue may cause problems in future marbling sessions.

CHAPTER THIRTEEN

Spalted Wood

Creating beauty from natural decay

SPALTED BIRCH BURL BOWL BY MARK LINDQUIST, 1987 COLLECTION OF ARTHUR AND JANE MASON

When wood is captured somewhere between the extremes of being completely sound and fully rotten, it can display magnificent beauty. The discoloration, prominent black lines and changes in texture that occur during the decaying process are known to woodworkers as spalting.

Spalting is a by-product of the rotting process that is carried out by a vast army of stain, mold and decay fungi. They are abundantly present in the air and soil, waiting for favorable conditions and a suitable host. Generally, wood moisture content of at least 25 percent, temperatures from about 40°–90°F, air and food (especially abundant in sap wood) are what the fungi need. A tree or branch freshly fallen onto a damp forest floor in warm weather is asking for it. Lighter colored woods offer the best canvas for nature's graphic work. Hard maple is viewed as the king of spalted woods, although sycamore, persimmon, red and white oak, elm, pecan, birch, buckeye, apple, magnolia, beech, holly, hackberry, box elder and the sapwoods of walnut and cocobolo are favored by woodworkers as well.

Sugar maple Homage Pot #1 by
David Elsworth, 1999

Spalted Soft Maple

Spalted Sycamore

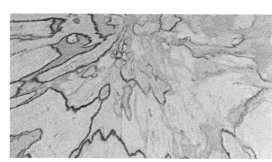

Spalted Holly (end-grain view)

Cabinet on Stand
English oak with
spalted bigleaf
maple panels by
Tim Patterson, stu-
dent, College of the
Redwoods, 1996

Where to Find Spalted Wood

You can purchase spalted wood—usually maple—from specialty lumber and mail order suppliers (see Sources, p. 62). Turning blocks are most easily found, but a few suppliers offer boards when they can get them.

Hunting spalted wood is like panning for gold—lots of searching for that one precious nugget. Logs rotting on the forest floor, dead limbs and entire dead standing trees are excellent sources. You can also hunt for hidden treasure at a community bone yard of removed trees, and don't overlook the bottom of your old firewood pile.

Make Your Own Spalted Wood

Woodworkers commonly use these methods to cause wood to spalt. They will work most effectively if the temperature is kept where the fungi will thrive, between 60° and 80°F. Monitor the spalting progress monthly—the optimal conditions you've created can make it happen fast.

- Place a freshly cut log section 2–3 ft. long upright on the bare ground. Put a shovel of dirt on the top end and cover it loosely with black plastic.
- Bury a log, freshly sawn green boards or green rough-turned bowls in damp sawdust containing pieces of rotten wood with active fungi. Keep the sawdust moist.
- Use plastic bags or plastic garbage cans to hold short sections of green wood or rough-turned bowls. Add-ing some soil or rotting sawdust may speed the process, although the fungi already present in the air or on the wood surface is probably enough to get it going. Leave the bags or cans with a small opening to allow for some air exchange.

How to Stabilize Spalted Wood

Remove those things the fungi need to grow, and you'll stop its progress. One method is to lower the wood's moisture content. Wood below 25-percent moisture content, when kept in low relative humidity, is not likely to decay or even stain. Accomplish this by air or kiln drying, placing smaller pieces in a microwave or finish turning if the piece was a rough-turned bowl. You can also raise or lower the wood's temperature. Spalting rarely occurs above 90°F and stops below 32°F. Some turners store blanks in a freezer prior to finish turning. Finally, you can restrict the air—no air, no decay. Logs submerged in water, for example, do not decompose from fungi. Tightly wrapping the wood in several layers of plastic will restrict the air and slow the growth of the fungi.

ELECTRON
MICROSCOPE
IMAGE BY ROBERT
BLANCHETTE,
UNIVERSITY OF
MINNESOTA

An active fungus colony surrounds itself with a chemical and physical barrier that defines its outer boundaries. Filaments of the fungus pack and swell in these regions and exude generous amounts of pigmented material that usually appear as black lines. The material in these "zone lines" protects the colony from attack by bacteria, insects, and other fungi, and assists in maintaining a desirably moist atmosphere. Inset: Electron microscope view of a fungus zone line in front of wood cell structures.

Claro walnut box inlaid with spalted end-grain sycamore, bookmatched to form a bird image by Del Stubbs, 1982

Working Properties

If you're lucky, you'll catch the spalting at the right time, before the cellular structure of the wood deteriorates, and you'll be able to work the piece without any trouble. Sometimes, however, the material will have areas that have become soft and punky. These areas have no strength and defy normal woodworking strategies. They will crumble, tear out in chunks or leave a wrinkled appearance when you try to cut or plane them. They refuse to be glued together, and leave you with a cratered, uneven surface when you try to sand. Though not suitable for joinery, these soft areas can often be stiffened enough to finish so the piece of wood can still be used decoratively.

You can saturate soft areas with a liquid hardener. Where the wood is only marginally soft, a spot coat or two of clear shellac or nitrocellulose sanding sealer may harden it sufficiently. A really punky spot will require cyanoacrylate (CA) glue (the thin, watery type) or a product made to stabilize rotten wood. There are a number of them sold as wood hardeners at hardware stores. It may take several generous applications to treat each bad spot. These hardeners are effective, but they have side effects. They fill the wood cells, so surfaces treated with them can't be glued and oil finishes don't take well because they can't penetrate. Solvent-based hardeners and CA glues darken the wood considerably. I like Protective Coatings Petrifier (see Sources, p. 62). It's a water-based hardener that doesn't discolor the wood, yet seals and stiffens effectively. It's an excellent choice for troublesome soft spots.

You should be able to work the stiffened surface with edge tools—make very light cuts—or with abrasives, taking care to provide a firm, flat backing for the sandpaper. Some turners use body grinders or stiffbacked sanding discs and work the piece while it's spinning on the lathe. For flat lumber, an abrasive planer is an excellent option, followed by a random orbit or pad sander. If you sand by hand, use a sanding block to give firm support to the paper.

Finishing

You are likely to encounter three problems when you finish spalted wood: Splotching, yellowing and excessive darkening. The whiter woods—which usually have the most dramatic examples of spalting—can

MORRIS CHAIR BY RICH GOTZ, 1998

WORKING SPALTED WOOD SAFELY

There is anecdotal and some medical evidence that substances from decaying wood are a health threat. Allergic reactions and some serious lung diseases have been traced to spores and fungi that inhabit rotting wood. The effect on an individual woodworker depends on his or her tolerance to the spores and fungi, the concentration of them in the environment and the length of exposure. Persons with weakened immune systems, lung illnesses or who show signs of allergic reactions to the spalted wood should avoid the material altogether. One must err on the side of caution when working spalted wood. Freshly sawn green material with active spores and fungi, or even air-dried material, is potentially the most hazardous. Kiln drying, by turning up the heat and driving out the moisture, will actually kill both fungi and spores. To avoid breathing spalted wood dust, I strongly recommend that you wear a respirator—not a nuisance mask—and have an effective point-of-origin dust collection system or a self-contained air filtration helmet. Avoid prolonged contact with your skin, and clean your work area thoroughly following any work with spalted wood.

Worm-spalted red maple bowl by Alan Lacer, 1998

Typical spalting differs from worm spalt, where the worm hole allows the fungus to enter and work from the inside out.

turn quite yellow with certain finishes, and because the soft areas act like end-grain or even a sponge, splotching or excessive darkening can result unless the piece is sealed first.

An effective weapon against splotching is clear, dewaxed shellac used as a sealer. (Spray cans of shellac are thinned and dewaxed.) Cover the entire piece with a thin coat and let it dry. Then recoat dull-looking areas until all surfaces have a uniform sheen. You can use almost any finish as a topcoat over dewaxed shellac after it's been sanded.

To minimize yellowing and darkening, use a surface film finish like clear shellac or lacquer. Waterborne finishes dry clear and don't yellow with age. If the piece is primarily decorative and has few, if any, soft areas, clear wax is appropriate.

If you don't mind the yellowing and darkening, use your favorite oil finish, but be prepared to make many applications to the softer areas. Experience has taught me that an oil-finished spalted piece will appear rather muddy and uneven at first, but will look better as the finish cures, which can take weeks or even months. Some oil finishes (such as General Finishes Sealacell Step 1, see Sources, below) are essentially a thinned, light-colored varnish, and will not yellow as much.

If you are looking for a challenge, and effects that often surpass the wildest woods from the tropics, spalted wood may be your ticket. Each block of wood has its own unique properties that must be judged and worked on its own terms. Use spalted wood and your work will never go unnoticed. Use it well, and you'll produce a real showstopper.

SOURCES ☙ **FLAT MATERIAL SUPPLIERS:** Search the web for sources of spalted wood for sale. A number of products for rotting wood are readily found in building centers, hardware stores and on the internet. Products such as P.C. Petrifier and Minwax's Wood Hardener work well on soft areas of spalted wood, as does a thin CA glue. **FOR FURTHER READING:** "Sculpting Wood" by Mark Lindquist, 1986, Worcester, Mass.; Davis Publications; $32.50; (800) 533-2847. Mark and his father Mel have been pioneers in working spalted wood and in popularizing its use as a decorative material. ☙ "Understanding Wood" by Bruce Hoadley, 1980, Newtown, Conn.; Taunton Press; $34.95; (800) 888-8286. ☙

CHAPTER FOURTEEN

French Polishing

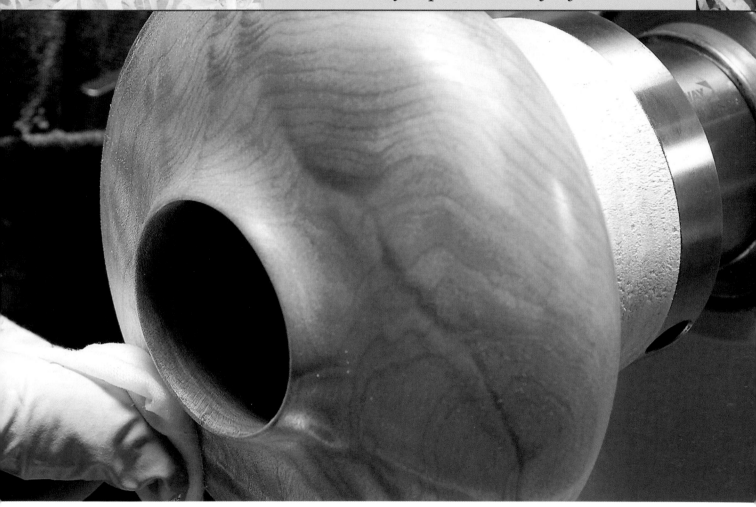

Six easy steps to a beautiful finish

French polish adds extraordinary depth to gorgeous wood. This finish is perfect for bowls, vessels, lamps and other turnings that aren't handled often or are exposed to moisture, alcohol or heat. It's easy to apply: Just hold a cloth moistened with the finish directly to your project as it spins on the lathe. What is French polish? It's simply shellac and a little oil applied with a pad. The oil acts as a lubricant when you apply the finish. French polish is available as commercially made products, also labeled as padding lacquer or friction polish, but I prefer to make my own from flakes, which guarantees freshness. You can achieve a variety of effects because shellac is available in a range of colors (see "Buying Shellac," page 64). Here's how you can mix your own French polish, choose different colors, apply it and rub it out.

BUYING SHELLAC

Shellac comes in a number of different colors, making it a versatile finish. You can use lighter shades of shellac to preserve natural color or use dark shades to add a warm color. I prefer to use lighter shades on light-colored woods and darker shades on dark woods. Shellac isn't darkened by adding pigment. Shellac is made from a resin that's naturally dark; bleaching the resin produces different grades of clearer finishes. Shellac is available in dried-flake form in a range of reddish brown, orange, yellow and pale blond colors (see Sources, page 65). Flakes have an extremely long shelf life. You can make any quantity of shellac by mixing the flakes with denatured alcohol. Shellac is also available at hardware stores in premixed form. Its shelf life is one to three years. Be sure to check the freshness date on the can, because aged shellac won't harden properly. Premixed shellac is only available in clear or amber colors.

Sand with Fine Grits

Thoroughly sand all surfaces of your project to eliminate torn grain, spirals and ridges. Start with #120-grit and progress through #150-, #180- and #220-grit sandpaper (**Photo 1**). If sanding scratches still show, continue with #320- or #400-grit sandpaper. Maple and cherry often require these finer grits. After sanding, remove the dust using an alcohol-moistened paper towel.

Mix the French Polish

You can use shellac flakes or premixed liquid shellac to make French polish. Either way, your goal is to make a 1-½-lb. cut, which is the equivalent of mixing 1-½ lbs. of flakes with 1 gal. of denatured alcohol. That's far too much finish for most projects, however. If you use flakes, dissolve 1-½ oz. of flakes with 1 cup of denatured alcohol. Premixed liquid shellac comes in a 3-lb. cut. To make approximately a 1-½ lb. cut, thin it with an equal amount of denatured alcohol.

The final ingredient of French polish is an oil, which acts a lubricant to prevent your applicator cloth from dragging or sticking. Add 1 tablespoon of mineral oil for every 3 liquid oz. of 1-½-lb.-cut shellac (**Photo 2**).

Apply the Finish

Adjust your lathe to run at a moderate speed, about 500 to 800 rpm, slower for large-diameter turnings. Make an applicator for applying the French polish from a densely woven, soft, white cotton cloth that has been washed many times to remove all lint. Soften the pad with alcohol before dipping it into the French polish.

Shake the French polish to suspend the oil, as though it were an oil-and-vinegar salad dressing. Turn on the lathe, saturate the cloth pad and flow on the finish (**Photo 3**). If the cloth grabs, add a half teaspoon of oil. Let this coat dry for 30 minutes before you sand it. The surface will feel dry right away, but don't grow impatient. If you rush it, the next coat will dissolve the first and you'll get nowhere in a hurry.-

Sand the first coat with #400-grit sandpaper and remove the sanding dust. Subsequent coats require less sanding. A synthetic sanding pad is all you need to achieve a smooth surface for the final coats (**Photo 4**).

Apply five or six coats. It's better to apply a number of light coats rather than a few heavy coats. Taking this approach prevents ridges or runs in the finish. Soften your cloth pad before each coat (**Photo 5**). Wait at least 30 minutes between coats. If your shop cools below 70°F, extend the waiting period another 15 minutes or so. Don't apply the finish in temperatures below 55°F.

Buff the Finish

After the last coat, you can leave the polish as is for a high luster. If you prefer to soften the luster, let it dry several days and rub it out with a finishing compound or fine abrasives (**Photo 6**). I like to use automotive polishing compound for this process because it costs little, is readily available and does a great job. Apply the compound with a soft cloth. Work gently until you get the look you're after. If the compound gets trapped in the pores, wash it off with naphtha or mineral spirits. Neither will harm the finish.

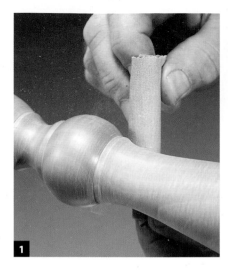

1

Sand your piece to eliminate flaws and sanding rings. Remove sanding dust using a paper towel moistened with denatured alcohol held against the workpiece while it's spinning.

2

French polish is a mixture of shellac and oil. Little oil is needed; it acts as a lubricant for the shellac.

AMBER SHELLAC

3

Liberally apply French polish from a moistened cloth to the spinning workpiece. Wait at least 30 minutes between coats.

4

Sand between coats using a fine synthetic sanding pad. Five or six coats produce a beautiful, deep finish. Amber shellac adds a warm tone to this walnut leg.

5

Your cloth will stiffen between coats. Soften the cloth by moistening it with denatured alcohol and then dip in the French polish.

6

French polish is naturally glossy. Rub out the finish with automotive polishing compound or fine abrasives if you want a soft luster instead.

SOURCES Shellac.Net, www.shellac.net Shellac flakes, $26.60 t0 $39.90 per pound. • Klingspor, (800) 228-0000, www.woodworking-shop.com Synthetic steel wool, ultra fine10 pack, #NW06254, $9. • Abralon synthetic sanding pads,500 grit, #1778, $3.99 ea; 1,000 grit, #1779, $3.49 ea.

PROJECTS

CHAPTER FIFTEEN

PROJECT 1 Game Call

Atrue American folk object, the game call gained enormous popularity in the late 19th century, when it became part and parcel of hunting. Poke around a bit and you'll find game calls for geese, turkeys, doves, crows, squirrels and even coyotes. But in all its many forms, the classic game call is the duck call.

Whether you hunt with a gun or a camera, a game call is a wonderful turning project. The parts that make the sound (called the "guts") are available in kit form or as separate parts (see Sources, page 71), so once you're set up for drilling and turning, it's easy to produce a number of calls in a short time. Play with different shapes or explore your own theories about dimensions and sound—I guarantee you'll have fun. But before you commit to a valuable piece of wood for that heirloom call, it's a good idea to work out the basic drilling, chucking, shaping and fitting, using blanks of common wood such as poplar.

Stuff You'll Need

In addition to the guts, you'll need two blanks of wood (**Photo 1**; see Sources). You can use contrasting woods or cut both blanks from one long piece. Any good, dry wood will do. Walnut is a popular choice (historically and with contemporary makers), and it's usually readily available. The recent development of resin-injected woods commonly used in pen-making has created a material not so prone to dimensional changes due to exposure to moisture—an unavoidable occurrence with mouth-blown calls.

You'll also need a 2" x 2" x 4" blank of poplar or other soft wood to create two jam chucks, and basic spindle-turning tools, including a spindle roughing gouge, a skew chisel, ¼" and ⅜" detail/spindle gouges and standard

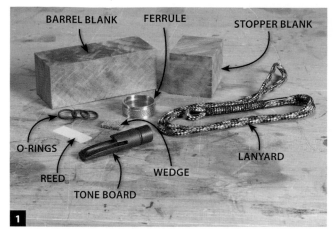

1 Cut blanks for the call's wooden parts. You'll also need three O-rings and the "guts"—the parts that create the sound. A ferrule and lanyard are optional.

2 Drill a hole through the blank that will be the call's barrel. This requires a scroll chuck to hold the blank and a drill chuck to hold the Forstner bit and its extension.

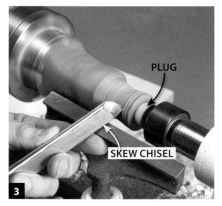

3 Reduce the diameter at the end of the barrel and add details after installing a tapered plug in the hole and engaging the tailstock. This end will be the mouthpiece.

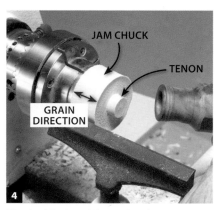

4 Flip the blank end-for-end and mount it on a jam chuck so you can work the other end. The hole in the barrel snugly fits a tenon turned on the jam chuck.

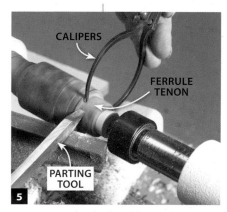

5 Turn a tenon for the ferrule, a metal band used to reinforce the joint between the call's two wooden parts. Ferrules commonly appear on older calls, but including one is optional.

and thin-kerf parting tools. Next on the list are a four-jaw scroll chuck and a drill chuck (a keyed chuck that mounts in the lathe's tailstock), ⅝" and ⅞" Forstner-style drill bits and E-6000 adhesive (see Sources). A lanyard and a ferrule are optional, but you'll definitely need O-rings if they don't come with the guts parts that you order (see Sources).

The Guts Rule

The guts play an important role in determining a call's diameter, because they mount in a hole drilled through one part (the stopper). As the guts come in different styles and sizes, this hole must be sized to fit. A larger hole drilled through the other part (the barrel) houses a tenon turned on the stopper. The call has to be long enough to house the guts; beyond that, its length can vary.

The call shown here is sized to house Arkansas-style single-reed guts, which require a ⅝" bore. I used a pair of 1¾" x 1¾" blanks to make this call: one 2" long with a ⅝" bore (for the stopper) and one 4" long with a ⅞" bore (for the barrel).

Turn the Barrel

The first step is to drill a centered ⅞" dia. hole all the way through the barrel blank, using the lathe or a drill press. To drill the hole on the lathe, mount the blank in a scroll chuck (**Photo 2**). The blank can be mounted square (as shown) or on a shouldered tenon. (This tenon has to be turned first, of course, after mounting the blank between centers.)

Drill the hole with a Forstner bit and a drill chuck. To keep from building up excessive heat, it's best to use a high-speed steel (HSS) or carbide-edged bit. Most of these bits are short, so you'll probably need a bit extension. Drill slowly and frequently back the bit out of the cut to clear the chips.

Next, shape the barrel's mouthpiece (**Photo 3**). Reduce the diameter to about 1¼". Flatten the end to facilitate mounting it for the next step and sand everything smooth—don't leave any sharp edges where your mouth will contact the call.

Remove the barrel and mount a 2" long poplar waste block in the scroll chuck, with its grain running parallel to the lathe bed. Turn a tenon on the waste block that's slightly

Complete the barrel by connecting the two ends. If you decide not to add a ferrule, leave extra thickness at the joint to keep the wood from splitting.

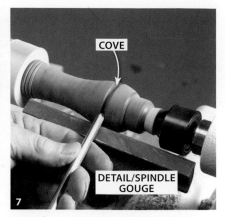

Cut a cove to house the lanyard. First, cut a shallow groove with a thin-kerf parting tool. Then use a small detail/spindle gouge to form the cove.

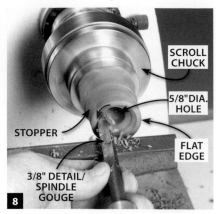

Flare the end of the call's stopper after mounting it and drilling through it, as for the barrel. Leave the edge flat for mounting on the jam chuck. This end sounds the call.

larger than the hole drilled through the barrel and about 1" long. Then carefully reduce its diameter to obtain a jam fit with the barrel (**Photo 4**). The fit should be tight enough to hold the barrel for turning but loose enough to allow it to be easily removed after it's been turned.

To support the barrel's free end, turn a short, tapered plug to fit inside its drilled hole and bring up the tailstock. (Another option is to install a live center with a cone-type point in the tailstock.)

The portion where the barrel fits onto the stopper requires special attention, because it may split if the parts swell or if the barrel takes too much force to install. The solutions are to leave this portion extra-thick or to install a metal ferrule to reinforce the joint (**Photo 5**). Size a tenon to fit the ferrule using outside calipers. Aim for a push-on fit and plan to glue on the ferrule using E-6000, a rubber-based adhesive that bonds permanently but stays flexible.

The barrel's final shape is up to you, but a curved form makes the call easy to hold (**Photo 6**). Although not essential, a lanyard reduces the chance of losing the call and frees up both hands for those moments of truth (**Photo 7**). Complete the barrel by finish-sanding it to #220-grit (or #320-grit if the #220-grit scratches remain visible).

Turn the Stopper

Drill a centered hole through the 2" blank as before, but use a ⅝" Forstner bit to match the hole to the Arkansas-style guts we've chosen. The tailstock end of this blank will be the exit for sound, so it's often flared like a horn for greater volume—in theory, anyway (**Photo 8**). Turn this end of the stopper about one-quarter of the way up the outside.

Remount the jam chuck you used for the barrel and resize its tenon to fit the smaller hole in the stopper. If the end of the stopper has been flared, you may have to lengthen the tenon to create a secure fit.

Install the stopper on the jam chuck and bring up the tailstock for additional support. Then turn a tenon to fit in-

side the barrel, with shallow grooves for two O-rings (**Photo 9**). Make the tenon about 1" long and size its diameter for a very slightly loose fit into the barrel. Space the grooves about ½" apart.

The O-rings may be slightly wider than the parting tool; if so, make a second cut to widen each groove. The depth of the grooves is also critical, as the O-rings must protrude slightly above the tenon to achieve an airtight fit with the barrel—but not so tight that the pieces have to be forced hard together (**Photo 10**).

Shape the tenon's shoulder to fit nicely against the barrel. Then finish-turn the outside of the stopper (**Photo 11**). Complete the job by finish-sanding the stopper to the same grit as the barrel.

Fowl-weather Finish

As moisture is a real enemy, whether from blowing the call or from the environment (cold and wet is often the norm for duck hunting), it's imperative to apply a moisture-resistant finish on both the inside and the outside of the call. Some makers soak their calls in linseed oil. I prefer to use a film-forming finish. Any high-quality varnish that's thin enough for wiping will work. I apply four coats of Waterlox Marine Finish, using a small brush to get inside the barrel. Allow the parts to dry for several days before assembling the call.

Get Quacking

Assemble the guts (the third O-ring fits in a groove on the tone board) and install them in the stopper (**Photo 12**). Use a bit of E-6000 adhesive, if necessary. Install the barrel and give the call a couple blasts. Does it sound like a duck? You can alter the sound by adjusting the reed and wedge on the tone board, but my advice is to ask someone familiar with duck calling to assist you with the call's initial "tuning" and to teach you some basic calls. That's much more fun than purchasing an instructional duck call CD.

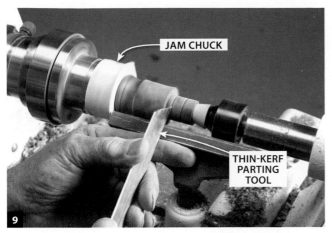

9 Cut shallow grooves for the O-rings after flipping the stopper, mounting it on a jam chuck and turning a tenon that's slightly smaller than the hole in the barrel.

JAM CHUCK

THIN-KERF PARTING TOOL

10 Install the O-rings to create an airtight fit with the barrel that's neither too tight nor too loose. This is a critical step! Adjust the fit by carefully increasing the depth of the O-ring grooves.

O-RING

11 Shape the middle section to complete the stopper. The end of this stopper flares like a horn on the outside to match the flared shape cut on the inside.

DETAIL/ SPINDLE GOUGE

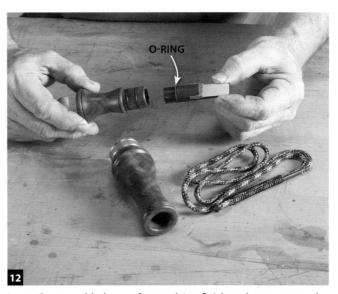

12 Insert the assembled guts after applying finish to the stopper and barrel and allowing it to thoroughly dry. Then install the barrel, add the lanyard and start quacking!

O-RING

SOURCES Web Foot Custom Calls, webfootcustomcalls.com, Duck Call Guts, #DS01, $4.10 ea. ☺ Hut Products, hutproducts.com, 800-547-5461, Deluxe Single Lanyard, #3002, $0.89 each, Dymondwood Duck Call Kit #3135 $12.99 ea.; O-rings, 10-pack, #3003, $0.99. ☺ Tho Game Calls, thogamecallsstore.com, 603-867-1018, Stippled Brass Band (Ferrule), 1-¼" OD x ½" wide, $5.99 each. ☺ Woodcraft Supply, woodcraft.com, 800-225-1153, E-6000 Adhesive, 3.7 oz. tube, #147109A, $6.50; Waterlox Marine Finish, 1 quart, #85W54, $42.50. ☺ Craft Supplies, woodturnerscatalog.com, 800 551 8876, HSS Forstner bits, 5/8" #979-310 $28.50, 7/8" bit #979-310 $30.90, bit extension in 3.5" #979-311 $26.75, No. 2MT adapter for these bits (replaces a Jacobs style chuck) #979-312 $43.25, or a Keyless drill chuck #104-578 $45.50, Oneway Talon Scroll Chuck #103-647 $234.95. ☺

CHAPTER SIXTEEN

PROJECT 2 — Natural-Edge Bowl

A project straight from the tree

A natural-edge bowl looks like it came straight from the tree. It's still got the bark on, and you can clearly see all the tree's growth rings. It's a project that gets you close to real, living wood.

All you need is a chainsaw (you can rent one for about $60 a day), a band saw, a standard lathe and two turning tools. You'll have to find a local source of winter-cut wood, or you can raid your own backyard or your neighbor's firewood pile. (The bark will stay on wood cut in the winter, but may fall off wood cut at other times of the year.) Before you turn a natural-edge bowl you should have some experience turning a "normal" bowl with a flat top because the uneven rim of a natural-edge bowl makes this turning project a bit trickier (see Learning From Mistakes, page 77).

For a heck of a good time at the lathe, sharpen your gouges and follow the steps on the following pages. When you've completed turning your bowl, put it in a double-thickness paper bag and let it sit for a week or two so it dries slowly. Then complete the sanding.

My favorite finish is wax or no finish at all. I feel that natural, unfinished wood best complements the bark edge. But to show off spectacular wood or protect the bowl from dirt and stains, use an oil finish. Avoid getting finish on the rough upper surface of the bark.

1

Visualize your bowl inside a log before sawing the log to length. Look for unusual shapes in the bark that may be included in the bowl's rim, but stay away from knots. They may check or distort your bowl.

END CHECKS

PITH

2

Crosscut the log with a chainsaw. Cradle the log in a thick bed of wood chips for safety. This way the log won't roll and your saw won't bite into the ground. First, cut off a thin slice to eliminate all the end checks. Then cut a blank that's about 1". longer than the diameter of the log. A bow saw will do, but you'll work up a good sweat! Caution: Chainsaws can be dangerous! Please follow all safety instructions. For more information, see Sources, page 77.

RISER BLOCK

3

Cut the log through the pith, on the bandsaw. If the pith is off center, you'll end up with two different-sized blanks, but that's OK. Feed the log fairly slowly. Use a 3/8" or ½", 4-tpi skip-tooth blade (see Sources). It may seem impossible, but a regular bandsaw can actually make this cut! However, you'll need a riser block to handle logs longer than 6".

TEMPLATE

4

Saw a round blank from the split log. First, nail a wooden template to the top of the log to guide your cut. Keep your fingers out of harm's way by standing to the side of the saw.

3" DIA. FACEPLATE

5

Fasten a faceplate to the bottom of the blank. You can find the approximate center of the blank with the template in Photo 4. Center the faceplate within a compass circle and fasten it with #12 sheet-metal screws. Unlike brittle drywall screws, they're unlikely to snap off when the blank is spinning on the lathe.

LIVE CENTER

6

Push the tailstock up against the top of the bowl. I like using a live center because it doesn't require lubrication, but a dead center works as well. Drive the point of the live center deep into the blank. It must penetrate the bark and bite into solid wood. Rotate the uneven blank by hand to make sure your tool rest is out of the way. Note: A heavy, out-of-round blank will cause your lathe to shake, but a standard-size machine can handle it. Set your lathe to its slowest speed and weigh it down with sandbags.

TURNING GREEN WOOD

Welcome to a whole different world from working with kiln-dried wood. Turning green wood like this is a completely different experience than turning spindles and knobs.

Here's what makes turning green wood so enjoyable:

- It's easy to cut. You'll be covered with long ribbons of shavings in no time. And your cutting edges last longer.

- It's fast. One evening is all you'll need to make one of these bowls.

- It's cheap. Almost any kind of wood will do (except softwoods like pine, which fuzz up). Forage through your wood lot or call a local tree trimmer. The stuff's out there at no cost.

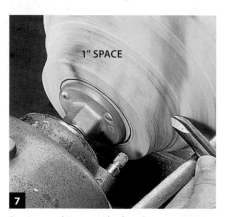

1" SPACE

7

Begin roughing out the bowl with a ½". bowl gouge, the tool you'll use for almost the whole project. First remove waste at the bottom third of the blank, cutting uphill, to help balance it. Stop about 1". above the rim of the faceplate.

IRISH GRIND BEVEL

I prefer the aggressive cut of an Irish grind on my bowl gouge, but it takes practice to use. With an Irish grind, the bevel is ground way back on the sides. Many turners re-grind standard bowl gouges to this shape (at left), but you can buy a new gouge with an Irish grind (see Sources).

8

Establish the diameter of the bowl's top. Begin each cut in the air, without touching wood, to the right of the top. Then sweep the gouge to the left. If you sweep right, you run the risk of lifting off the bark. Stop the lathe to make sure you've turned below the bandsaw cuts all the way around the blank.

WASTE

9

Shape the base of the bowl. Direct your gouge to cut from the top of the bowl down into the middle of the blank, creating a valley. The wood to the left of the valley supports the bowl for now, but is essentially waste. Now that the blank is turned completely round and is balanced, reduce the diameter of this waste so it's about ½" larger than the faceplate.

10

Smooth the side of the bowl with a light shear-scraping cut. This finishing cut avoids lifting the bark when done with a bowl gouge that has an Irish grind. Otherwise, take very light cuts with a scraper.

TIP Consolidate loose bark, should you have any, with cyanoacrylate (CA) glue (see Sources). It's the best glue to use on wet, green wood. It dries in a minute so you can go right back to turning. Use thin CA glue for flaking bark and medium CA glue for filling the gaps among loose chunks.

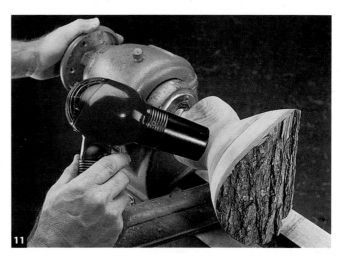

11

Heat the outside of the bowl with a hair dryer. Rotate the bowl by hand. After a couple of minutes the wood is dry to the touch and ready to sand. Green wood will load fine sandpaper if it's not lightly dried like this first.

12 Power sand the outside of the bowl. Move the tool rest out of the way, then go through #120-, #150-, and #180-grit paper. You can sand by hand, but it's much slower.

13 Hollow the inside of the bowl, starting at the center. Gradually enlarge the diameter of the hollow. Leave the center of the bowl fairly shallow for now. Note: This is a job suited only for a long-handled, sturdy bowl gouge because the cutting edge hangs far over the tool rest (see Sources).

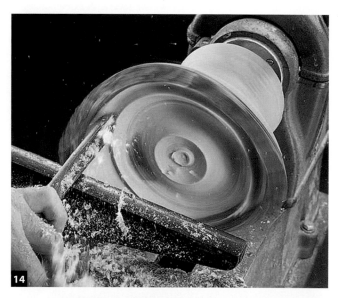

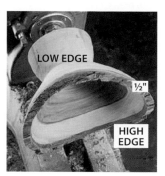

Turn the rim and wall of the bowl about ½-in. thick. Cut the saddle-shaped rim in two stages. First, establish the width of the rim's high edge. Second, push your gouge deeper into the bowl to cut the low edge. You'll have to stop the lathe now and then to see if the entire rim is the same width. Finish hollowing the inside of the bowl. I leave it unsanded for now and wait until after the bowl is completed and air-dried, then I sand with small sanding discs mounted on a drill and also by hand.

14

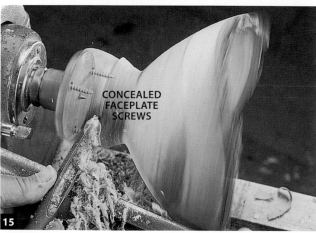

15 Reduce the base of the bowl until it's about the same diameter as the faceplate. That's far enough, because the last thing you want to do is inadvertently hit one of the faceplate screws buried in the waste! Remove the bowl using the following tip.

CONCEALED FACEPLATE SCREWS

TIP

DEAD CENTER

Remove the bowl from the lathe and mark its center. Although there are many different methods, one surefire way is to put a dead center in the headstock and screw the bowl back on for a few revolutions. Dimple the bottom of the bowl with the point of the dead center, then unscrew the faceplate.

LEARNING FROM MISTAKES

Dang it! I couldn't get a rim of equal thickness on my first natural-edge bowl. I made the lower rim (at A) too thin and then tried to go back and cut the upper rim (at B) thinner to match it. But I couldn't get a smooth cut because the upper rim fluttered and vibrated. What was going on? I took an old turner's advice and sawed the bowl in half. He said that if I looked at a cross-section of my bowl I would figure it out. He was right! I saw that consistent wall thickness is the key. A lower rim that's too thin leaves the upper rim with little support, and that's why it fluttered. I've learned to stop the lathe often as I gradually cut the lower rim. I'm very careful not to take too much off. Only when the bowl is stopped can I actually see and compare the widths of both rims.

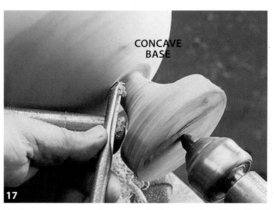

Re-mount the bowl with a reverse-chucking jig made from glued-up scrap. Round the end of the scrap block to fit the bowl. The glued-on, 1/8-in.-thick router mat provides enough friction to spin the bowl without marring its inside surface.

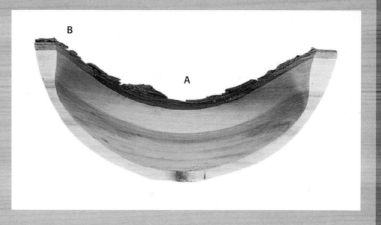

Undercut a concave base on the bowl so it will sit flat. Switch to a 3/8-in. detail gouge, take light shavings and reduce the neck of the waste block to about 3/4-in. diameter. Remove the bowl from the lathe.

Knock off the waste block with a sharp blow from your gouge handle. The block easily snaps off because the grain is very weak. Clean up the bottom of the bowl with a carving gouge and you're done!

SOURCES Packard Woodworks, (800) 683-8876, www.packardwoodworks.com, 1/2 bowl gouge standard grind #100122 $65; Side Grind 1/2" bowl gouge #100180 $93; 3/8" detail gouge #100108 $38.50; Cyanoacrylate glue: #121001 Thin Hot Stuff $10 for 2 oz; #121002 Medium Hot Stuff $10 for 2 oz. ⊙ Woodworker's Supply (800) 645-9292 www.woodworker.com, 1/2" 4-tpi skip-tooth bandsaw blades, prices vary according to length. Highland Woodworking (800) 241-6748 www.highlandwoodworking.com

CHAPTER SEVENTEEN

PROJECT 3 Green Wood Bowl

How to turn freshly cut wood

Making a functional object directly from raw material in its natural state is incredibly satisfying. Just ask any potter. For woodworkers, green woodturning captures that feeling. You literally start with a log and end up with a beautiful bowl. If you've never turned green wood before, you're in for a treat. Green wood is easier to turn than kiln-dried wood. It cuts cleaner and produces very little dust. To top it off, the wood itself often costs nothing.

Cut the log along the marked line. A ½" wide, 3 to 4 tpi skip tooth blade is a good choice for a 14" bandsaw with riser blocks. If the log is too big to cut on your bandsaw, use your chainsaw or split the log with a wedge.

Cut green bowl blanks in lengths that are equal to the log's diameter, plus one inch. Start by lopping off a short section to eliminate any end checks. Mark a line through the pith where the log will be split into two bowl blanks.

Material

The process works best if the wood is wet and freshly cut. Storm downed trees, areas being cleared for development and tree service dumping sites (often called "bone yards") are all good sources of green wood. For ease of handling and cutting, choose logs or limbs that are smaller in diameter than your lathe's swing. Almost any species is worth trying, but here are some of my favorites: maple, walnut, butternut, ash, birch, locust, white oak, cherry, beech, Osage orange, and pear. My rule for green bowls is to try whatever is locally available—you may be pleasantly surprised by the abundance of material in your own backyard.

Tools and Supplies:

- ½" bowl gouge (from a ⅝" rod)
- 1-¼" to 1-½" heavy scraper (usually ⅜" thick)
- Jacobs style chuck
- A ⅝" to 1" bit
- Double ended calipers
- Vernier style caliper
- Sanding discs and soft pads (5" and 2" dia.)
- Flexible shaft tool or flexible shaft for a drill
- ⅛" router mat material
- CA glue

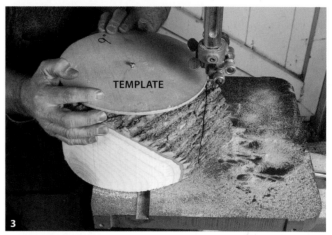

Round up the blank using a ¼" plywood template as a guide. I keep a set of these discs in ½" increments. Simply nail the template on the bark edge and follow the shape.

Locate the faceplate on the blank's flat surface. This will eventually be the inside of the bowl. Center the round template on the blank and use the nail hole to mark the center. Then draw a circle that's slightly larger than the faceplate's diameter.

5 Screw the faceplate into what will be the opening of the bowl. The screws should penetrate the wood at least 1" for initial rough turning.

6 Rough the bowl with a bowl gouge. Point the flute in the direction of cut and keep the bevel rubbing on the wood. The tailstock adds support.

7 Remove the tailstock and flatten the bowl's bottom with a scraper. The bottom must be at least 1" larger than the faceplate.

8 Draw a series of circles with a pencil to aid in mounting the faceplate for the next step. One of the circles will be close enough to the size of your faceplate to center it. Remove the bowl and remount the faceplate on the base.

9 The bowl is now mounted with the base towards the headstock. Cut the bowl's height so the pith is removed. Use the gouge in a scraping fashion with the bevel facing away from the wood and the bottom edge scraping.

Safety First!

Wet logs weigh a lot! You don't want one flying off the lathe. Use a faceplate that's made from one piece of steel and is at least ⅜" thick at the screw hole flange. For bowls less than 10 inches in diameter, I use a 6-hole, 3"-diameter faceplate. The type of screw is also critical: Use #12 sheet metal screws. Avoid dry wall, deck and wood screws. Be sure the faceplate sits flat on the log's surface—if it doesn't, use a small hand plane across the grain to create the desired fit. Last but not least, be sure to wear a full-face shield—goggles are not sufficient for bowl turning.

Avoid a Splintered Rim

If you run the tool off the ends of the blank into air (most commonly at the rim area), the fibers will break off along the edge—much like sawing through a board that is not supported on the back side of the cut. Solution: Work from air into the wood for about the first 1" or so of material. (**Photo 11**)

10 Begin the final shaping. Establish a base with enough waste for the screws. Concentrate on perfecting the upper two-thirds of the bowl. Work from small to large diameters to reduce tearout.

11 Finish with a shear-cut. Place the gouge high on the piece and keep the bevel rubbing. You can tell a good shear cut by the thin, wispy curls of wood. Work up to an inch of the rim, then from air into the rim.

Start the hollowing process by drilling out the center of the bowl. The hole gives a place for the tool to end each cut and eliminates the need to constantly check the depth. Use a 5/8"–1"-dia. bit mounted in a Jacobs-style chuck. Drill to a depth that is ½" less than the finished depth will be.

Hollow the bowl's interior. Start an inch or so back from the drilled hole. Roll the tool on its side to about a 45° angle and cut with the bevel rubbing. Work from large to small diameters. Continue this backing up process until the walls are 3/8"–½" thick.

Shape the rim with a scraper before you finish hollowing. Green bowls change shape rapidly once they are hollowed, making the rim nearly impossible to shape later. Here, I'm rolling the rim to round it like a bead.

Establish the bowl's final depth with a heavy scraper. Use the scraper for the bottom and at the transition a little up the sides. Scrapers cut poorly across end grain, so rely on the gouge for cutting the bowl's sides.

Remove the extra material around the faceplate and base of the bowl. Then, remove the bowl from the lathe—but don't unscrew the faceplate just yet.

Reverse chucking is a way to mount the bowl backwards in order to finish off the underside of the base. Start by mounting a dead center in the headstock. Then screw the bowl back on the lathe so the pin marks the center of the base. Remove the bowl from the lathe and unscrew the faceplate.

Mount a 2" thick block of wood to your faceplate. True the sides and flatten the face. Slightly round the corners where the sides meet the face.

Glue a piece of router anti-slip pad to the chuck. I use CA glue on the wood and an accelerator on the rubber for an instant bond. The inside of the bowl will be held against the rubber with pressure from the tailstock.

Use calipers to mark the depth of the hollow on the outside of the bowl. It's good to know where the bottom of the bowl is as you cut the base. Set the bowl over the chuck and bring the tailstock forward to engage the center mark you made earlier on the base.

Cut away the waste block where the screws were fastened. Refine the final shape of the base and the bottom third of the bowl with light, finishing cuts.

Undercut the bowl's base to create a rim for the bowl to sit on. This looks better than a flat bottom. Watch the bottom mark (made by holding a pencil on the mark made earlier) so you don't cut too deep.

Break off the remaining nib with a rap from a tool handle. It takes little effort to break the nib. This leaves a small area to be cleaned up by hand.

Sand the bowl after it has dried for 4-5 days. Use a soft foam backed disc mounted on the lathe with a drill chuck. Keep the bowl moving to avoid creating flat spots. Start with #100-grit and work through #220-grit.

Sand the inside with a smaller foam disc. A flexible shaft that attaches to your drill or a flexible shaft tool such as a Foredom works well for getting inside the bowl.

Finishes

Is your bowl functional (made for food) or decorative? If it's decorative, choose any finish that gives the look and feel you prefer. My favorite finishes for functional bowls are mineral oil, walnut oil and pure tung oil. Mineral oil looks great on light colored wood, as it adds no color of its own. However, it never dries so renew it regularly, especially after washing. Walnut oil adds a little color and will dry in time. It's available at health food stores. I also like pure tung oil. It adds a deeper color that looks great on dark woods and it will dry.

TIP Every green bowl will distort as it dries—I think this adds character. Too often green-turned bowls dry so rapidly they crack. Slow down the drying process by placing the completed bowl in a two paper bags. Store it in a cool damp location.

CHAPTER EIGHTEEN

PROJECT 4 Lumberyard Bowl

Kiln-dried wood requires a different approach than green wood

Although most bowls are turned from green material, working with kiln-dried lumber has its advantages. You don't have to deal with checks and cracks or significant distortion. Sanding is far easier and you can apply finish immediately. However, turning dry wood has its own challenges and real differences compared with turning wet wood. And because wet wood often costs nothing, dry wood—especially thick stock—usually costs more. So, if you're up for a challenge, have money to burn and a burning desire to turn a bowl, you're in luck—this story is for you.

Choosing Stock

Rough sawn kiln-dried hardwood lumber is available in thicknesses ranging from 4/4 (1") to 16/4 (4"). Sizes 8/4 and thicker make decent bowl material. Thinner stock is excellent for turning plates and platters. Hardwood lumberyards typically stock various species in 4/4, 5/4, 6/4 and 8/4 sizes and one or two species in 10/4, 12/4 and perhaps even 16/4 sizes.

Some lumberyards allow buying a portion of a board. For example, cutting 4' from the end of a 12' board—or 2' from a 10' board—leaves a salable 8' length. So before you buy an entire board, ask if the yard will sell one end.

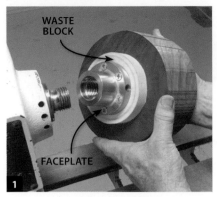

Maximize the blank's usable thickness by gluing a waste block on its bottom to hold the faceplate's mounting screws.

Establish the bowl's maximum diameter by trueing the blank. Cut from the outside to the center on both the left and right, so you don't chip out the edges.

Establish the bowl's maximum height by leveling about 1" of the top. To make this cut, roll over the gouge and use a delicate scraping action with its bottom edge.

Traditional furniture and cabinet woods such as walnut, ash, mahogany, hard and soft maple, beech, cherry, birch and white oak are excellent choices for this type of turning. Some pines, cypress and cedar may also have merit.

Prepare the Wood

Cut the wood into square blanks. The wider the board is, the larger the bowl's diameter can be. Decide which side will be the top (the inside of the bowl). Hollowing into the bark side of the blank (against the curve of the wood's annual rings) usually creates fairly straight grain patterns. Hollowing into the pith side of the blank creates curving patterns that I find more interesting.

Flatten the blank's bottom face. Then locate its center and use a compass to draw the largest possible circle. Mark the center point that the compass leaves, so it's easy to find. Then head to the band saw and saw the blank into a disc.

To make the best use of your stock, it's important to choose a mounting method that minimizes wood loss. I usually use a faceplate that screws into a waste block of poplar or other hardwood scrap that's glued to the blank's flattened bottom surface (**Photo 1**).

Cut the waste block into a disc that's about 10% larger than the faceplate's diameter. Use the center point from the circle drawn earlier on the blank to draw a second circle that matches the waste block's diameter. Use this circle to locate the waste block. Glue on the block using yellow or white glue, clamp it securely and allow it to dry overnight. Draw a centered circle on the waste block to locate the faceplate. Then attach the faceplate directly to the block, using No. 10 or No. 12 sheet metal screws or SPAX screws.

Use the Right Tools

In almost every case, the correct tool is a bowl gouge made from ½" or ⅝" diameter high-speed steel rod (see Sources, page 86). Do not use a spindle roughing gouge. Supplement the bowl gouge with a round-end bowl scraper for areas that are hard to reach with the bowl gouge or that just require

light finishing or blending (see Sources).

True the Blank

Screw the blank/faceplate assembly onto the lathe's headstock and bring up the tailstock for extra support. Set the lathe at slow speed—the larger the blank, the slower the speed. (For roughing, I typically set the speed below 600 rpm.) Then use the bowl gouge to true the blank (**Photo 2**).

Next, level the top of the disc, using a scraper or a bowl gouge rolled over to a scraping angle (**Photo 3**). As most of the top will be hollowed, you only need to level about 1" in from the edge. When you make this scraping action, make sure the top edge of the gouge doesn't contact the wood.

Shape the Outside

Determine the bowl's profile. The sweeping "U" shape shown here is relatively easy to create (**Photo 4**). If you're new to bowl turning, it's a great shape to start with.

This blank is face-grain mounted, so in order to work "with the grain" while shaping the outside, you have to turn from smaller to larger diameters. Using the bowl gouge, make successive cuts, starting at the bottom edge of the blank and working toward the top to gradually reduce the diameter and create the bowl's "U" shape. As before, do not run off the top. Stop about ½" from the edge, switch directions and work back from the rim. This eliminates any chance of chipping out the top edge.

Turn the base to near its final dimensions—unless you decide it will be smaller than the faceplate.

To improve the surface after the shape has been roughly determined, hone the edge of your bowl gouge so it's razor-sharp and then make progressively lighter and lighter cuts. To go one step further, try shear cutting (**Photo 5**). Long, twisted shavings appear when you achieve this cut.

Power-sand

This is the best time to sand the outside of the bowl. Holding sandpaper on the bowl as it spins tends to produce rings

4

Shape the outside of the bowl by making multiple passes. Work from smaller to larger diameter. Stop just short of the top edge and finish by cutting in from the top.

5

TWISTED SHAVINGS

Refine the surface by making a shearing cut. Hold the gouge at about a 45° angle to the surface. Rub the bevel, cut lightly and watch for long, twisted shavings.

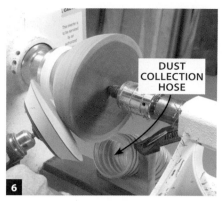

6

DUST COLLECTION HOSE

Sand the outside using a padded disc and a drill. This method creates a much better result than holding folded sandpaper against the surface.

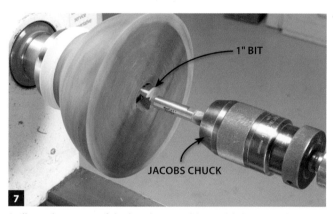

1" BIT

JACOBS CHUCK

7

Drill out the center of the bowl to roughly establish its depth and provide clearance for the gouge. This step also eliminates the wood at the center, which is difficult to turn.

GROOVE

8

Begin hollowing the interior by making a series of wider and deeper concave cuts. Establish a groove to support the gouge's bevel and work backward from the hole toward the edge.

that can be tough to remove. One solution is to power-sand using padded discs in a drill (**Photo 6**; see Sources). Any reversing drill will work; a drill with an angled head is a luxury. Set the drill to rotate so the abrasive spins up to meet the bowl (rather than spinning in the same direction as the bowl). You may have to adjust the rotation depending on the area being sanded. Use a hard padded disc for grits below #180 and a soft pad for #180 and above. If your tool work was well done, start with a #120-grit disc and sand through finer grits until there are no visible scratches.

Hollow the Interior

Mount a Jacobs chuck in the tailstock and drill a hole just large enough to provide an air pocket for the bowl gouge to work into (**Photo 7**). In most cases, ½" to 1" dia. bits are sufficient.

To work with the grain while hollowing a face-grain mounted bowl such as this one, you must work from larger to smaller diameters. The process requires making light, concave cuts toward the drilled hole at the center, with each cut progressively wider and deeper (**Photo 8**). Picture the blank as though it consists of a series of small bowls that get progressively larger. Begin by hollowing the smallest bowl

and work backward until you reach the intended thickness of the "final" bowl.

Stop to determine the shape of the rim before the wall thickness is less than 1" (**Photo 9**). Rolled, dropped, coved, tapered out or tapered in (as shown)—these are a few of the options that look better than an ordinary flat-topped rim.

As you near the final wall thickness, use double-ended calipers (see Sources) to help make the thickness consistent from the bottom of the bowl to the top. Cracking isn't an issue with kiln-dried material, so you can leave the walls a bit thicker and heavier than if you were working green wood. However, the heavy weight and feel of a thick wall often distracts from a nice form. Depending on the bowl's diameter, wall thickness between ¼" and ½" is both strong and more elegant in look and feel, in my experience.

Making a uniform and flowing cut with the bowl gouge to blend the bowl's lower interior wall with the bottom is desirable—but difficult. Using a heavy scraper is easier (**Photo 10**).

Sand the rim with folded paper, but try power-sanding the inside, using a 2" to 3" soft padded disc held in a drill (**Photo 11**; see Sources).

TAPERED-IN RIM

9

Establish the shape of the rim before completely roughing out the interior, while there's still enough wall thickness to support the cut.

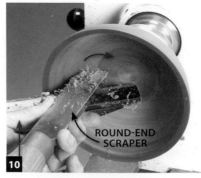

ROUND-END SCRAPER

10

Use a scraper to blend the lower sides and bottom. Position the tool rest close in and hold the scraper with the end of its handle slightly elevated.

SOFT PAD

OVERSIZED DISC

11

Power-sand the inside of the bowl. An oversize sanding disc mounted on a smaller soft pad conforms to the concave contour and leaves a scratch-free surface.

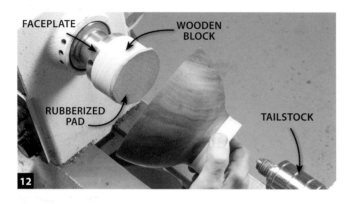

FACEPLATE

WOODEN BLOCK

RUBBERIZED PAD

TAILSTOCK

12

Remount the bowl between the tailstock and a wooden block covered with a rubberized pad. Called "reverse chucking," this step allows you to complete the bowl's base.

13

Finish turning the bottom of the bowl. After refining its lower outside profile, undercut the base so the bowl sits on a rim.

Complete the Bottom

In order to maintain good workmanship when finishing the bottom of the bowl, reverse chucking—turning the bowl around so you can get at the bottom—is absolutely essential. Several commercial and turner-made chucks are available for this purpose, but a very simple version for shallow bowls like the one shown here is a block (usually 1¾" thick) that's screwed to the faceplate, trued round and faced flat, and then covered with a soft, grippy material, such as a routing pad (**Photo 12**; see Sources).

Place the bowl over the block and bring up the tailstock center to lightly support it. Then center the bowl while turning the lathe by hand. As the bowl rotates, position a pencil near the base to mark the high spot. Slightly reposition the bowl and recheck until the pencil mark is continuous. Then secure the bowl with firm pressure from the tailstock center.

Turn the base and lower portions of the bowl, leaving a tapered tenon (about ½" in diameter for this size of bowl) to keep it securely mounted (**Photo 13**). I think a concave base with a rim looks much better than a simple flat base. It also tends to sit better. Finish-sand the lower sides using the padded disc. Use folded paper inside the rim.

Remove the bowl from the chuck with the small tenon attached. (This tenon is all that remains of the waste block.) Orient the bowl to access the tenon's end grain and give it a sharp rap—the tenon should easily snap off. Carve and sand the area at the break to the same quality as the rest of the bowl.

Apply a Finish

If a bowl is more decorative than functional, choose a finish for its appearance. Film finishes such as wipe-on poly, shellac, water-based finishes and lacquer give the wood a pleasant range of sheen (also called luster). Oil-type finishes (oil varnish blend, polymerized oils, mineral oil, walnut oil, tung oil, boiled linseed oil) add color and emphasize the grain. All common wood finishes are food-safe once they've cured (or aren't harmful to begin with, as with mineral and walnut oil).

SOURCES The Sanding Glove, thesandingglove.com, 800-995-9328, Velcro Disc Holder, 5", #SM-5F (firm), $15.95, #SM-5S (soft), $15.95; 2", #SM-2S (soft), $8.95; Norton Dri Ice Ceramic Disc Assortment, 5", #DRI-500AP, $26.95; 2", #DRI-200AP, $13.95. ⊚ Craft Supplies USA, woodturnerscatalog.com, 800-551-8876, Bowl Gouges, Bowl Scrapers, Outside Shear Scrapers, Double-End Calipers, Jacobs Chucks. ⊚ Grizzly, grizzly.com, 800-523-4777, 1/8" Router Pad, #W1320, $10.95.

CHAPTER NINETEEN

PROJECT 5 Toothpick Holder

Here's an attractive little project to learn the ins and outs of hollowing end grain. Its thin shaft and delicate details also present an opportunity to fine-tune your spindle-turning skills. And when you're finished, you'll have a nifty conversation piece for the dining table, especially if you turn the toothpicks, too (just kidding!).

Prepare the Blank

Begin by mounting a blank that's about 2-½" square x 5" long between centers on the lathe. You can use virtually any type of wood, as long as it's relatively dry and doesn't contain any pith.

Round the blank into a cylinder using the roughing gouge.

Using either a parting tool or a skew chisel, turn a short tenon on one end of the blank so you can mount it in a scroll chuck (see Sources, page 89). Make sure that the tenon fits in the scroll chuck without bottoming out (reduce the tenon's length) or having to extend the jaws too far beyond the chuck's body (reduce the tenon's diameter). Also, be certain that the tenon's shoulder is slightly concave. Remove the blank from between the centers.

Install the scroll chuck and mount the blank (**Photo 1**).

True the cylinder if the mounting process has created any variation. Bring up the tailstock for extra support during this operation.

A Toothpick-friendly Shape

Determine the cup's depth with a toothpick (**Photo 2**). The cup shown here will be about 1-½" deep, but feel free to experiment, depending on how far you want the toothpicks to extend above the holder.

Mount a Jacobs-style chuck (see

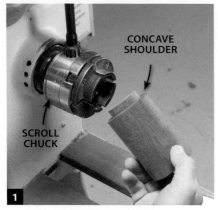

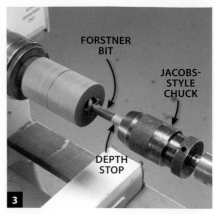

1 Mount the blank in a scroll chuck after turning a tenon on one end. The tenon's shoulder must be slightly concave.

2 Use a toothpick to set the depth of the hollow cup. Mark the line all the way around the blank.

3 Drill out the cup, using a Forstner bit and a Jacobs-style chuck. The bit's taped-on depth stop matches the line on the blank.

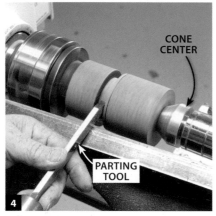

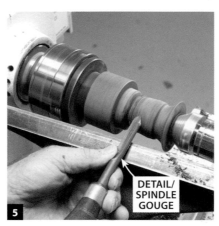

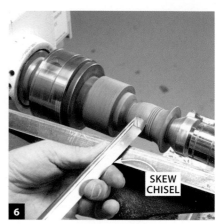

4 Establish the bottom of the cup by cutting in slightly below the line marked earlier. Support the blank with a cone center.

5 Use a detail/spindle gouge to roughly shape the outside of the cup, including the flared rim.

6 Refine the bowl's shape and add decorative elements such as tiny beads with the gouge and the skew chisel.

Sources) in the tailstock and install a ⅝" Forstner bit (see Sources). To avoid scorching the wood, this bit should be carbide-tipped or made of high-speed steel. Use tape to mark the drilling depth on the bit.

Turn on the lathe at slow speed. Then slowly advance the tailstock to drill the hole (**Photo 3**). Go slowly to avoid overheating the bit or the wood. Retract the bit often to clear the chips.

Use a parting tool to establish the bottom of the bowl on the outside of the blank. Cut in about ¼" away (on the headstock side) from the depth line drawn earlier (**Photo 4**). Reduce the diameter by no more than one-third at this point. Support the blank's tailstock end with a tapered cone center (see Sources). The cone fits inside the hole that's just been drilled.

Begin to shape the outside of the cup (**Photo 5**). Be very careful not to reduce the diameter too much at this point; doing so will make it much more difficult to hollow the cup's inside. Start at the upper rim—I like a flared rim on this type of holder, but this is an excellent opportunity to play with a variety of curves, both concave and convex.

Add interest by using a skew chisel to create one or several small beads (**Photo 6**).

Back off the cone center. Then hollow the cup with a ½" or ¾" round-nose or left-side radiused scraper (**Photo 7**). Hold the scraper flat on the tool rest, with the back end of its handle slightly elevated. In order to work with the grain, insert the tool without engaging the wood and cut only as you pull the tool out of the hole. It's best to hollow the cup in stages. Start with the upper third, then move to the next third and finally to the bottom. The final pass starts at the bottom, moves up along the side and over the rim.

Refine the cup's inside surface by shear scraping, a finishing process used prior to sanding that removes very little wood but results in a finer surface than the initial shaping. Put a fine burr on the curved-edge scraper and tilt the tool in the direction you want to move (**Photo 8**). At approximately a 45° angle you'll notice a change in the chips being produced—and improved surface quality.

Establish the holder's overall height by cutting in with

LEFT-SIDE RADIUSED SCRAPER

7

Hollow the cup with a radiused or round-nose scraper. Insert the tool without touching and engage the near side as you draw it out.

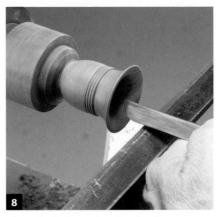

8

Clean the hollowed surface by shear scraping. Raise the scraper onto a corner at 45°. Then work the near side, as before.

9

Shape the base and begin to reduce the stem's diameter with the detail/spindle gouge. Work from large to small diameters.

10

Shape the bottom of the cup and its transition to the stem by working in the opposite direction.

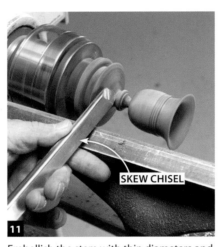

SKEW CHISEL

11

Embellish the stem with thin diameters and delicate details.

12

Part off the completed holder with a parting tool or the skew and a light touch to grasp the holder as it separates.

the parting tool. Then use the detail/spindle gouge to begin shaping (**Photo 9**).

Use the same movement—from large to small diameters—but from the opposite direction to shape the bottom of the cup (**Photo 10**).

As toothpicks weigh next to nothing, push your skills to the limit by turning the stem very thin and adding small details (**Photo 11**).

Finish-sand the outside of the holder to #220-grit.

Separate the completed holder from the blank, using the parting tool or the skew chisel (**Photo 12**). The parting tool is easier to use, but the skew leaves a better surface.

Make sure the bottom of the holder is flat by rubbing it on a piece of sandpaper adhered to a flat surface. I sand the bottom to the same grit as the outside surfaces.

A toothpick holder doesn't need much protection, so you can use almost any finish. Your top priority is the way the finish looks.

SOURCES Packard Woodworks, Inc. www.packardwoodworks.com, (800) 683-8876, Oneway Talon 4-Jaw Scroll Chuck, #112670, $206.95 , Threaded Insert for Talon (for a specific lathe thread), #112606, $24.95; Oneway Live Center #2 MT (includes cone center), #112622, $120; Jacobs-Style #2MT Keyless Chuck, #111022, $37.95. ☺ Highland Woodworking www.highlandwoodworking .com, (800) 241-6748, Freud 5/8" Carbide-Tipped Forstner Bit, #472004, $26.99. ⌒

CHAPTER TWENTY

Wine Goblet

Sharpen your end-grain hollowing skills

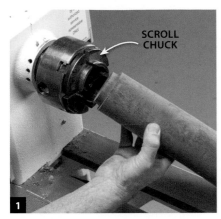

1 Securely mount a blank with a turned tenon into a scroll chuck. A secure mount comes from the tenon's large gripping surface and its shoulder, which rests on the top of the chuck's jaws.

2 Cut in below a line marked to indicate the cup portion of the goblet to provide clearance for shaping the bottom of the cup.

3 Shape the bottom portion of the cup with the detail/spindle gouge. Switch to the roughing gouge to refine the cup's flatter upper portion.

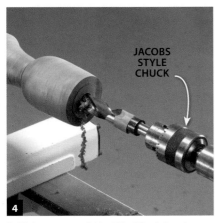

4 Drill the cup to within ½" of final depth, using a Jacobs style chuck mounted in the tailstock.

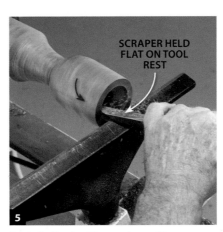

5 Begin hollowing the cup by making sweeping cuts with a thick round-nose scraper, working from the sides of the pilot hole back towards the rim. Make ever-deepening cuts to open the inside.

6 Work near the rim to establish the wall thickness. Make the same sweeping cuts, working from the inside out.

Drinking from a wooden Goblet is a unique experience, because its weight and feel is distinct from goblets made of other materials. But is it practical? Of course! With the right wood and finish, it's perfect for anyone who loves wood!

Tools and Materials

Almost any lathe will do for this project—even a mini lathe. A four-jaw scroll chuck (see Sources, page 93) is a great asset for mounting the blank for hollowing. You'll need standard spindle turning tools, including a roughing gouge, a detail/spindle gouge, a skew chisel and a parting tool. You'll also need a tool for hollowing the cup. I recommend using a round-nose scraper (with either a side- or full-round profile) that's ½" to 1" wide and ⁵⁄₁₆" to ³⁄₈" thick.

Steer away from really soft woods such as basswood, pine, cottonwood, etc. and look for harder woods such as cherry,

walnut, maple and oak. Many exotic woods are also suitable. Finding large enough turning blanks may be the biggest challenge—I like to start with blanks that are 2-½" to 3" square.

A wooden goblet's usability turns on the finish. With some woods the wrong finish can allow wine to literally seep right through the cup. Epoxy, pre-catalyzed lacquer (sometimes sold to turners as "melamine") and varnish are good choices that seal the wood well and are not affected by alcohol.

Securely Mount the Blank

Select a square blank that's about 9" long. Mount the blank on the lathe between centers and turn it to a cylinder using the roughing gouge. Select which end will be the base and which will be the cup. Use a parting tool or a skew chisel to turn a tenon on the base end to fit the scroll chuck. Size the diameter of this tenon to provide the chuck's jaws with an effective grip

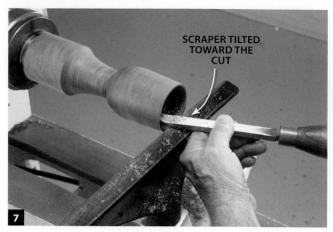

SCRAPER TILTED TOWARD THE CUT

7

Finish hollowing the cup by making light passes from the bottom to the top edge with the scraper tilted toward the cut. Then sand the inside of the cup and the upper part of the outside.

SPINDLE/DETAIL GOUGE

8

Ease the transition between the cup and the stem by adding a bead detail. Sand the detail. Then establish the final shape at the base of the cup.

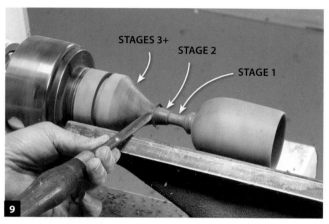

STAGES 3+
STAGE 2
STAGE 1

9

Cut in slightly at the base to establish the goblet's overall height. Then turn the stem in stages, working from the cup to the base and sanding completed areas as you go.

SKEW CHISEL

10

Complete the base and add details, using the detail/spindle gouge and the skew chisel.

over a large surface area. Remove the blank and mount your scroll chuck onto the headstock. Then, using plenty of pressure, mount the blank securely within the jaws (**Photo 1**).

Shape the Cup

Decide the cup's height and mark it on the blank. You may want to measure glass goblets that you like to find a pleasing balance between the cup and the goblet's overall height. Or simply experiment by drawing different lines on the blank. I like a 40-to-60 ratio between the cup and the overall height.

Begin the rough shaping by cutting in below the line to provide clearance (**Photo 2**). Do not cut in too far—about half the diameter of the cylinder is as deep as you should cut at this point. Reducing the diameter too much will leave too little support for hollowing the cup.

Roughly shape the outside of the cup. Its bottom is normally rounded like the side of a bead (**Photo 3**). Don't cut in too far as you refine the shape—leave plenty of stock at the bottom for support during the hollowing process. Switch to

the roughing gouge to shape and refine the sides of the cup. They may be straight as shown here, or gently rounded.

Hollow the Cup

It's much easier to hollow the cup if you drill it out first (**Photo 4**). Use a ½" to ¾" drill bit to create working room for the turning tools. Drill to a depth about ½" less than the ultimate final depth, to allow refining the bottom of the cut.

Use a thick round-nose scraper to open the cup (**Photo 5**). To work with the grain, you must work from smaller to larger diameter. In this case, that means working from the center of the cup towards the sides and top edge—"pulling out" rather than "pushing in," as with face-grain bowl turning.

Open the cup in stages, gradually reducing the wall thickness more towards the top of the cup than the sides (**Photo 6**). Work to a wall thickness near the top of ³⁄₁₆" to ¼"—you'll be able to further reduce the wall thickness as your end-grain hollowing skills improve.

Switch to the detail/spindle gouge to further refine the

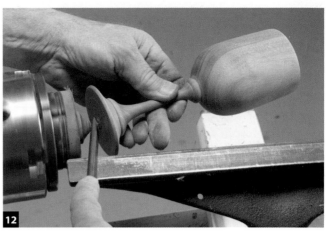

Refine the rim of the base by making an angled cut on the bottom edge, using the long point of the skew chisel.

Part the goblet from the waste material after cutting into the underside of the base at a slight angle to create a concave bottom surface, so the goblet will sit flat.

shape of the bottom on the outside of the cup. Reducing the outside diameter around the bottom and at the base of the cup provides a better sense of the wall thickness when you refine the interior walls—but be careful about reducing the outside shape to its final diameter, as you still need some support to finish hollowing the inside.

Switch back to the round-nose scraper to finish turning the inside of the cup (**Photo 7**). Work to achieve the best surface you can prior to sanding by using a technique called "shear scraping." Work from the bottom and up the sides with the scraper tilted to the left, in the direction of the cut (around 45°), making light, consistent movements across the wood's surface.

When you're satisfied with the surface finish from the turning tools, finish-sand the inside of the cup and the flat part of the outside. Start with #120-grit and work through #320-grit. Note: Waiting to sand the cup after the goblet's stem has been turned to a small diameter is a bad idea—it courts disaster.

Shape the Stem and Base

Finish turning the bottom of the cup (**Photo 8**). The stem can flow right into the cup, or you can add a detail at the transition point. Finish-sand the bottom of the cup.

Establish the goblet's height by cutting in with a parting tool about ¼" deep on the chucked end of the blank. Then slowly create the stem and the base by clearing away the remaining waste in short segments, finish-sanding as you go (**Photo 9**). When the stem and base are nearly complete, decide whether to add a detail (**Photo 10**). Finish-sand any remaining areas to #320-grit.

Parting Off

Cut a small chamfer at the bottom edge of the base (**Photo 11**). This cut creates a subtle shadow line that slightly lifts the base. Prepare to part off the goblet by alternating between removing the waste with a parting tool and shaping the underside of its base with the skew chisel or the detail/spindle gouge. Create a shallow undercut from the rim towards the center, so the goblet will sit only on the rim (**Photo 12**). Continue the slight undercut until you part off the completed goblet into your hand. Sand the underside of the base by hand or with a soft flexible pad mounted in a drill or rotary tool.

Apply a Durable Finish

Use an alcohol- and liquid-resistant finish. Of the three options mentioned earlier, I prefer the working properties, durability, look and feel of a high-grade varnish finish, even though it dries slowly and takes a long time to fully cure.

Create an excellent wiping varnish by mixing equal parts of Behlen's Rock Hard Tabletop Varnish (see Sources) and odorless mineral spirits. Apply at least five light coats inside the cup and three to four coats on all other areas. Allow each coat to dry for at least eight hours and lightly sand between coats. Wait 20 to 30 days before using the goblet, to allow the finish to adequately cure. I often go by the sniff test: If I detect any solvent odors inside the goblet, it needs more curing time.

SOURCES Oneway Manufacturing, oneway.ca, 800-565 7288, Oneway Talon Chuck, #2985, $232. ⊚ Woodcraft, woodcraft.com, 800-225-1153, Behlen's Rockhard Tabletop Varnish, #154369, $25.99 per qt. ⌒

CHAPTER TWENTY-ONE

PROJECT 7 Letter Opener & Butter Knife

Household utensils a cut above the rest

Metal has long since replaced wood as the preferred material for household utensils. But that doesn't change the fact that opening letters and spreading butter can be accomplished effectively with wooden tools. So, here's a chance to make a pair of useful utensils that will stand out beautifully from the tarnished crowd, especially in the eyes of a woodworker. Why two separate projects in one article? Because the techniques used to create each one are similar.

Choose closed-grain hardwood for both projects. The letter opener requires durable, sharp edges and the butter knife will be much easier to keep clean if the wood doesn't contain large open pores. Hard maple is an excellent choice—so are cherry, pear, apple, Osage orange and a host of exotics, including goncalo alves, olive, ebony, and purpleheart. Even laminated bamboo flooring material will work

for the letter opener, although you may have to glue several pieces together to reach the necessary thickness.

Both projects are evenly divided between turning operations and contour sanding. Basic spindle turning tools are all you'll need for the turnings: a spindle roughing gouge, a spindle/detail gouge, a parting tool and a skew chisel. If you are adept with the skew chisel, you can complete both projects with it alone.

To shape the blades, you'll need a Jacobs-type chuck that fits your lathe's headstock and a 5" firmed-backed sanding disc holder (see Sources, page 96). If you want to add curves to the blade of the butter knife, as I have, you'll need a 1" or 2" sanding drum that fits into the Jacobs chuck You'll also need #80-, #120-, #150- and #220-grit paper for the sanding disc and a #100-grit sleeve for the sanding drum.

The how-to steps for both projects are basically the same,

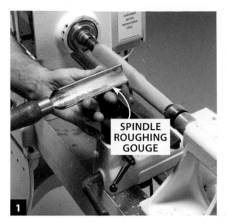

Many steps in making a letter opener and a butter knife are the same. Start both projects by turning the square stock into a cylinder.

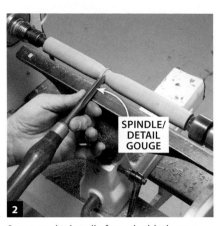

Separate the handle from the blade area by rolling a bead. Cut in with a parting tool or skew chisel. Then roll the bead with a spindle/detail gouge.

To make a letter opener, shape the blade portion to look like an asymmetrical ellipse, using the skew chisel or spindle/detail gouge.

Shape the handle to a form that fits nicely in your hand—this is a great opportunity to try different shapes.

Detail the handle. One option is to lay out a series of small beads with the long point of the skew. To roll the beads, use either the skew or the spindle/detail gouge.

Turn both ends to a small diameter with the long point of the skew. Then carefully part off the turning at the headstock end. This leaves only a bit of waste to cut through at the tailstock end.

with a few minor variations. So, I'll show how to turn and shape the letter opener first. Then I'll explain the variations used to turn and shape the butter knife.

The Letter Opener

Start with 1¼" squares of wood that are approximately 10" long. Mount a blank and turn it to a cylinder (**Photo 1**).

Determine where the handle will transition to the blade. Make the blade portion longer, rather than dividing the parts evenly, and mark the transition by creating a bead (**Photo 2**).

Traditional metal letter opener blades often swell from the tip, so turn the blade portion to look like an ellipse—an asymmetrical "ellipse" looks the best (**Photo 3**).

When shaping the handle, the top priority is always a comfortable grip. Here, the handle echoes the blade's elliptical look (**Photo 4**). A gradual taper from the end to the bead also forms a comfortable grip.

The handle's surface can be detailed or left smooth. A series of small beads can make the handle easier to grip. Vary the beads' sizes for interest, wider in the middle and gradu-

ally narrowing towards the ends (**Photo 5**).

Finish-sand everything but the blade area to #220-grit.

Remove the letter opener from the lathe and cut the waste material from both ends, using a coping saw or Japanese-style saw. Alternately, you can save some sanding by using the skew chisel to part off the letter opener at the headstock end (**Photo 6**).

Shape the blade by sanding. One way to reduce the amount of sanding dust raised during this step is to cut away most of the waste wood with a small saw earlier, while the letter opener is still on the lathe. The alternative is to plan to capture a lot of dust. Position a dust collection hose near the headstock and be sure to wear an effective dust mask (rated at NIOSH 95).

Mount the Jacobs-type chuck in the headstock and install the 5" sanding disc holder with #80-grit paper attached.

Work the blade slowly into the basic shape. Then start tapering from the middle to the edges to create the double-sided wedge shape (**Photo 7**). For the opener to work effectively, the edges of the blade must be fairly sharp. If the

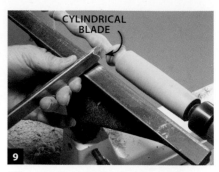

Install a sanding disc holder to finish shaping the letter opener's blade. On both sides, create tapers from the center to the edges and from the handle to the tip.

Complete the letter opener by sanding with the grain to remove cross-sanding marks from the blade.

Although a butter knife's handle may be differently shaped, the main differences from the letter opener are that the knife's blade is shorter and turned to a cylinder.

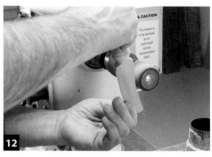

Whenever you turn a handle, it's a good idea to stop during the process and check the way it feels in your hand.

The butter knife's blade tapers from the handle to the tip, and from the top to the bottom. Only the bottom edge tapers to a point.

Shape the butter knife's blade on a sanding drum, to add interest. A concave curve on the top edge complements the curve on the front at the bottom.

#80-grit paper cuts too aggressively, switch to #100-grit. Switch to #120-grit when you near the final shape; switch to #220-grit to complete the disc sanding.

Finish-sand the blade by hand, following the grain (**Photo 8**).

Test the opener on several sealed envelopes. You'll discover that (1) a certain level of edge sharpness is required to cut the paper, and (2) properly shaped wedges aid the cutting process by easing the envelope open. You may need to do some re-shaping to achieve optimal results.

The Butter Knife

Turn the blade area to a cylinder, instead of an ellipse, and experiment with a variety of shapes for the handle (**Photos 9 and 10**).

When shaping the blade with the 5" disc, taper from the topside down, to create an edge at the bottom (**Photo 11**). This edge doesn't have to be as sharp as the edges on a letter opener. Generally speaking, butter knife blades are a bit thinner, usually about ⅛" thick along the top edge of the

blade, and more consistently thick from end to end.

Use a sanding drum to make the blade look more interesting (**Photo 12**). After shaping these curves, you may have to return to the disc to refine the edge.

Finishes

Almost any finish will work for the letter opener. Wipe-on poly or gel varnish would be good choices if you prefer a film-forming finish. For an oil finish, choose an oil-varnish blend or a drying oil such as linseed oil or tung oil.

The butter knife is a little different, as it will be washed and used with food. The first option is no finish—just let the knife take on the natural look it acquires through use. For a more finished look and a little protection against staining, try an oil finish such as pure mineral oil, walnut oil or tung oil. (Make sure the product you use contains no toxic additives.) For still more protection, apply coats of wipe-on or gel-type varnish. These finishes will be food safe once they've fully cured, which may take several weeks.

SOURCES Craft Supplies, woodturnerscatalog.com, 800 551 8876, Keyless Drill Chuck #104-578 $45.50 ⌬ The Sanding Glove, www.thesandingglove.com, (800) 995-9328, 5" Firm Disc Holder #SM-5F, $15.95. ⌬ Rockler Woodworking and Hardware, www.rockler.com, (800) 279-4441, 15 Piece Sanding Drum Kit #42937, $18.99. ⌬

CHAPTER TWENTY-TWO

Ice Cream Scoop

Turn a scoop handle that evokes nostalgia

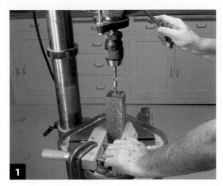

1

Use dense hardwood for the scoop's handle. Start by drilling a hole for the scoop's stem in the end of the handle blank.

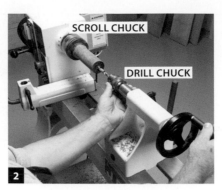

2

Another option is to drill the hole on the lathe. This method requires turning the blank to a cylinder and then replacing the tailstock center with a drill chuck. The mark left by the tailstock center locates the bit.

3

Once the hole is drilled, you have two options for re-mounting the blank: A cone-shaped live center or a small tapered plug. The cone centers itself; the plug fills the hole, so you can mount a standard live center.

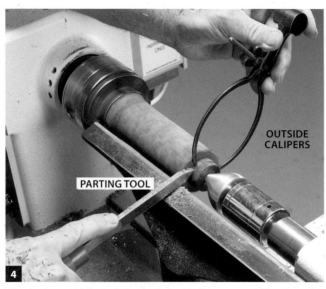

4

Turn a tenon to house the scoop's ferrule in two steps. First, match the ferrule's outside diameter. Then carefully reduce the diameter until you can drive on the ferrule.

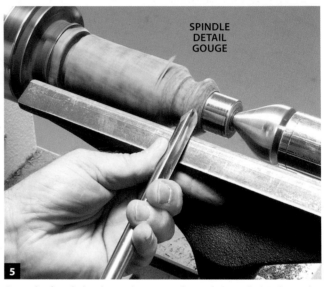

5

Once the ferrule has been driven on, shape the area behind it with the spindle detail gouge, working from large to small diameters. I like to start with a wide, tapered flange.

In simpler days, soda jerks quickly and efficiently dished perfect servings of ice cream with sturdy wooden-handled scoops. Once you've collected the metal parts (see Sources, page 100), a small block of wood and a little turning skill, I'll show you how to create a classic ice cream scoop that will make you the envy of jerks everywhere.

How-to

Select a block of dried hardwood about 1-¾" square and 6" in length. The handle must have a certain level of strength, so stay with domestic hardwoods as cherry, hard maple, walnut or yellow birch. Exotic woods such as purpleheart, black palm (used here), bubinga, rosewood and goncalo alves are also good choices.

Drill a ⅜" dia. by 1-¼" deep hole for the scoop's stem. If the end of the blank is properly squared, this operation is easily performed on a drill press (**Photo 1**). Another option is to mount the blank on the lathe and turn it to a cylinder, using a spindle roughing gouge. Then replace the tailstock center with a drill chuck to drill the hole (**Photo 2**).

Mount the drilled blank on the lathe with the drilled hole facing the tailstock. If you have a cone-type live center, simply run the cone into the drilled hole (**Photo 3**). Another option is to turn a tapered wooden plug that fills the hole and provides a surface to engage the tailstock center. The plug should protrude about ½", so you can remove it when you've finished turning the handle.

If the blank you've mounted is still square, turn it to a cylinder, using a spindle roughing gouge.

Fit the brass ferrule to the blank. The ferrule is 1" long, so mark that length on the blank with a pencil. Turning the correct diameter is a bit trickier. Start by turning the tenon to match the outside diameter of the ferrule (**Photo 4**). Before you use the outside calipers for any lathe work, be sure to round the ends.

6 Reduce the diameter behind the flange to create the neck. From this point on, remove the handle often to check how it feels in your hand.

7 Start to shape the end of the handle. Be sure to leave sufficient waste, so you don't whack into the chuck.

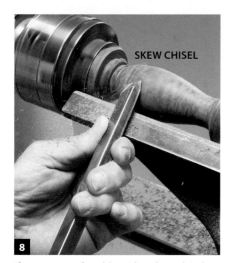

SKEW CHISEL

8 If you are comfortable with a skew chisel, use it to finish shaping the handle's rounded areas. You can shape the entire handle with the spindle detail gouge, but the skew leaves a smoother surface.

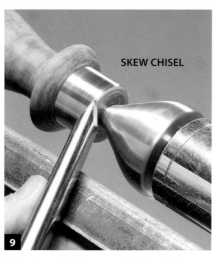

SKEW CHISEL

9 Trim the end of the tenon flush with the ferrule. Use the skew chisel long-end-down or a thin-kerf parting tool.

10 Finish-sand the handle. Start with #120-grit; if turning marks remain, drop back to #100-grit. Sand to #220-grit, or further if you still see sanding scratches. Sand the brass ferrule to the same grit.

Next, create a short taper on the end of the tenon. Keep checking until the ferrule just starts to go on. Turn the ferrule a few times around the tenon to create a burnished surface. When you start the lathe you should be able to "see" the diameter you are targeting. I try to achieve a very tight driven-on fit. Unless the tenon's length is exactly the same as the ferrule, you may need another ferrule to drive the first one home. Another option is to turn the tenon to a slightly loose fit and glue on the ferrule with epoxy. If you use epoxy, wait for several hours before completing the turning.

Shape the handle with a spindle detail gouge (**Photos 5, 6 and 7**). This is an organic process: Remove the handle frequently, to see how it feels in your hands—the perfect shape is the one that feels right. Most of my handles end up about 5-½" long, with maximum diameters near 1-⅝". Switch to the skew chisel to finish shaping the rounded areas (**Photo 8**).

If the ferrule's tenon protrudes, use either a skew chisel

(long point down) or a thin-kerf parting tool to turn the end flush with the brass (**Photo 9**).

When you're satisfied with the handle's feel and appearance, sand it—and the ferrule, too—to at least #220-grit (**Photo 10**).

Cut the handle from the waste. I usually remove the blank from the lathe and free the handle by sawing with a coping or Japanese saw. Then I finish sanding the end of the handle by hand.

Apply the finish (**Photo 11**). For the best protection against water and washing, use a film finish such as a gel varnish or polyurethane. Wipe on at least three coats, with light sanding with #320- or #400-grit sandpaper, #0000 steel wool, or a very fine abrasive pad, such as white Scotch Brite. For a more natural look, use pure tung oil or even boiled linseed oil as the finish. Again, apply at least three coats and wait until the finish is completely dry before using the scoop.

TIPS FOR USING

Before you attack that frozen ice cream, immerse the scoop's business end in a cup of hot water for a couple minutes. Use the side of the scoop to dish the ice cream—don't dig in with the front, like a shovel. If you're serving a gang of kids, or a gaggle of soda enthusiasts, dip the metal in the hot water periodically, to keep it warm.

After your ice cream social, wash only the brass part of the scoop. Don't submerge the wood and don't ever run the scoop through a dishwasher. Following washing, towel the scoop dry and then leave it out to air-dry, so any moisture that remains evaporates.

Glue the metal scoop into the handle with epoxy (**Photo 12**). Use a rag dampened with lacquer thinner or acetone to remove any epoxy that squeezes out. Prop the scoop upright for about one hour for the glue to set, and allow at least one day before use.

11

For a finish, I wipe on polyurethane or pure tung oil. I think tung oil looks better, but polyurethane provides somewhat better protection.

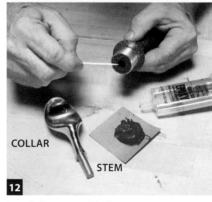

12

COLLAR

STEM

Install the scoop. Work a generous amount of epoxy into the hole. Insert the scoop's stem and bed its collar against the end of the handle.

SOURCES Rockler Woodworking and Hardware, www.rockler.com, (800) 279-4441, Brass Ice Cream Scoop Hardware Kit (includes scoop and ferrule), #29848, $13.99. ☺ Oneway Mfg.,www.oneway.ca, (800) 565-7288, #2MT Live Center with Cones, #2064, $121; Talon Chuck, #2985, $232. ☺ Packard Woodworks, www.packardwoodworks.com, (800) 683-8876, #2MT 1/2" Keyless Chuck, #111022, $37.95

CHAPTER TWENTY-THREE

PROJECT 9 Wooden Plate

A great way to make use of offcuts

One of my woodworking friends defines "offcuts" as boards that are too short to be useful, but too good to be thrown away. That explains why he always has a big stack of unused short boards. As a woodturner, I view those offcuts as prime material: Short, thin boards are perfect for making plates, platters and saucers. The process is fairly simple, because all three objects are really just shallow bowls. You don't need a big lathe, either, because wooden plates don't have much mass. The only tricky part is mounting the blank so you can turn both sides, and I'll show you a method that simplifies the process.

Use Almost any Board

Almost any offcut or short board will work, or is at least worth trying, as long as it is free of checks (cracks) and pith (the material at the very center of the tree). The board should also be relatively dry—plates and platters made from wet wood are much more likely to warp. Any traditional hardwood used in furniture making is suitable. Maple, cherry, oak (especially quartersawn or riftsawn), walnut, hickory, butternut, birch, and beech are all good choices. So are cypress, cedar and pine. You can also use local woods you have cut yourself. These projects are also a good way to test the turning qualities of exotic woods. The plate's diameter depends on the width (or length) of the board, of course, but it's ultimately limited only by your lathe's capacity. For starters, I recommend turning a plate with a diameter between 7" and 10". As the plate will be hollowed into the board's face grain, the board's thickness is another consideration. Hardwood lumber is available in a variety of thicknesses on the rough: 1", 1-¼" and 1-½" thick

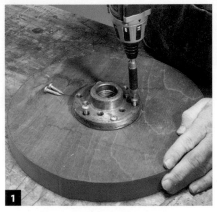

1 Mount the bandsawn blank for turning. The back of the plate will be turned first, so fasten a faceplate on the front of the blank. The screw holes will disappear later, when the front—or "open" side—of the plate is shaped.

2 Use a bowl gouge to true up the edge of the blank and make it round. Avoid splintering the blank's faces by working the edge from both sides. Start at the outside and move to the center.

3 Flatten the back side of the blank. Work from the center to the outside. Start with the bowl gouge; then switch to a square ended scraper to level the surface.

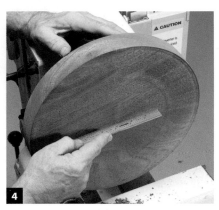

4 Use a straightedge to check the leveled surface. The center area must be absolutely flat, so you can successfully remount the faceplate when it's time to turn the plate's open side.

5 Use the bowl gouge to shape the back side of the rim. Work from small to large diameter. As you shape the outside, consider your intentions for the inside shape.

6 Mark a circle on the spinning blank, slightly larger than the faceplate. Then remove the blank from the lathe and the faceplate from the blank.

boards all make good plate and platter material. If you plan to turn a small saucer (6" dia. or less), you might even use a board as thin as ½".

Mount the Blank Backwards

Mounting the blank is the first challenge, because plates and platters tend to be on the thin side.

Fortunately, there are several good options that don't rely on cutting or screwing into the turning blank. This story shows my favorite mounting method, which involves using special double-sided tape. However, you should use this method only after you have turned a number of bowls and have developed a sound technique with bowl gouges.

The best strategy is to remove the blank after turning one side and remount it to turn the other side. I prefer to turn the back of the plate first, so I start by mounting the blank "backwards," with it's front face oriented toward the headstock (**Photo 1**). I'll use the double sided tape when I remount the blank.

The tape you use must have a super-strong grip. Do not substitute garden-variety tape from the hardware store, or even carpet tape. For the tape to adhere properly, the blank must be flat, clean, unfinished, dry and absent of oily resins. If the wood is oily or resinous (teak, cocobolo, or bocote, for example), scrub the surface with lacquer thinner or acetone.

Turn the Back Side

Start by truing up the blank's edge (**Photo 2**).

Next, true up the blank's back side and determine the size of its base (**Photos 3 and 4**). The center area must be absolutely flat.

Shape the back side of the plate (**Photo 5**). This shape should roughly mirror the shape you have in mind for the plate's open (front) side.

Draw a circle on the base to mark the faceplate's next location, so when you reverse the blank, it will remain ac-

HIGH-STRENGTH DOUBLE FACED TAPE

7

Remount the faceplate on the outside of the blank, using the centered circle and high-strength double faced tape. Trim the tape to match the faceplate.

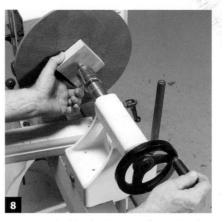

8

Remount the blank. Then use the tailstock and a block to clamp the taped joint. The block isn't glued; it's used to distribute the clamping pressure. Allow one hour for the tape's bond to fully strengthen.

9

Sand the back of the rim using a cushioned disc and a drill set to rotate clockwise. Before sanding, remove the clamp block and reposition the tailstock so it continues to support the plate.

ROUGHED OUT BEAD

10

Always work from the outside edge towards the middle when shaping the open side of the blank. Start by creating the rim. It can be flat, curved or detailed. Here, cutting in with a parting tool roughs out a bead.

11

Roll the bead using a detail/spindle gouge. Complete each side separately, by starting at the center and working to the edge.

12

Remove waste beyond the rim, using the bowl gouge. Plunge down and toward the center, using the bowl gouge. This step provides clearance, so you can complete the rim.

curately centered (**Photo 6**).

Remove the blank; then remove the faceplate. Make sure that the faceplate is absolutely clean of rust and residue by wiping or scrubbing it with lacquer thinner. Cover the faceplate with the double sided tape and mount it on the outside of the blank (**Photo 7**).

Remount the blank on the lathe—its open side now faces the tailstock. Use a block of wood and the tailstock center to clamp the blank/faceplate assembly (**Photo 8**).

Complete the back side of the rim by power sanding, using a drill and a 5" cushioned disc (**Photo 9** and Sources). Power sanding is a fast and effective way to true up any slight irregularities.

Turn the Open Side

Determine the shape of the rim: bead, flare, rolled edge or just a gentle transition into the bottom of the plate. If you intend to do a bead, lay it out with a parting tool (**Photo 10**).

Finish the shape with a detail/spindle gouge (**Photo 11**).

Use the bowl gouge to shape the plate's interior. Work from the rim towards the center, one section at a time (**Photo 12**). The goal is to complete the turning for each section as you go (**Photo 13**). Consider the wall thickness as you create the transition from the rim to the bottom of the plate. Cut in decisively—it's difficult to go back and rework this shape later, due to the lack of support (**Photo 14**). Leave the tailstock in position until only a 2" dia. section remains at the center. Remove the tailstock and peel this area down (**Photo 15**).

The bottom of the plate's interior is usually flat or curves gently to the center. Remember that you often have very little thickness to work with on these projects, so don't overdo the hollowing—leave the bottom of the plate at least ³⁄₁₆" thick. I normally shape the bottom with the bowl gouge (**Photo 16**), followed by very light scraping with a square ended scraper (**Photo 17**). Once the open side of the

13 Complete the rim. It can be tapered or flat and wide or narrow, depending on your taste and the shape you've created on the outside of the plate.

14 Establish the plate's depth. Cut in decisively from the edge of the rim, plunging down and towards the center.

15 Remove the waste at the center, using the opposite side of the gouge and working in the opposite direction. Plunge in and down to full depth. Back off the tailstock to complete the job.

16 Make a light, cleaning cut with the bowl gouge to blend the transition between the previous two cuts. Switch to a square ended scraper to level the surface. Then finish-sand this side of the plate.

17 Remove the plate from the faceplate with a slow, steady pull. Remove any tape or residue that remains with mineral spirits. Finish-sand the back side of the plate by hand.

18 Apply your chosen finish. This is pure tung oil.

plate is turned, complete the process by sanding. I prefer to sand this side by hand, especially if it has beads and other fine details.

Apply the Finish

Removing the plate or platter from the taped faceplate can be challenging, because of the strong bond. The key is a steady, even pull for 20 to 30 seconds (**Photo 18**). If the project has turned out to be on the thin side, work some mineral spirits or naphtha into the area of the tape and wait a few minutes. Then try the slow and steady pull—don't force it.

Clean the bottom with mineral spirits or naphtha; then sand lightly by hand.

For functional objects that will be well cared for, I like to use food safe oil finishes, such as pure tung oil, walnut oil or mineral oil. Tung and walnut oils will eventually dry; mineral oil never dries. For stain resistance, I suggest using a film-type finish, such as a wiping varnish. Plan to apply at least four coats. Once they've fully cured, these finishes are food safe.

SOURCES Craft Supplies, woodturnerscatalog.com, 800 551 8876, Double-sided Tape #104-982, $27.50. The Sanding Glove (www.thesandingglove.com, 800 995 9328, 5" Disc Holder #PSM-5M $15.95; 30 Piece Norton DryIce 5" disc assortment #DRI-500-AP $26.95.

CHAPTER TWENTY-FOUR

PROJECT 10 Spinning Top

%)) *A two-piece varation of a classic toy* ((%

Most of us picture a spinning top as a simple wooden toy that stands upright when it spins. But in other parts of the world, the perception can be quite different. In Japan, for example, it is said that there are over one thousand different types and variations of tops.

I'm going to show you how to create one of those variations, a spinning top that's made out of two pieces of wood, instead of one. This miniature project offers a great opportunity to try your hand at precision turning. It also gives you the chance to add interest by using contrasting woods or even non-wood materials. And if one piece breaks, you can disassemble the top and install a replacement part.

Despite their diminutive size, you can make these tops

on any lathe, and you only need four tools to create them—a spindle roughing gouge (¾" to 1-¼"), a narrow parting tool (³⁄₁₆" to ¼"), a ⅜" spindle detail gouge and a skew chisel. If you are adept with your skew chisel, you can complete the entire project with it alone. You'll also need a ¼" drill bit and a Jacobs-type chuck that mounts into your tailstock (see Sources, page 108). Using a scroll-type chuck to hold the pieces is most convenient, but it's not necessary (see "No-Frills Mounting," page 108 and Sources).

The wood you use is part of the design. Choose a hard, dense wood for the top's shaft, as both the spinning point and the finger-gripping area will be made from this material. Good choices for the shaft include hard maple, cherry,

1

Use the tailstock center to hold the blank for the disc-shaped top bodies in position as you tighten the scroll chuck.

2

Round the blank with the spindle roughing gouge.

3

Cut in with the narrow parting tool to establish the disc.

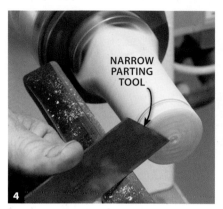

4

Exactly center a tiny recess in the disc's face.

5

Use the recess and a Jacobs-type chuck mounted in the tailstock to drill a hole through the disc. This hole must be precisely centered for the top to spin without wobbling.

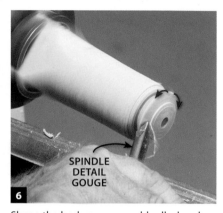

6

Shape the body as you would roll a bead. Start at the edge and cut toward the center, rotating the gouge as you go. When shaping the back, don't cut all the way to the center hole.

Osage orange, and numerous exotic woods such as ebony, bubinga, goncalo alves and bloodwood. Make sure this wood is well dried. For the top's disc-shaped body, you have many more options. Choose woods that contrast well in color or figure, again on the drier side. If you intend to chatter the body (I'll show this option), be sure and pick a very hard wood such as hard maple or one of the exotics mentioned above. To explore non-wood possibilities, consider materials such as solid surface composites, hard plastics, antler or even soft metals.

These tops operate by spinning them with your fingers, so they should be less than 1-¾" in diameter. Most of the finger-spun tops that I make measure 1-¼" to 1-½". Also, you should plan to make these tops in multiples, because you can easily turn three to five of the disc-shaped bodies from a single blank.

Turn the Body

Cut a square blank of wood, approximately 4" long. Mark the center of one end of the blank.

Mount the block loosely in the scroll chuck, with the marked center towards the tailstock.

Engage the point of the tailstock center on your mark, to hold the blank perfectly centered while you tighten the chuck (**Photo 1**). Then back off the tailstock.

Round the blank using the spindle roughing gouge or your skew chisel (**Photo 2**).

Use the parting tool to establish the disc's thickness—usually between ¼" and ⅜" (Photo 3). Then mark the center of the disc's face (**Photo 4**).

Install a Jacobs-type chuck and drill a ¼" hole, precisely centered and about 1" deep (**Photo 5**).

Shape the body on both sides, using the spindle detail gouge (**Photo 6**). A slightly rounded body is more appealing than one that is cut straight in. Take care to cut the outside face cleanly. It will be the most visible part of the top. Finish-sand this face, unless you want to enhance it by adding chatter marks.

If you want to add chatter marks, you'll need a chatter tool (**Photo 7** and Sources). Learning to use this tool takes practice, so experiment on scrap materials, or plan to sacrifice a few top bodies as you get the hang of it. Here's a tip: a chatter tool makes a high-pitched noise when it's working

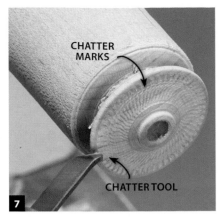

7 CHATTER MARKS / CHATTER TOOL

Create interesting texture with a chatter tool. A chatter tool's thin shaft is designed to vibrate when it contacts the wood, causing its tip to leave squiggly marks on the surface.

8

To chatter the top of the body, move the tool rest back and hold the chatter tool as shown. Start near the center and draw the tool toward the edge.

9 JAPANESE PAINT PEN

Accentuate chatter marks with color. Use a delicate touch to color only the high points, or flow the color into the crevices and then sand lightly, to remove the color from the high points.

10

Free the completed body by cutting in with the narrow parting tool. Catch the body in your hand or let it to fall onto a paper towel draped over the lathe's ways, and you're ready to go again.

11

To finish turning the body's bottom face, turn it around and re-mount it on a stub spindle that you've turned on a scrap block.

12 SKEW CHISEL

Complete the bottom face with light cuts and finish-sanding.

properly. The lathe's speed, how hard you push, and how fast you draw the tool across the surface all effect the chatter pattern. (**Photo 8**).

Another option is to add rings of color, using Japanese paint pens, such as Tombow dual brush pens (**Photo 9** and Sources). Color adds interest to both chattered and smoothly sanded surfaces.

Part off the top body, either catching it in your hand or allowing it to fall into a paper towel (**Photo 10**).

Turn as many top bodies as the blank allows, until about 1" remains protruding from the chuck.

Using the narrow parting tool, turn a ¼" dia. spindle on a scrap block, so you can mount the bodies backwards, to finish the bottoms (**Photo 11**). This spindle should be slightly longer than the bodies' thickness. The goal is a fit that's snug enough to allow working the body, yet free enough to allow removing the body when it's done. Turning this spindle is actually great practice for an upcoming step—turning the hub that secures the body to the shaft. Finish the bottom face of each body to the same level as its top face (**Photo 12**).

Turn the Shaft

I turn the shafts one at a time. Start by mounting and truing a blank (**Photo 13**).

Rough out the shaft's components (**Photo 14**). I usually make the hub a bit longer than the body's thickness, and the gripping area (for spinning the top) about 1-¼" long. I like to make the gripping area pretty slender, but not less than ⅛" dia. Finish-sand the gripping area.

Create a cradle to seat the body (**Photo 15**).

Size the hub (**Photo 16**).

Shape the bottom, but don't cut it off just yet (**Photo 17**). Finish-sand the bottom. Do not sand the hub, where the body mounts.

Use the skew chisel or the narrow parting tool to cut the shaft from the blank, leaving the bottom's spinning point slightly rounded.

Assemble the top (**Photo 18**). If the fit isn't quite tight enough, a small amount of glue will hold the two pieces together.

NO-FRILLS MOUNTING

Here's how to mount both blanks without using a scroll chuck. Shape the end of the blank for the top's body to a #2 Morse taper, so it fits snugly inside the drive shaft. Turn a concave shoulder on the blank, so it nests firmly against the driveshaft threads. Use the knockout bar for removal.

To mount the blank for the shaft, simply jam a 9/16" square length into the driveshaft. You can chamfer the corners at the end if you want, to make it easier to get started. Again, use the knockout bar for removal.

SKEW CHISEL

13

To create the top's shaft, start with a ½" square x 3" long blank mounted in the scroll chuck. Turn the blank round with the spindle roughing gouge or skew chisel. Then taper the end.

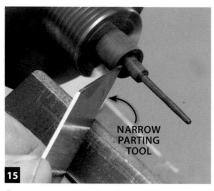

NARROW PARTING TOOL

15

Create a cradle to seat the disc-shaped body by hollowing the shoulder with either the skew or a narrow parting tool.

SKEW CHISEL

17

Shape the bottom like the outside of a tiny bowl, and create the spinning point as you part off the shaft. The spinning point's tip should be slightly rounded.

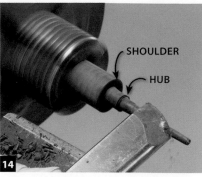

SHOULDER

HUB

14

Rough out the shoulder that will seat the top's body, the hub that it will mount on, and the gripping area for your fingers. Reduce this area to a diameter that's smaller than the hole in the top's body.

16

Here's the tricky part. Turn the hub's diameter to snugly fit the hole in the body—tight enough to hold the body on, but not so tight that you can't remove it. This step requires patience and lots of test fitting.

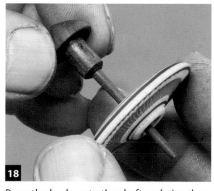

18

Press the body onto the shaft and give the top a spin.

SOURCES Packard Woodworks, www.packardwoodworks.com, (800) 683-8876, Oneway Talon Scroll Chuck #112670 $206.95 + #112606 $24.95 adapter for your lathe; Talon Spigot (small) Jaws #1122671 $40.95; Jacobs-Type Chuck #2MT, #111012 $36.95; KC Chatter Tool #105301 $49.95. ⊙ Dick Blick, www.dickblick.com, (800) 828-4548, Tombow Brush Pens, set of 10 bright colors #21334-2219, $15.99. ◠

CHAPTER TWENTY-FIVE

PROJECT 11 Classic Wooden Bat

Learn how to beat the chatter

The crack of a baseball against a wooden bat is a wonderful sound seldom heard today. Too often it's been replaced by the metallic "clink" of an aluminum bat. Baseball has its roots in balls, gloves and shoes made from animal hides, and bats made from trees. It seems an odd place for high tech equipment to intrude. Making a wooden bat returns you and your kids to the real, old-time baseball.

The Right Wood

Almost every common wood has been used for bats at one time or another. However, a few species dominate the history of the sport. Traditionally northern ash has been the wood of choice, but currently— at least in the pros— it is a neck-and-neck race with hard maple. A few bats are still made of hickory and beech. For this project, I suggest buying a blank of ash or maple that has been graded for bats (see "Sources", p. 112). The reason is not only superior performance, but also safety. A bat made from a graded bat blank is less likely to break in use.

MAJOR LEAGUE BAT — 2-¾" MAX
42" MAX (32" - 36" TYP.

ADULT SOFTBALL BAT — 2-¼" MAX
34" MAX (38 OZ. MAX WEIGHT

LITTLE LEAGUE BAT — 2-¼" MAX
33" MAX (26" - 32" TYP.

FIG. A
Note: These numbers are only guidelines. Because of the ever changing and sometimes localized nature of bat regulations, it's best to check with your local league officials for specific bat dimension limits.

1 If you're starting with a purchased round blank, mark the center on both ends with a plastic center finder. On a square blank use a ruler across the diagonals to find the centers.

2 True the cylinder's entire length with a spindle-roughing gouge. This step is necessary because the blank may be warped, or your center marks aren't perfect. Take light cuts. You don't want to remove too much stock.

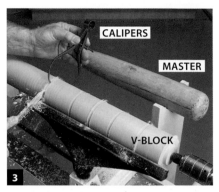

CALIPERS
MASTER
V-BLOCK

3 Size the bat with calipers and a parting tool. Transfer diameters from a drawing or an existing bat (called a master) onto the blank. Lightly push the calipers into the work as you reduce the diameter with the parting tool until the calipers just slip over the cut.

Bat blanks are graded differently from regular furniture grade lumber. First, only straight-grained wood from slow-growing trees of moderate size make the grade. The blank must have tight, evenly spaced growth rings and be free of flaws like knots. The best blanks are often split from the log rather than sawn in order to follow the grain perfectly. Extra care is taken in the drying of bat blanks to create an even distribution of moisture throughout the entire thickness.

Tools and Supplies

To make a full-size baseball bat you will need a lathe that can handle lengths up to 36" between centers. For Little League bats a lathe with shorter capacity will work just fine. It is best to have a live center at the tailstock end, and drive with either a spur or cup drive. If you are duplicating a bat, you will need to fabricate a simple V-block system to hold the master bat (the one being duplicated) directly behind your blank (**Photo 3**).

The bat can be turned with three tools: a spindle- roughing gouge (1-¼" to 1-¾"), a parting tool (¼" wide) and a spindle/detail gouge (⅜" or ½"). If you are comfortable using a skew, a large one (1" to 1-½") can be added as an option for smoothing the shape and rounding the end of the barrel.

Complete your supplies with a pair of locking outside calipers. Make sure the caliper's points are fully rounded smooth. Sharp points can catch when used to size your bat. Round the points with a file and smooth with sandpaper. A pair of dividers is helpful—although optional—for sizing the knob's width. A plastic center finder is helpful in locating centers on round bat blanks (see "Sources").

Prepare the Blank

Determine the type of the bat you intend to turn: Major League, softball or Little League. This can be based on an old favorite you'd like to duplicate or from scratch using a drawing based on regulations dimension (see Fig. A, p. 110). The blank should be 1 to 2 inches longer than the finished bat to allow for waste at both ends.

Mark the centers on the blank (**Photo 1**) and mount it on the lathe. I place the barrel end of the bat at the tailstock. Then I true the cylinder to the axis of the lathe (**Photo 2**).

Shape the Barrel

Shape the widest part of the bat, called the barrel, first. You want to preserve the thick diameter on the blank as long as possible to avoid chatter from vibration. Start by making guide diameters on the first third of the blank with calipers and a parting tool (**Photo 3**). Set the calipers about ⅛" wider

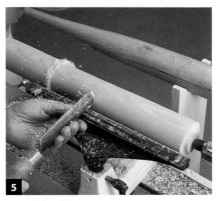

Use a spindleroughing gouge to "connect the dots". The goal is to join and blend the different guide diameters to create a smooth cylinder that tapers towards the handle.

Take light cuts and create level transitions as you approach the final shape of the barrel. Work from the large diameter to the small to minimize tearout.

Roll over the end of the barrel with a detail/spindle gouge. Shoot for a smooth, gradual curve like the master has. Leave about a ½" by 2" diameter waste area near your live center for now.

Spiraling or chatter is a big challenge for the bat maker. Spiraling results from the wood flexing, or the tool bouncing or a combination of both. As the bat gets thinner, the problem becomes more pronounced.

Support the work with your hand to reduce spiraling. This is a safe and common practice. Make sure there is little gap between the tool rest and the wood. Keep your hand pressure on the back of the blank.

A steady rest is an alternative to the hand-support method. It virtually eliminates chatter and spiraling because the work is supported on three sides at once. A steady rest requires a smooth area for the wheels to run upon.

than the desired diameter to allow for final shaping and sanding. If you're duplicating a bat, place the master directly behind the mounted blank.

Next is a process of connecting the guide diameters with the spindle-roughing gouge (**Photo 4**). Shoot for smooth transitions between the guide diameters (**Photo 5**).

Go ahead and roll over the end of the barrel at this time (**Photo 6**).

Shape the Handle

Mark and shape the middle third of the bat in the same way you shaped the barrel. When you reach the last third of the bat, remove some of the waste material towards the knob end first to give you some working room. Spindle work is best done from larger to smaller diameters because it produces the least amount of tearout. As you reduce the diameter of the bat, you will experience chatter. This usually shows up as spiral marks on the surface of the wood (**Photo 7**). To reduce chatter, use a sharp tool and keep it firmly planted on the tool rest. Take light cuts. Avoid pushing hard

or you're bound to get chatter from the flexing blank. Even with all these tactics, you will need added support as the handle narrows. The traditional method is to support the narrow area with your hand (**Photo 8**). Another option is to employ a steady rest (**Photo 9**). I use a steady rest when I get to about the middle of the blank.

Continue the process of cutting and connecting the guide diameters working from the large diameters on either end towards the narrowest point on the handle (**Photo 10**).

Shape the Knob

As you approach the end of the bat, go ahead and lay out the knob area. Establish the knob's width and diameter (**Photo 11**). Then reduce the diameter on the knob's right side, blending into the handle. Leave a ½" to 1" length of waste material past the end of the knob.

After the handle area is completed, finish off the knob by rolling away the corners with the spindle/detail gouge (**Photo 12**).

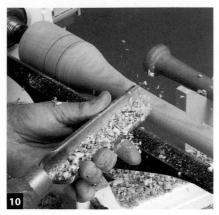

10 Work the area to the right of the knob. Cut from the large diameter towards the small diameter (also known as cutting downhill). This produces the smoothest cut with the least tearout.

11 Establish the width of the knob with a pair of dividers. I keep the wood on either side of the knob as fat as possible until the handle area is almost complete. This helps reduce spiraling from a flexing blank.

12 Roll the knob using the spindle/detail gouge. Start at the widest portion of the knob and ride the bevel of the gouge down to the handle or waste block. The open or U-shaped portion of the gouge faces the direction of the cut.

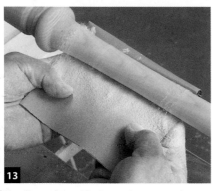

13 Sand your bat with the tool rest, steady rest, and master bat removed. Start with #100-grit followed by #120, #150 and #180-grit paper.

14 Add a customized look to your bat by burning in your own brand. The brand is always placed on the face grain portion of the bat (see inset) to give the hitter a point of reference for positioning the bat.

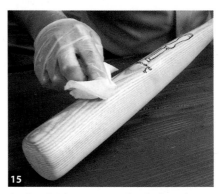

15 Apply a finish to give a richer look to the bat as well as some protection against moisture.

Finishing Touches

Sand the entire piece, working through the different grits up to #180 (**Photo 13**). Turn the waste material on both ends down to slightly larger than your lathe centers. Remove the bat, cut the waste off with a handsaw (such as a small Japanese saw), and finish sanding the ends of your bat by hand or a disc on the lathe.

Most bats have brands to indicate how the bat should be held. Always swing the bat with the label up to reduce the chances of breakage.

The goal is to hit the ball on the radial grain, or what some woodworkers call the edge grain—rather than the tangential or face grain. So, put your brand on the grain that looks like chevrons rather than the edges of plywood. Use a woodburning tool to put whatever name or symbol you wish to use as your brand (**Photo 14**).

I recommend finishing your bat (**Photo 15**). A finish gives the bat a nicer look as it brings out the grain. Plus it offers some protection from moisture. All types of finishes have been used for bats, including shellac, lacquer, varnish (water-based or oil-based). For this bat I am using a wipe-on poly; three coats is sufficient. Some players prefer the handle area to be free of finish—for better gripping and applying pine tar.

Now, it's time to hit the field!

SOURCES Craft Supplies, woodturnerscatalog.com, 800 551 8876, ash bat blanks #104-359 $18.95 or #25.95 in hard maple; woodburner #1040671 $85.95 (other models available). Oneway, oneway.ca, 800 565 7288, Spindle steady #3280, $144.95.

CHAPTER TWENTY-SIX

PROJECT 12 Wooden Fishing Lures

*Turning the body
is half the fun*

1

Most lures are simply shaped, so they're easy to turn with a skew chisel or detail/spindle gouge. Cylinders and elliptical shapes like this one are typical. Sizes vary, depending on the type of fish you want to catch.

SKEW CHISEL

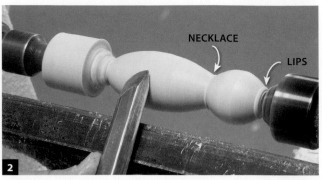

2

NECKLACE

LIPS

Embellish the basic shape to create variations. Adding a head and unique details, such as lips and a necklace show individuality that's not always found on factory-made lures.

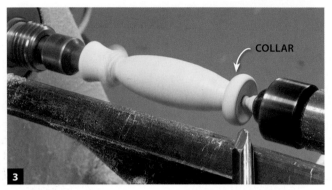

3

COLLAR

Add a hollowed-out collar to create additional sound and surface disturbance. The hollow shape makes the lure chug and pop as it's pulled across the water. To hollow the collar, cut in with a skew chisel, long point down.

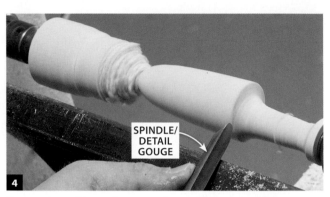

4

SPINDLE/ DETAIL GOUGE

Create a lure with an offset snout by turning on two different centers. Turn the body with the blank centered between the ends. Then offset the blank's mounting point at the tailstock end to turn the snout.

W hen I picked up Dudley Murphy and Rick Edmisten's *Fishing Lure Collectibles* (see Sources, page 116), my interests in fishing, antiques and wood turning met head-on: Now I'm hooked on making wooden fishing lures. I know this passion is somewhat irrational, because plastic lures are abundant and economical—and they catch fish. I make my own wooden lures because it's fun. I love recreating old patterns as much as I love to explore my own theories on catching fish. I enjoy testing unusual shapes and unique finishes. And I can report first-hand that catching a fish with a lure I've made myself is delightful. You should try it yourself.

I like to fish for bass, musky and pike, which are all known to feed at the surface, so most of the lures that I make are designed to skip across the water. These "top water" lures can be made from almost any wood that holds screws well. (There's nothing worse than having a trophy fish escape because it was able to rip out the screw that anchored the hook to the lure!) I usually work with poplar and start with 1-½" to 1-¾" square blocks. My bass lures range from 2" to 5" in length, while my musky and pike lures tend to be 5" to 11" long.

Use Your Imagination

Usually, turning a wooden lure is basic spindle work, but the shapes you can experiment with are almost endless. Mimic a minnow or a small fish, a crawfish, a frog, a mouse, a bug, or a bird. Sometimes the turning doesn't resemble anything specific from nature.

Most lure shapes are turned between centers with basic tools (**Photos 1 and 2**). If you're adept with a skew chisel, you can complete most of the work using it alone. Use the skew or a ½" round-nose scraper to create a detail that gives the lure more "action" (**Photo 3**). Use a ⅜" detail/spindle gouge and turn from two different centers to create a lure with an unusual face (**Photo 4**).

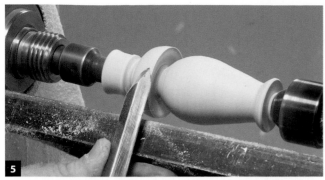

5

Create your own designs. I call this one the "Leapin' Lacer." The turning is just a squat-shaped ellipse with hollowed collars at both ends. But to a largemouth bass, the completed lure will look like a tasty frog (Photo 10).

6

Most lures take ten minutes or less to turn, so it makes sense to turn multiples, whether they're unique or all the same. Leave the waste attached for now—it makes painting much easier.

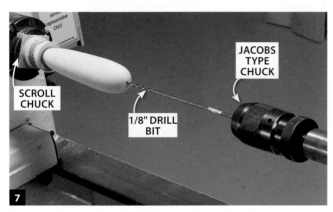

SCROLL CHUCK

1/8" DRILL BIT

JACOBS TYPE CHUCK

7

To strengthen any lure, drill all the way through and mount the hook on stainless steel wire. Install the lure in a scroll chuck and drill from the tailstock end, using a long bit and a Jacobs-type chuck.

8

Here's the lazy man's painting method—just hold the brush and let the lathe do all the work. Run the lathe very slowly and thin the paint so that it flows evenly onto the lure.

Refer to old lure shapes you find appealing, or use your imagination to dream up your own shapes (**Photo 5**). Whatever the shape, it'll take only minutes to complete, so you might as well turn several at a time (**Photo 6**).

To eliminate any chance of a fish ripping out the hook, attach the hook to a length of stainless steel wire (.030"—.040") that runs all the way through the lure (**Photo 7**). Drill a ⅛" hole and glue in ⅛" aluminum tubing to house the wire. Then insert the wire and use pliers to create loops at both ends for tying on the lure and for mounting the hook. This through wire also creates a nice foundation for adding propellers, beads and other details.

What Fish Want

To attract fish, wooden lures are usually painted, and they almost always have eyes—as far as I can tell, fish just don't appreciate plain wood.

Historically, lures were brush-painted, dipped, marbled or sprayed. Red was often used as the primary color, or for details, in the belief that predator fish would view it as blood, a sign of injury. Examples decorated with real frog skin have

also been documented. All of these options are open to the contemporary lure maker (except, perhaps, the frog skin option). I usually use a variation of the brush-painting method to apply paint while the lure is still on the lathe (**Photos 8 and 9**). Epoxy paints are the most durable, but they take a long time to dry, which makes applying multiple colors a lengthy process. I often use acrylic paints for the color coats, followed several days later by a coat of clear epoxy paint, for durability.

Another option is to carve or sand the turned body, before or after painting, to make the lure attract more piscean

SKEW CHISEL

9

Turn down the waste material at both ends, after the paint has dried. Then part off. This step shortens the time it takes to produce finished surfaces on the ends.

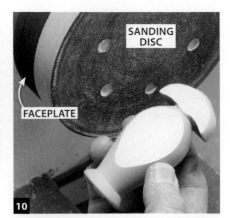

SANDING DISC

FACEPLATE

10

Flattening one side on a sanding disc transforms the turned body of the "Leapin' Lacer" into a frog—especially from a largemouth's viewpoint. Adding hardware (and occasionally lead weights) ensures that the lure will orient correctly in the water.

11

Attach eyes, hooks, weights and other hardware to complete each lure. Outsmarting fish isn't always easy, so use both your experience and imagination. And don't hesitate to change hardware that doesn't seem to work.

attention as it moves across the water. Carving the head end of a lure will make it wobble or dive, much like hollowing on the lathe. A bit of sanding can dramatically change a turned lure's appearance (**Photo 10**). Viewing historical examples is a great way to get ideas for additional shaping (see Sources).

Eyes really do make a difference—just ask anyone who casts a lure. Eyes can be painted on or dotted, or they can be small tacks or nails that are driven in and then painted. You can also buy eyes made of glass or plastic, adhesive backed or with stems for gluing into a hole—or even doll eyes with loose pupils, for that "come hither" look that may help you hook the big one.

Please the Consumer

An almost endless array of options exists for mounting hooks and adding the final touches that make a piece of wood irresistible to fish (**Photo 11**). You can buy hardware (see Sources), strip it from an old lure, or make it yourself from

metal or plastic. You can keep it simple or go for broke by installing hooks wrapped with fur or feathers, eyelets, diving lips, spinners, propellers, fins, collars, glass and metal beads, wire, spacers, cup washers, weights and split rings. The bottom line during the entire lure-making process is to think like a hungry fish, because ultimately, hungry fish will be your greatest critics.

"LEAPIN' LACER"

SOURCES Dudley Murphy and Rick Edmisten, *Fishing Lure Collectibles: An Identification and Value Guide to the Most Collectible Antique Fishing Lures Vol. I (2nd Ed)*, Collector Books, 2001. ☞ Barlow's Tackle Express, www.barlowstackle.com, (972) 231-5982; Jann's Netcraft, www.jannsnetcraft.com, (800) 346-6590; Moore's Lures, www.mooreslures.com, (715) 356-6834. ☞

CHAPTER TWENTY-SEVEN

PROJECT 13 Bocce Balls

Practice turning spheres freehand

SHOP-MADE CHUCKS

You have to make three different concave holding chucks to turn these balls. For the headstock side you need two different sizes that fit into your scroll chuck or a recess in a scrap block on your 3" faceplate (a "jam chuck," see **Photo 2**). On the tailstock side, make a chuck that slips over your live center (two styles are shown as examples). This tailstock chuck works for both size balls.

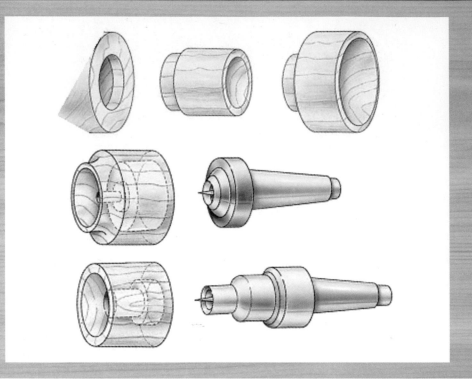

Freehand turning of a near perfect wooden sphere without flat spots or bumps is a wonderful challenge for a turner. Whether it's for croquet, furniture drawer knobs or simply as a decorative object, the wooden sphere is a wonderful exercise in developing a form, tool control and understanding grain direction.

We've chosen to make wooden balls for the ancient game of bocce ball. Originating in the Middle East some 7,000 years ago, the game was popular with ancient Greeks and Romans. It hit its heyday in 16th-century Italy, where it was something of a national sport. Much of the vocabulary and manner of play stems from this period.

Bocce Ball Essentials

To play the game you have to make either five or nine wooden balls, in two sizes. One ball, the "pallino" or target ball, should be approx. 2-¼" in diameter, in a contrasting or colored wood. The other balls, or "bocce" that are tossed, should be approx. 4" in diameter. Create either a full set with eight bocce or a half set of four, with one-half of each set in distinctive colors or patterns to identify two sides or teams. Within each team you may want to create a crisscross or other pattern to distinguish individual bocce balls.

Wood to Turn

Turn the bocce balls and pallino from a dense hardwood such as hard maple, birch or white oak in either solid or laminated stock. If you laminate, choose glue that is water-resistant and doesn't "creep" at the seams such as plastic resin or polyurethane.

Here's What You Need:

- Hard maple, 4x4 by 1" (makes four bocce balls; buy twice this amount for a full set of 8). Each ball blank should be 4-½" long.
- Hardwood, 2-¼" by 2-¼" by 2-¾" (for one pallino).
- Basswood (or poplar) 3" by 3" by 2" in length (headstock side holding chuck for larger ball); two pieces 2" by 2" by 2" (headstock side holding chuck for smaller ball and for tailstock-side holding chuck that fits over the live center).
- ½" detailing gouge ground to a fingernail shape, roughing gouge, parting tool, ½" to 1" round-nose scraper, ½" or larger skew chisel.
- Outside calipers with a minimum capacity of 4-½"
- Dividers or compass.
- Either a scroll chuck or a 3" faceplate with 1-½"-thick piece of face-grain poplar or soft maple.
- Live center for tailstock, spur center for headstock.
- Jacobs chuck and appropriate bit for fitting tailstock-side chuck to your live center.
- Acrylic paint in two colors and a small, stiff brush.
- Wood dye.

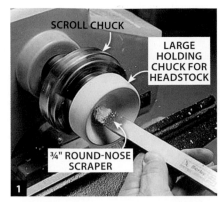

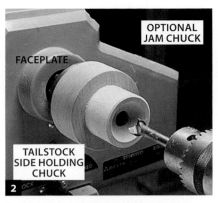

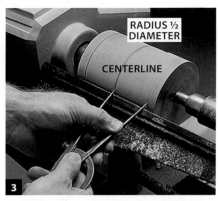

Begin by turning a chuck to hold the balls as they are turned. This one is for the larger balls, and is held at the headstock. Work from the center out with your round-nose scraper to produce a smooth surface. Make a smaller chuck for the headstock to hold the pallino.

Turn another holding chuck for the tail-stock. It needs to fit over a live center so it can spin freely. Drill or turn out the center of the chuck to match the outside diameter of the live center. Each live center requires a slightly different design. The chuck must be centered and fit snugly.

Lay out the size of the ball with dividers or a compass after roughing out the blank to a cylinder. Mark the centerline (red) and two radius lines (blue) that are equal to half the dia. of the cylinder. After marking, reduce the waste outside of the radius lines to approx. 1" in dia.

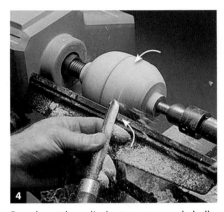

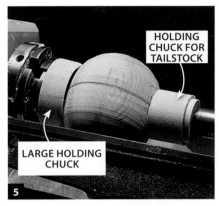

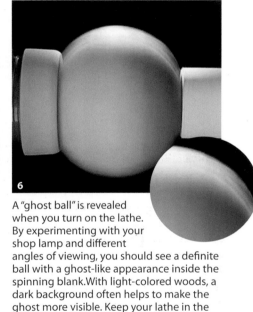

Rough cut the cylinder to a very crude ball form using a ½" detail gouge. Don't be too zealous in trying to hit the perfect sphere at this point—it is far too easy to cut below the curves of the final sphere. Allow considerable waste material to be trimmed away in the next step.

Mount the rough ball between the two holding chucks with the red centerline turned 90° so it's parallel to the bed or axis of the lathe. Rotate the lathe by hand a few times to be sure both sides of the red line are in alignment. When all seems right, firmly secure the block by tightening the tailstock.

A "ghost ball" is revealed when you turn on the lathe. By experimenting with your shop lamp and different angles of viewing, you should see a definite ball with a ghost-like appearance inside the spinning blank. With light-colored woods, a dark background often helps to make the ghost more visible. Keep your lathe in the slower speed ranges (400 to 600 rpm).

The Rules of Bocce Ball

Official bocce ball is played on a court of fixed dimensions, often with walls and backstops. What most of us play is an informal version or "lawn bowling." Here are the basic rules:

- There are two teams, played with two, four, or eight players. In games of two or four players, you can get by with only four bocce balls. The game is a bit more interesting, though, if you play with a full set of eight balls.
- By a flip of a coin or some other means, choose one side to roll the small ball (pallino) out into the playing area. All throws must be made behind a real or imaginary foul line.
- The side that placed the pallino rolls one bocce ball as close to the pallino as possible (even touching it). This becomes the "point ball."

- The opposing side rolls all of its bocce balls to see if it can come closer to the pallino than the "point ball."
- The starting team rolls the remainder of its bocce balls to see if can come closer to the pallino than any of their opponents' balls.
- Points are awarded after all bocce balls have been thrown. A point is awarded for each ball closer than any of the opponents' to the pallino. Games are played to 12, 16 or 21. Often the winner must win by at least two points.
- Yes, you may hit the pallino, your own team's previously thrown bocce or the bocce of the opposing team!

For more information, go to www.bocceballrules.net

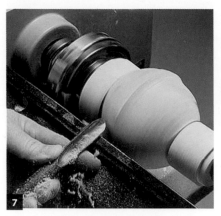

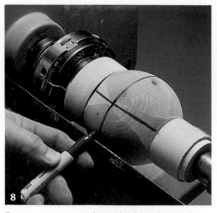

Turn down to the ghost ball, using a ½" detailing gouge with a fingernail shape. Work from smaller to larger diameters on both sides of the centerline (the ball now has the same grain orientation as a face-grain bowl). Go slowly and gently, with a mixture of cutting and light scraping actions to remove waste surrounding the ghost ball.

Draw a new centerline (the blue line) when you're finished turning.

Continue turning with the blue line positioned parallel to the lathe's axis. The grain is again as we started (indicated by the red line), so work from larger to smaller diameter in order to work with the grain. Gently turn away the waste that was held in the holding chucks. Again, use the ghost ball as a guide.

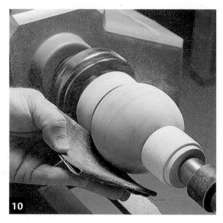

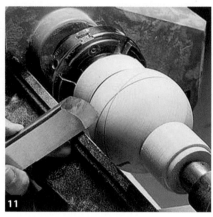

Sand to further refine the shape and remove minor imperfections. Randomly reposition the ball five or six times, sanding lightly between each change of position.

Cut narrow grooves on the larger balls with the long point (toe) of the skew chisel. Create a crisscross pattern by changing the axis of the ball. With the lathe spinning, color the grooves with unthinned acrylic paint applied with a stiff brush. Light sanding removes excess paint. The single pallino (smaller ball) is usually not grooved and can be dyed a bright color for high visibility..

SOURCES Constantines, constantines.com, 954 561 1716, Hard maple 4 x 4 x 18" (makes 4 bocce balls), $35.25, hard maple 2 1/2" square 12" long for the pallino, $7.95.. ☺ Woodcraft Supply, (800) 225-1153, www.woodcraft.com, yellow powdered dye for the pallino #123837 $11.49, plus shipping. ℘

CHAPTER TWENTY-EIGHT

14 Heirloom Awl

~∽ *An exercise in basic toolmaking* ∼~

Metal and wood are the basic ingredients in most woodworking tools. As woodworkers, we're familiar with working wood, but what about metal? Actually, the level of metal working required to make some woodworking tools is pretty basic. If you've never made your own tools, give this project a try. There's something enormously satisfying about using a tool you made yourself.

We chose the scratch awl for this article because it's an everyday tool that's easy to make. This project will teach you the basic principles of heat-treating steel and turning a wood handle with a metal ferrule. This awl will be the first

milestone on your custom tool-making journey.

Note: This project involves metal grinding and working with an open flame, be sure to follow these basic safety guidelines:

- Thoroughly clean the work area of all wood shavings and dust before using the torch or grinding the steel.
- Keep a fire extinguisher on hand for emergencies.
- If possible, do the heat-treating outside.
- Wear eye protection for all grinding operations.
- Never use motor oil for the heat-treating process.

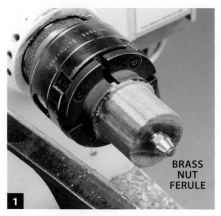

1

Round the handle blank and fit the ferrule on the end. You can use different materials for a ferrule; this one is a solid brass nut with a tapered end section.

BRASS NUT FERULE

2

Rough in the basic shape of the handle with the detailing gouge. The shape and size of the handle is up to you.

3

Turn away the flats of the nut and shape the ferrule with a detailing gouge. Cutting brass and copper on the lathe is similar to cutting wood. However, take light cuts.

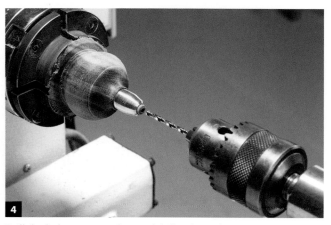

4

Drill the hole to accept the steel drill rod. Use bits 1/64" larger in diameter than the drill rod to allow room for the epoxy.

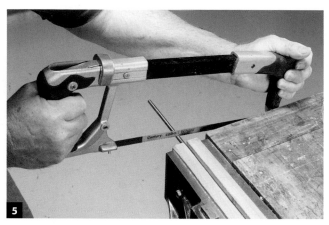

5

Make the awl's steel shaft from a piece of drill rod. Cut it to length using a hacksaw.

What You Will Need:

- Fire extinguisher
- ⅛", ³⁄₁₆" or ¼" dia. drill rod in oil hardening steel
- Propane or MAP gas torch
- Quart of olive oil
- Locking pliers
- 8" or 10" mill file
- Electric drill
- 10" Grinding disc on ¾" plywood or MDF.
- 2" x 2" x 4" piece of dry hardwood
- Copper plumbing coupling, brass or copper pipe, brass nut, or brass compression nut for the ferrule material
- Metal can with a lid
- Lathe tools: roughing gouge, detail gouge, parting tool, and optional skew chisel
- Scroll chuck
- Sandpaper (usually #100, #150, #180 and #220)
- Jacobs style chuck for your lathe's tailstock
- A drill bit that's ¹⁄₆₄" larger than the drill rod
- Epoxy
- Optional; Tempilstik in 450°–50)° range

Turn the Handle

Pick any strong hardwood for the handle: cherry, hard maple, oak, walnut, hickory, ash, rosewood, goncalo alves, purpleheart, etc. (Now, aren't you glad you saved all those little pieces of really cool wood?) Determine the desired diameter and length of the handle. Be sure to allow for the length of the ferrule.

Mount the wood into the scroll chuck and create a cylinder with the roughing gouge.

With the parting tool, cut a small cylinder on the end to fit the metal ferrule (**Photo 1**). Take care to achieve a tight fit. The ferrule stock can be a copper coupling (¼" to ½" depending on the look you desire), brass nuts, brass or copper pipe. If you're using a brass nut, simply thread it onto the wood.

Shape the handle with the detail gouge or skew chisel (**Photo 2**). The possibilities are endless and depend on the handle style, the size of your hands, and whether the tool is meant for delicate or heavy service. I seldom make any two the same. Take the opportunity to add your own fine detailing to distinguish your awl from production versions. When

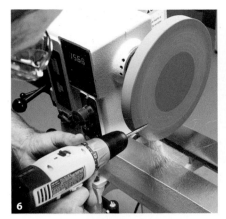

Shape a tapered point on the shaft using a drill and a lathe mounted abrasive disc. With the drill running, grind the point on the near lower quadrant of the spinning disc. Wear eye protection!

Harden the shaft by heating the pointed half to an even cherry red color. Hold the shaft in a pair of locking pliers.

When the steel is evenly bright red from the point to the middle, quickly quench and stir it in a can of olive oil.

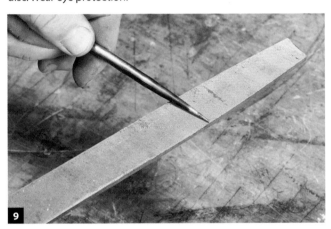

Test the hardness of the shaft by running it along a file. The hardened part should skate off the file, not bite in.

Sand the steel to a bright, clean surface with #220-grit paper. Wash it with soap and water to remove oil residue first.

satisfied with the shape, finish sand to #220-grit.

Shape the ferrule with the gouge (**Photo 3**).

Use a Jacobs chuck to drill a 1-½" (minimum) deep hole for the steel shaft (**Photo 4**).

Part the handle off the chuck and hand sand the end. You can leave the handle unfinished or use a drying oil.

Make the Steel Shaft

Drill rod is too soft to use as a tool. On the other hand, soft steel is easy to work so we'll leave it that way for now and tackle the hardening later.

Cut the drill rod with a hacksaw to the desired length of the awl shaft (**Photo 5**). I normally use 3" to 6" lengths. Choose a length and diameter that fits the desired look of the awl.

To shape the point on the business end of the shaft, first chuck it in a drill. Then, run the drill as you hold the shaft against a spinning lathe mounted grinding disc (**Photo 6**). Run the lathe at low to medium speed (400 to 800 rpm). Don't try and put a delicate point on the steel at the stage. It will just get burned off in the heat-treating process. And

don't worry if you "blue" the steel at this juncture as over-heating is only a concern once the steel is heat-treated.

Get the torch and can of olive oil ready. With the shank held in a pair of locking pliers, fire-up the torch and apply heat to the steel. Twirl the rod as if you were slow cooking a marshmallow (**Photo 7**). Try for an even, bright cherry-red color from the middle to the point, then quickly dunk the hot steel into the olive oil and agitate rapidly for about 30 seconds (**Photo 8**). Note: Never use motor oil for this as it gives off toxic fumes and can even ignite.

Use a mill file to test the shank tip hardness (**Photo 9**). If the steel does not pass the file test, reheat and quench again.

Hand-sand the shaft to achieve a clean bright surface (**Photo 10**).

The second phase of heat-treating is called tempering. This is where the degree of final hardness is established. Tempering involves reheating the hardened area to a specific temperature, then quenching it immediately in water. The higher the temperature the softer the shaft will be. As the end user, you are free to determine the degree of hardness you want in your tool. You may want an awl that is very

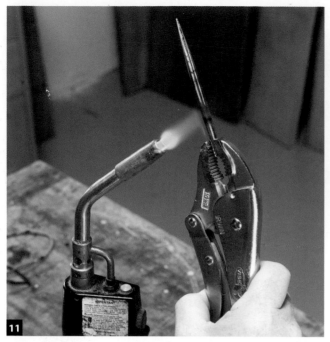

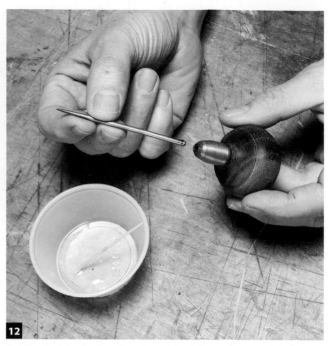

Temper the shaft with a torch held just below the heat-treated area. Keep the flame there and rotate the shaft until the hardened area is a uniform dark gold or bronze color. Then, quickly quench it in water.

Set the shaft in the handle using a bit of slow set epoxy. Put the epoxy in the hole with a toothpick. Rotate the shaft a bit as you push it in to evenly distribute the epoxy.

hard and can scratch deep lines in hard wood. The down side is a very hard shaft will have a brittle point that's prone to breaking. At the other extreme you can temper the shaft so the point won't break but it may bend so easily that the awl becomes useless. I suggest making a couple of awls, each tempered to different temperatures to see what best fits your needs.

The tempered "sweet spot" for my awls is a temperature around 450°–500°. There are three ways to achieve this:

A. Heat the steel slowly with a torch well back of the hardened area (**Photo 11**). When the hardened area turns a gold or bronze color, quench immediately in water to stop the process.

B. Use a temperature-indicating substance such as Tempilstik. Choose a Tempilstik that fits your desired heat range. Rub the area around the point with the wax-like stick. Then, heat the shaft as described in option A. When the steel reaches the desired temperature, the Tempilstik will smoke and liquefy. At this point, quickly quench the shaft in water.

C. The easiest, but slowest method is to bake the steel in

a conventional oven for about 30 minutes at 450° Be sure to preheat the oven and place the steel on a cookie sheet. Elevate the steel with rolled up pieces of aluminum foil so it will heat evenly. Remove the steel from the oven and let it cool. There's no need to quench a shaft that's been cooked in an oven.

Wood + Steel = Awl Done

If you need a sharper point on the awl, place it back in the drill and lightly shape the tapered area on the disc mounted on the lathe (use a finer grit for this, such as #150 or finer). Do this slowly, as bluing the point may make the tool too soft for your purposes.

Mount the steel in the handle (**Photo 12**). I put a small amount of epoxy down in the hole, and then push the handle down over the steel with the point in a scrap piece of wood. Use the awl for a while; you may find you want one harder or one more flexible—you decide based on your tempering temperatures.

SOURCES MSC, www.mscdirect.com (800) 645-7270, Oil hardening Drill Rod 3-ft., 1/8", #06000087, $2.10, 3/16-in., #06000160, $2.93, ¼", #06000160, $3.52, Tempilstik in 488° temperature, #93312023 $19.02, 10-in. Abrasive Disc for Steel in #120-grit, #88592480 $6.80 each. ⊚ Home Centers and Hardware Stores, Propane or MAP gas torch, locking pliers, brass nuts and copper couplings and epoxy. ⌒

CHAPTER TWENTY-NINE

PROJECT 15 Lidded Box

∞〕 *Beauty and usefulness—a perfect fit* 〔∞

FLAME SHE-OAK

BLEACHED WENGE

CHERRY

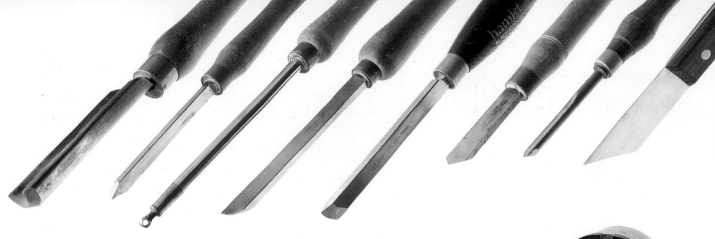

Of all the different forms of woodturning, I find the most delight in creating lidded boxes. The satisfying snap of a well fit lid as it closes, the beauty of the shape and the wood combined with the usefulness of a lidded container just do it for me. Turning a lidded box is a demanding project, but anyone with a few bowls and some spindle work under their belt can produce these wonderful objects. All it takes is a methodical approach and sound technique.

A lidded box presents two unique challenges. One is creating the perfect fit between the lid and base. Think of it as a precise joint that's designed to come apart.

The other challenge is hollowing end grain. End grain can be up to five times harder than side grain and is prone to tear out. Even experienced bowl turners are surprised when they first try hollowing end grain. Fortunately, these problems can be overcome by switching from a gouge to a scraper when hollowing end grain. If you fall in love with lidded boxes, you might consider purchasing a ring or a hook tool that's designed specifically for cutting end grain.

Why hollow end grain when you can make a box from face grain? The answer is simple: an end-grain box is more stable. That means your lid will fit well all year long. Face-grain turnings change shape more dramatically with changes in humidity causing the lid to fit perfectly one day and fit too tight the next. If you want a loose fitting lid and a different grain look, then a face grain box is acceptable.

For this story, I will take you through the entire process of making an end grain box with a snug, friction-fit lid. We'll cover chucking the parts in different manners, cutting end grain, tight tolerances, hollowing in a narrow space, creating the desired "perfect fit," and dealing with a joint designed to come apart.

What You'll Need:

TURNING TOOLS:
- A spindle-roughing gouge for shaping; I prefer a 1-¼" for boxes.
- Parting tool: either ³⁄₁₆" or ¼".
- Ring Tool for finish cuts on end grain.
- ½ in. side profile heavy-duty scraper.
- Skew chisel; a ½" or ⅝" is best.

SOURCE: PACKARD WOODWORKS, WWW.PACKARDWOODWORKS.COM, OR (800) 683-8876.

- Spear point scraper; ¾" or 1"
- ⅜" or ½" shallow gouge; also called a detail, spindle or fingernail gouge.
- Thin-kerf parting tool.

ACCESSORIES:
- A scroll chuck with serrated jaws such as the Oneway Talon or Stronghold or a Vicmarc VM100 or VM120.
- A drill chuck to fit the lathe tailstock.
- A ⅝" to 1" in diameter twist or bradpoint drill bit.
- Outside calipers with a 4" capacity. Important: be sure to roundover the points.
- 6" steel ruler.
- Vernier or dial calipers.

TIP The dimensions for the box Alan turned for this story are approximate. Keep in mind that for a turner, exact dimensions are less important than the overall look and proportion. Each piece of wood is unique and thus dictates its own dimensions.

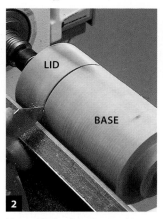
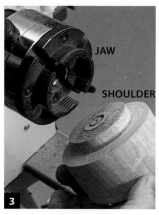

1 Turn your blank into a cylinder then cut tenons on each end with a parting tool. Use a caliper to size the tenon to fit your scroll chuck.

2 Use a thin-kerf parting tool to separate the lid from the base. This tool removes as little material as possible and helps maintain the grain match at the joint.

3 Mount the lid blank on your scroll chuck. Push the tenon all the way in so the shoulder sits firmly on top of the jaws.

4 Rough out the inside of the lid with a ½" side scraper. Hollowing end grain is best done from the center out to minimize tear-out.

Choosing Your Wood

If you are new to box making I suggest using walnut, soft maple or cherry. These woods are easy to turn and make fine looking boxes. Select a piece that's 3" square and 5" to 6" long. The wood needs to be dry throughout, as you can afford very little dimensional change as you turn these boxes. Move up to exotic domestic or imported woods as you gain experience.

Prepare the Blank for the Chuck

Mount your blank between centers as you would for spindle turning. Create a cylinder with the spindle roughing gouge.

Cut tenons on both ends of the cylinder (**Photo 1**). Set your outside calipers to a size that fits the jaws of your scroll chuck. Cut the tenons slightly shorter than the depth of the scroll chuck's jaws so the tenons don't bottom out before the chuck is tightened. The shoulder should be 90° to the tenon in order to seat firmly in the jaws.

Separate the lid from the base (**Photo 2**). On a 5"-long box I normally make the lid blank about 1-¾" long.

Shape the Inside of the Lid

Mount the lid blank into your scroll chuck (**Photo 3**).

Rough shape the inside of the lid (**Photo 4**). I think a lid looks better when it has a smaller diameter than the base so I leave enough wall thickness to allow for downsizing the outside diameter later on. For a 1-¾" high lid I hollow to about 1-¼" deep, generally following the outside shape I intend to give the lid. Leave the wall thickness about ⅜" where the mortise will be cut.

For the final passes, use a ring or hook tool designed to solve the problem of cutting end-grain cleanly (**Photo 5**). An alternative is to shear scrape with your side scraper. Simply tilt the scraper at a 45° angle and take a very light cut, just a little above center.

Cut the lid's mortise with the spear point scraper (**Photo**

5 Make the finish cuts with a ring or hook tool to leave a smooth surface.

6 Cut the lid mortise with a spear point scraper held flat against the tool rest. Finish with light cuts and the tool held at a 45° angle (shown). This is known as a shear scraping cut.

6). The sides of the lid at the opening are often referred to as the mortise because it fits over the tenon on the base. This area of the lid must be cut as clean as possible and left untouched by sandpaper. Sanding will change the circularity of the mortise ever so slightly and result in a poor fit. I plan on a ⅜" tenon on the base so the lid mortise is cut ½" deep.

Check that the mortise does not taper in towards the center (**Photo 7**). I strive for either a straight wall or a very slight taper away from center. Finish off this area with a light shear scraping action. Don't sand the mortise, or you may distort it.

Remove the lid from the lathe. Measure the inside diameter and depth of the lid with a Vernier or dial caliper. Record the diameter on paper but lock the setting for the depth on the calipers.

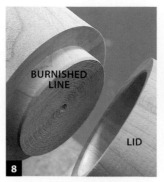

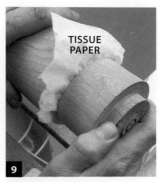

7 Check that the mortise does not taper in towards the center of the lid by holding a rule against the mortise. The perfect mortise will position the ruler so that it sits parallel with the lathe bed.

8 Mount the base in the jaw chuck. Cut a tenon that tapers so the lid just fits on the end. Twist the lid to create a burnished line then shave the tenon down to that line. The fit has to be tight so the lid won't spin as it's turned on the base.

9 If you inadvertently cut the base tenon too deep, the lid will spin or come off when you shape the box. A tissue paper shim will fix a fit that's a tad loose.

10 Use the points on a dial or Vernier caliper to mark the depth of the interior hollow on the lid. Be sure the calipers are laying flat on the tool rest.

11 Shape the top of the lid with a shallow gouge. Let your creativity be your guide for the top design. Shoot for a 3/16"–¼" thick top.

12 Use a spinderoughing gouge to shape the rest of the box. A groove cut with a parting tool marks the bottom of the box.

13 Use a skew chisel to cut a slight chamfer on the bottom of the box. This softens the sharp corner and creates a small shadow under the box to give it a visual lift.

14 Cut a shallow Vgroove at the joint with a skew. This detail helps disguise slight changes in circularity that may show up at the joint over time.

Mount the Lid on the Base

Mount the base blank into the chuck. Make sure it is seated securely.

Create the rough tenon on the base with a standard parting tool. Set your calipers ¼" larger than the mortise. Once you're within ¼" of your finished tenon size, it's time to slow down. You will be amazed how much you can take off with a light cut. That's because pushing the parting tool in 1/16-in. actually removes ⅛" from the tenon's diameter. Plan on making 5 or 6 light cuts, turning off the lathe and checking the fit after each cut. At this point you need a tight fit on the lid because the outside of the box is turned with the lid in place. The objective is to create a fit that is tight enough to hold the lid on the base while turning but still loose enough to pull off when ready to hollow the base. This is not the final fit of the lid. We'll get to that later. To simplify "creeping up" on the fit, cut a tenon that tapers slightly in towards the end (**Photo 8**).

If, after all your best efforts, you end up with a fit that's a tad loose, use a tissue paper shim to tighten it up (**Photo 9**).

Turn the Outside of the Box

With the lid now firmly mounted on the base, begin shaping the outside of your box. Use the measurement from step #9 to mark the depth of the hollow on the lid (**Photo 10**). I start the outside of the box by shaping the lid first (**Photo 11**).

With the lid to your liking, establish the overall height of the box. Use a parting tool to mark the bottom with a ¼" deep groove. Start on the long side, then nibble away at the height until the box's proportions look the way you want. Play with different ratios using your eye rather than exact measurements. I like a ⅓ lid, ⅔ base ratio.

Shape the sides of the box (**Photo 12**). I make my boxes with a little asymmetry: the lid has a smaller diameter than the base with a slight curve in the side. This entails working from both ends towards the joint in order to keep working with the grain.

Cut a chamfer on the box's bottom (**Photo 13**).

Make a V-shaped cut at the joint (**Photo 14**).

Sand the outside of the box up to #220-grit. If "ringing" (telltale sanding scratches encircling the box) is a problem—as it often is with cherry and maple—you may have to sand to #400-grit.

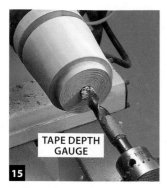

15 TAPE DEPTH GAUGE

Drill out the base's interior using a drill chuck in the tailstock and a 5/8" to 1" drill bit. Mark the desired depth of the base interior with a piece of tape.

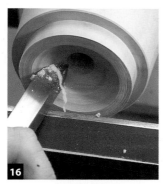

16

Use a side radius scraper to continue hollowing the base. Start in the drilled opening and work from the center out.

17 BLANK

Part the base off from the blank. Be sure to leave enough wood on the base so the bottom can be scooped out in the next step.

18 BLANK — RIM

Turn the base around and mount it on a tenon cut on the remaining blank stock. Use the ring tool to cut from the center out to create a concave bottom with a small rim.

Hollow the Inside of the Base

Remove the lid from the base. If the smooth surface makes it hard to get a grip, try using one of those rubber gadgets for removing jar lids.

Drill the base interior to establish a finish depth (**Photo 15**).

Hollow the base (**Photo 16**). Complete both the bottom and sides with a shear scraping action.

Sand the inside of the box. Do not touch the outside of the tenon with sandpaper.

Final Fit the Lid

At this point the lid is too tight for use. With a parting tool, take extremely light cuts from the tenon to loosen the fit. Turners refer to them as "dust cuts" because you barely remove any wood. There are any number of ways to fit the lid to the base: loose, light suction, snap, or tight. The "correct" fit is the one targeted by the turner. If you would like to remove the lid without picking up the piece, then a loose fit is in order. If you want the closest thing to a locking lid then a tight fit is appropriate.

Shape the Bottom of the Base

Part the base off from the blank stock (**Photo 17**).

Use a parting tool to cut a tenon on the blank stock left in the chuck. The tenon is sized to fit the base opening in the same way the base tenon was sized to fit the lid. You want a tight fit that will hold the base while you finish the bottom. This is often referred to as jam chucking.

Run the lathe at a slow speed (under 500 rpm if possible) and shape the bottom of the box with the ring tool (**Photo 18**). As an alternative, use the ½" side radius scraper—but with very light shear scraping cuts. Be sure to note how deep you hollowed the inside of the base. If there is enough wood at the bottom of the base then make this concave area fairly deep to lighten the feel of the box. Shoot for a bottom thickness of ³⁄₁₆" to ¼".

Pull the base off the jam chuck, place the lid on the base and admire your workmanship.

Thoughts on Finishing

If the box is a light colored wood, such as maple or holly, I use either wax or white shellac. Both of these products can be applied while your box is on the lathe. For darker woods, such as cherry and walnut, I use pure tung oil or an oil and varnish blend. The blend is one part varnish, one part pure tung oil and one part boiled linseed oil.

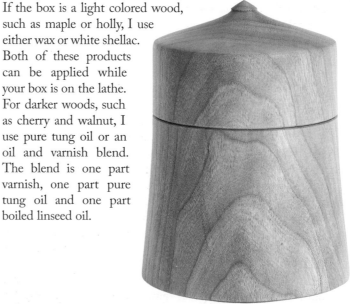

TIP To create a snap fit, remove a small amount of wood from the bottom half of the tenon near the shoulder, leaving a fairly tight fit in the upper half. The snap is created when the first sensation of resistance is felt in putting on the lid followed by little or no resistance as it is seated. Like all of the tenon to mortise tolerances in box making, go at this in the tiniest increments to achieve the desired fit—it is very hard to put wood back on.

CHAPTER THIRTY

PROJECT 16 Lowrider Box

Challenge yourself—make an unusual lidded box

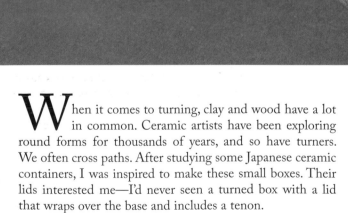

When it comes to turning, clay and wood have a lot in common. Ceramic artists have been exploring round forms for thousands of years, and so have turners. We often cross paths. After studying some Japanese ceramic containers, I was inspired to make these small boxes. Their lids interested me—I'd never seen a turned box with a lid that wraps over the base and includes a tenon.

Start With One Blank

Make the box from a blank that's about 3" to 4" in diameter x 4" long; the grain must run the length of the piece. Just about any wood will do, as long as it's good and dry. I'll be using mesquite, which is perfect for a lidded box. Mesquite tends to stay quite round after it's turned.

Mount the blank between centers and round it into a cylinder with a spindle roughing gouge. Using a parting tool and outside calipers, create tenons that fit your scroll chuck on both ends of the blank.

One portion of this blank will be the box's lid; the other portion will be its base. Making both parts from a single blank guarantees that the wood's figure nicely flows from one to the other when the box is assembled. To lay out the lid, mark a line about 1-¼" from one of the ends of the blank.

Your next task is to cut the blank into two pieces, separat-

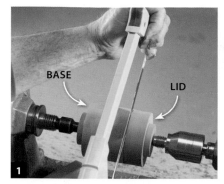

1 Turn a cylinder that includes both lid and base. With the lathe running, cut through the cylinder to separate the lid from the base.

2 Shape the underside of the lid. Using a detail gouge, form the lip that overhangs the base, then turn a tenon inside the lip.

LIP
TENON

3 Hollow the tenon using a half-round scraper. To scrape with the grain, move the tool from the hollow's small diameter to its large diameter.

TENON

4 Remove the lid, then set a divider to 1/8" less than the diameter of the lid's tenon.

5 Install the base in your scroll chuck, then use the divider to mark the tenon's approximate diameter while the work is spinning.

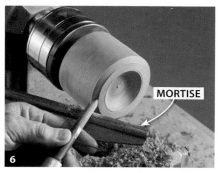

MORTISE

6 Use a detail/spindle gouge to shape the top of the base. Use a half-round scraper to begin hollowing a mortise to fit the lid's tenon.

---

ing the lid from the base. There are two ways you can do this: Part it with a thin-kerf parting tool or saw it with a hacksaw (**Photo 1**). Both methods minimize the amount of wood lost to the kerf, so there's the least amount of interruption in how the figure flows.

If you choose the hacksaw method, use a saw with a heavy, rigid frame. (Don't use anything else!) Install a high-quality 18 teeth per inch, bi-metal blade and orient the teeth so they're pointing away from you. Remove the lathe's tool rest and run the lathe at a moderate speed of 400 to 600 rpm. It's also important to wear a full face shield with an ANSI Z87+ rating.

Here's how to proceed: First, cut a shallow "V" shape on the marked line using the long point of a skew. (This is an optional step, but it's very helpful.) Sight along the "V" to position the saw at a right angle to the lathe's axis, then place the middle of the saw's blade in the "V." If the saw bounces or fights you, it's not quite square—reposition it. Apply moderate downward pressure. Once you've cut about ¾" deep, you can push and pull the saw back and forth to speed up the process. When the cut is nearly complete, you'll hear a hollow sound. At this point, stop sawing and turn off the lathe. Remove the blank and cut or twist it apart. If you cut all the way through while the blank is spinning, don't worry; the pieces won't fly off!

Shape the Lid's Underside

Mount the lid in a four-jaw scroll chuck. Determine how much of the lid you wish to overhang the base. Let's call this overhang the "lip." On your first box, make the lip about ½" wide. (If the lip is wider, you'll have a harder time back-hollowing the interior portion of the base underneath the lip.) You'll also be cutting a tenon next to the lip. The tenon should be ¼"–⅜" long.

Cut the lip and tenon at the same time, using a freshly sharpened ⅜" detail/spindle gouge (**Photo 2**). When shaping the lip, move the gouge from left to right. This results in cutting against the grain, so cut slowly to minimize tearout. Be sure to cut the outside edge of the tenon parallel to the lathe's axis.

Hollow the inside of the lid using a ½" half-round scraper (**Photo 3**). As the lid will be quite thin, cut only ½" deep. Sand the entire underside of the lid.

Move On to the Base

Mount the base portion of the blank in the scroll chuck. Measure the outside width of the lid's tenon using a set of dividers, then close up the dividers by about ⅛" (**Photo 4**). Set the lathe to a low rpm and place the dividers on the tool rest, approximately centered on the blank. Lightly touch the left leg of the dividers to the wood, leaving a shallow scored line.

7 Gradually increase the mortise's diameter using a small parting tool—make diagonal cuts until the tenon barely fits, then finish with a straight cut.

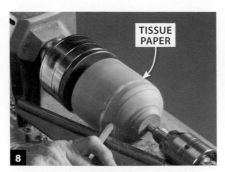

8 Place the lid on the base, then shape the lid's top. If necessary, insert a piece of tissue paper between lid and base to ensure a tight fit.

TISSUE PAPER

9 Shape most of the base with the lid in place, using a detail gouge. It's best to see both pieces together to create a pleasing overall form.

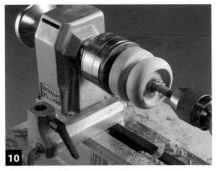

10 Remove the lid, then drill the base to roughly establish the depth of its interior. This step also simplifies hollowing the base.

11 Use a half-round scraper to hollow most of the base's interior.

12 Switch to a bent round-nose scraper to create a concave area under the base's rim. When you're done with all turning and sanding, part off the base.

(A word of caution: Never touch the wood with the divider's right leg. The wood's rotation will kick the dividers back at you.) If the dividers are centered, the right leg will be positioned immediately above this line. If the right leg is off a bit, reposition the dividers and score a new line. When both legs indicate that the dividers are centered, push the left leg into the blank a bit deeper to clearly mark a diameter (**Photo 5**).

Using a ½" half-round scraper, make a mortise by removing the wood inside the scored line. Cut about ⅝" deep in the center and right up to the line. Using a detail/spindle gouge, begin rolling over the outside of the base, but only about 1" back from the mortise (**Photo 6**). To cut with the grain, move the gouge from the outside of the blank toward the mortise. This area will be underneath the lid's lip, so it should be slightly convex.

Gradually widen the mortise using a parting tool (**Photo 7**). Take it easy, holding the tool diagonally to create a taper. Remember, every cut you make effectively doubles the size of the mortise. Removing ¹⁄₃₂" from one side of the mortise, for example, actually widens the mortise by ¹⁄₁₆". The taper allows you to find the correct diameter without overshooting too far.

Test-fit the lid's tenon to the mortise quite often. Once the tenon just starts to enter the opening, turn off the lathe and rotate the tenon on the mortise. The tenon will lightly burnish the mortise, leaving a mark to guide you. The goal is to achieve a tight enough fit so you can mount the lid on the base in order to turn both as a pair. If you accidentally make the mortise slightly too wide, place one layer of tissue paper between the lid and base. If one layer is insufficient and the lid is still loose, start over and make the base shorter.

With the lid now securely in place, bring up the tailstock with a flat-faced center, or use the center's normal point covered with a small piece of wood. Use the detail/spindle gouge to shape the outside of the lid first. I prefer a gentle low dome with a continuous curve (**Photo 8**).

Cut a small chamfer on the lower edge of the lid's rim so you'll be able to lift the lid from the base when the box is complete. Shape the lid right up to the tailstock center. Slide away the tailstock and complete the final shape. Sand the outside of the lid to completion.

Set in with a parting tool to establish the height of the box—I usually make the visible portion of the base twice as tall as the lid—then start rounding towards the bottom and up to the rim of the lid. Remove the lid and refine the upper half of the base using very light cuts with a detail/spindle gouge (**Photo 9**). When you're done, sand the outside of the base.

Next, mount a Jacob's style chuck and a 1" Forstner bit in the lathe's tailstock. Drill to about ¾ of the final inside depth of the base (**Photo 10**). Using a half-round scraper, hollow as

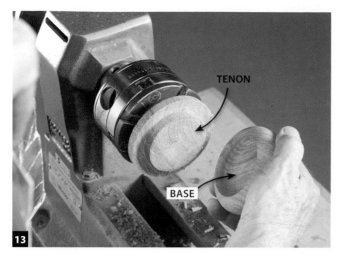

Turn a snug-fitting tenon on the remainder of the original blank in order to reverse-chuck the base.

Complete the underside of the base using the half-round scraper. Raise the scraper on edge, as shown here, to make the final finishing cuts.

much of the inside as you can reach, aiming for a wall thickness of ¼" or less (**Photo 11**).

At some point, you will find there are areas that can only be worked with a bent scraper (**Photo 12**). This tool can be aggressive, so work slowly. Strive to achieve the same wall thicknesses as elsewhere on the box. Take the inside to the final depth, then finish its surface—where possible—by shear scraping. (In shear scraping, the tool is held at a 45° angle or higher and is tilted in the direction of the cut). Completely sand the inside.

Fine-tune the lid's fit; it should be just loose enough to come off by itself. (You shouldn't have to hold on to the base to remove the lid.) To do this, widen the mortise ever so slightly with a half-round scraper. In addition, refine the final shape and diameter of the lower edge of the base using a detail/spindle gouge. Sand this area, then part off the base.

Reverse Chuck the Base

There is one more crucial step in completing a well-turned box: Finishing its bottom. A good bottom should be turned smooth, not left rough or merely sanded smooth off the lathe. To do this, you'll use "reverse chucking," a process that holds a piece backwards, with its bottom facing out.

Turn a tenon to fit the base's mortise on the remainder of the original blank or on a new piece of wood (**Photo 13**). The tenon should fit tight enough so the base doesn't spin when you turn it, but not so tight that you'll have to pry off the base when you're done.

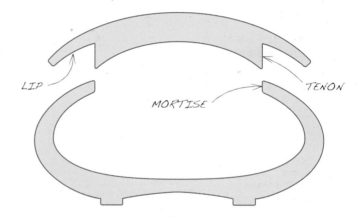

Cut the bottom lightly with the half-round scraper. For this tool to work its best, form a small hook on its end with a burnisher and shear scrape (**Photo 14**). I prefer making a bottom that has a slightly concave surface and a small rim about ¼" wide. Make the rim by light scraping with the skew chisel held parallel to the bottom face. Once you've completed this work, sand the bottom.

Apply a finish, then sit back and study the piece. Is it too tall? Too squat? Make some more and experiment with different diameters and proportions. Explore the possibilities of this wonderful form.

SOURCES Packard Woodworks, packardwoodworks.com, 800-683-8876, ½" half-round scraper #100127, $49, ¼" bent scraper, #103381, $43

CHAPTER THIRTY-ONE

PROJECT 17 Reading Glasses Case

Protect your "cheaters" in style

Sooner or later everyone's eyes need a little help—especially for reading or close work. One popular solution is to buy a pair of "cheaters," those stylish reading glasses that are available in bookstores and practically everywhere else. How to protect these delicate, inexpensive glasses—especially the compact versions—is always an issue.

A turned wooden case with a friction-fit cap is a perfect solution. It's a unique gift that fits in pockets, purses and briefcases. It can also hold more than glasses. It would make an outstanding one-cigar humidor, for example, if you used the appropriate wood. In either case, this project provides an opportunity to develop skills in end-grain drilling, turning delicate details and creating just the right fit between the base and the cap.

Materials and Tools

A 1-½" square by 9" to 10" long block of wood should be more than adequate, although the glasses' size is the ultimate determinant (the glasses shown here measure $^{11}/_{16}$" x ¾" x 5-⅜"). Almost any wood will work, but stronger woods such as maple, cherry, cocobolo, purpleheart, goncalo alves and boxwood will allow creating thinner walls. Make sure the wood is at the drier end of the spectrum.

A spindle roughing gouge, a spindle/detail gouge, a parting tool, a thin-kerf parting tool and a skew chisel will suffice for turning. You'll need a scroll chuck equipped with a small set of jaws to hold the wood for drilling (see Sources, page 137). You'll also need two high-speed steel or carbide Forstner-style drill bits. An extension to allow drilling deep

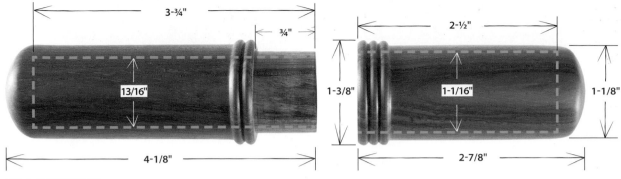

FIG. A DIMENSIONS

3-¾" ¾" 13/16" 4-1/8"

2-½" 1-3/8" 1-1/16" 1-1/8" 2-7/8"

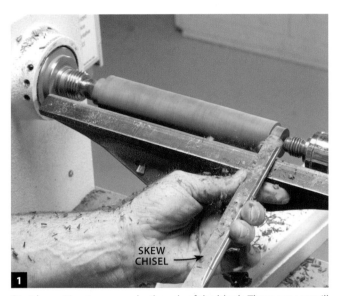

SKEW CHISEL

1 Start by cutting tenons on both ends of the blank. These tenons will be used later, when the cap and base pieces are drilled out.

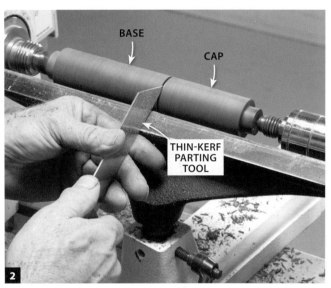

BASE CAP

THIN-KERF PARTING TOOL

2 Separate the cap from the base by cutting in with a parting tool. Stop just before cutting through. Then twist the blank to break the pieces apart.

holes and an adaptor/holder with a #2 Morse taper end, designed to mount in the tailstock quill, can be purchased with the bits (see Sources). The glasses and the wall thickness of the case determine the bit sizes. For the glasses shown here, I used a 1-¹⁄₁₆" dia. bit to drill out the case's slip-on cap and a ¹³⁄₁₆" dia. bit to drill out its base (Fig. A, above).

Determine the Proportions

Mount the blank between centers and knock down the corners using the spindle roughing gouge. Then turn tenons at both ends (**Photo 1**). These tenons will be used later, to mount the cap and base blanks in the scroll chuck. The tenons should be about ¾" long and about 1" in diameter, and their shoulders should be slightly concave.

Lay out the base and cap on the blank. Their overall lengths depend on the depth of the holes drilled in them. Use your glasses and the overlap of the friction-fit joint to

calculate the depth of these holes. I normally allow ¾" for the joint on both parts (the tenon is on the base; the mortise is in the cap), and I drill into the base far enough to house the glasses by about two-thirds their length, so they won't easily fall out when the cap is removed. For the glasses shown here, I drilled a 3-¾" deep hole in the base and a 2-½" deep hole in the cap.

The overall lengths of each part must be longer than the drilled holes, of course—by at least ¼". Decide which end of the blank will be the cap and which will be the base. When you mark the dividing line on the blank, allow about ½" additional length on both parts for shaping their ends, finish sanding and parting off.

Use a parting tool to separate the cap and the base (**Photo 2**). Although not essential, a thin-kerf parting tool minimizes the wood loss, resulting in a slightly better grain match between these two parts on the completed case.

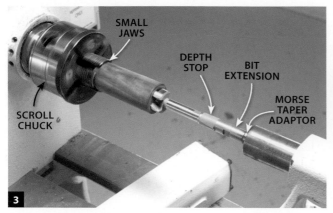

3. Drill out the cap with a Forstner bit attached to an extension for deep drilling and an adaptor for mounting in the tailstock. Slowly advance the tailstock to move the bit into the spinning blank.

4. Face off the cap's rim by scraping with the skew chisel. The rim must be flat or taper slightly to the inside. Mark the depth of the drilled hole on the blank.

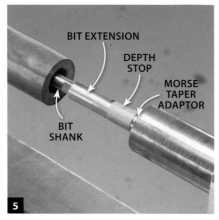

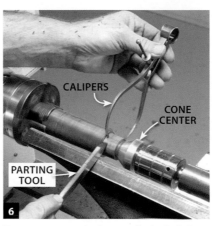

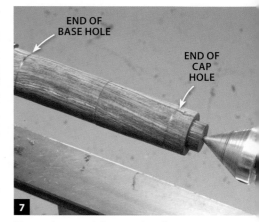

5. Follow the same procedure to drill out the base. Use a smaller Forstner bit and drill the hole about two-thirds as deep as the glasses are long.

6. Turn a tenon on the base to fit the hole in the cap. Start oversize and reduce the diameter to create a very tight fit. A cone center supports the drilled-out end.

7. Mount the cap. Make sure that the assembled joint does not slip and that the ends of both drilled holes are marked. Bring up the cone center to support the end of the reassembled blank.

Drill the Holes

It's much easier to fit the tenon on the base to the hole in the cap than vice versa, so start with the cap. Mount the cap blank in the small jaws of the scroll chuck. Then lightly face off the end with a parting tool or skew chisel—this makes it easier to center the drill bit. Drilling holes on the lathe is different than ordinary drilling because the workpiece rotates instead of the bit. Mount the large Forstner bit and its extension in the tailstock quill, using the Morse taper adaptor or a Jacobs-style chuck. Then drill into the cap by slowly advancing the bit (**Photo 3**).

The cap's rim must be perfectly flat or tapered to the inside, so scrape it lightly with the skew chisel (**Photo 4**). Mark the hole depth on the outside of the cap blank. Then remove it from the chuck and mount the base blank. Lightly face off the end. Then install the small Forstner bit and its extension and drill into the base (**Photo 5**).

Turn the Tenon

I install a cone-type live center in the tailstock to support the

base blank while turning the tenon. Another solution is to fill the drilled hole with a piece of wood that's slightly tapered (like a bottle's cork), so you can use a standard live center.

I like the sure feel that a ¾" long tenon gives the case's friction-fit joint. Use a parting tool and outside calipers to turn the tenon (**Photo 6**). Be sure to round the calipers' ends, so they don't catch and get launched at you by the spinning blank. Set the calipers about ⅟₁₆" oversize and then reduce the diameter in very small increments. Stop frequently and use the cap to check the fit. The goal is to create a very tight fit, so the joint won't slip—but not so tight that you can't remove the cap without breaking the wood.

Shape the Outside

Mount the fitted cap on the base and bring up the tailstock for support (**Photo 7**). Then establish the final outside lengths, which are based on the depths of the holes drilled in both pieces (**Photo 8**). Turn the case to a cylinder with the spindle roughing gouge and add details with the skew chisel or detail/spindle gouge at the same time (**Photo 9**). This

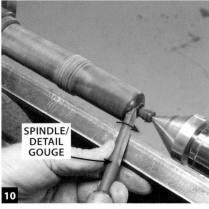

8 Turn the case to a cylinder after establishing the ends by cutting in with the parting tool about ¼" beyond each end mark.

SPINDLE ROUGHING GOUGE

9 Create tactile surfaces and disguise the joint by adding decorative details such as the beads shown here, using the skew.

10 Round the end of the cap by making rolling cuts with the spindle/detail gouge. Then finish-sand both the cap and the base.

SPINDLE/ DETAIL GOUGE

SKEW CHISEL

11 Use the skew to part off the cap. Then remove the cap from the base and finish-sand its parted-off tip.

SKEW CHISEL

12 Tune the joint's fit by removing a tiny amount from the tenon with a peeling cut. Ideally, you'll hear a vacuum pop when you pull off the cap.

time the goal is to leave just enough wood for strength in both length and diameter, so the case doesn't feel excessively heavy. Obviously, the hole in the cap ultimately determines the outside diameter.

Round the end of the cap and finish-sand the entire case (**Photo 10**). Part off the cap, remove it from the tenon, and hand-sand its parted-off tip (**Photo 11**).

Final Details

Fine-tune the fit between the cap and the tenon by adjusting the tenon (**Photo 12**). Make a peeling cut (not a scraping

action) to lightly remove a very small amount of wood. The goal is a piston-like fit. You should feel resistance between the parts; ideally, you'll hear a vacuum pop when you pull them apart (the same sound you hear when pulling a cork from a bottle).

Round and finish-sand the end of the base using the same method used earlier on the cap. Then part off the base and hand-sand the tip. Apply the finish of your choice. I often use pure tung oil, especially for darker woods. For the cocobolo case shown here, I simply applied paste wax.

SOURCES Craft Supplies, woodturnerscatalog.com, 800 551 8876, Maxi Cut HSS Forstner bit 13/16" #979-310, 1 1/16" #979-310 $$32.95, 3 1/2" bit extension #979-311 $26.95, No. 2 MT RotaStop adapter (alternative to a Jacobs style chuck) #979-312 $43.25. Oneway Manufacturing, www.oneway.ca, (800) 565-7288, Oneway Talon Chuck, #2985, $232; Spigot (small) Jaws, #3016, $40.95.

CHAPTER THIRTY-TWO

PROJECT 18 4-in-1 Screwdriver

Buy the parts; turn the handle

You just can't beat the look and feel of a beautifully turned handle. I love commercially made multiple-tip screwdrivers because they cut down on the clutter in my tool drawers. I don't care for their plastic handles, though, so I make my own from wood. It's easy to crank out these screwdrivers in any shape or size. They make great gifts. All you need is a chunk of your favorite wood, a drill chuck for your lathe's headstock and a $5 to $7 hardware kit that contains two double-ended bits. This is a terrific project for a larger mini-lathe and takes less than an hour to complete.

Drill a 5/8"-dia. starter hole in a square blank. Make the hole 1 in. deep.

PLUG

Turn a tapered plug to fit in the hole. Put the plug in the hole and mount the blank on your lathe. The plug's center bears against the point of the live center in the tailstock. You may use a metal cone-type center as well.

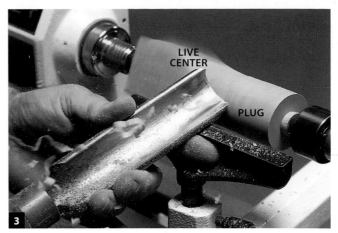

Turn the blank into a cylinder using a spindle-roughing gouge.

Select a Dense, Tough Wood

Pick a wood that's beautiful and durable. Hard maple, white oak, hickory, cherry, apple or Osage-orange are good domestic options. Purpleheart, cocobolo, tulipwood, goncalo alves, ipe, olive, black palm and Brazilian cherry are imports I also like. Avoid softer woods, such as poplar, pine, cedar and basswood. They scratch easily and won't stand up to the daily rigors of driving screws or any of those jobs you're not supposed to do with screwdrivers.

Materials

- One 1-¾" x 1-¾" x 6" hardwood blank
- One hardware kit (see Sources, page 141)

Tools

- Drill press
- ⅝" and ⁷⁄₁₆" twist drill bits
- Spindle-roughing gouge
- ⅜" or ½" detail or spindle gouge
- ³⁄₁₆" or ¼" parting tool
- Jacobs chuck with Morse taper to fit your lathe's headstock

Cost

- About $7, not including wood

Hardware

The hardware kit contains a brass ferrule, a knurled insert, a hollow stem and two double-ended bits. Two different kits are available (see Sources). Rockler's kit is used and shown here. Check instructions with other kits for specific dimensions.

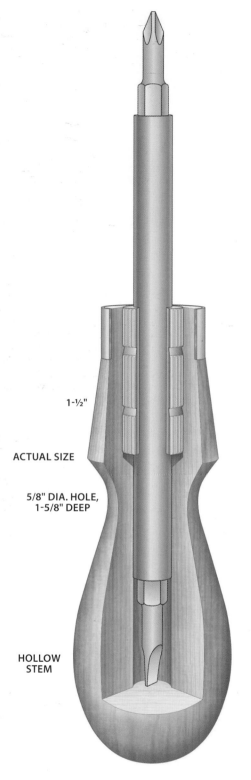

1-½"

ACTUAL SIZE

5/8" DIA. HOLE,
1-5/8" DEEP

**HOLLOW
STEM**

FERRULE

BITS

INSERT

4

Cut a tenon using a parting tool. Set calipers to the ferrule's outside diameter. When the tenon matches this diameter, continue to remove small amounts of wood. Turn off the lathe and remove the handle often to check the ferrule's fit. Smooth caliper edges before using.

5

Use a soft mallet to tap the ferrule onto the tenon. Insert the plug and mount the blank back on your lathe with the ferrule in place.

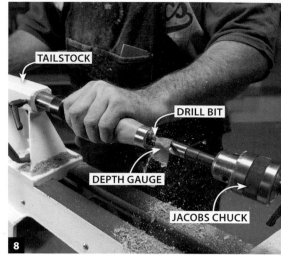

6 Shape the handle using a spindle or detail gouge. Sneak up to the ferrule using very light pressure. Avoid cutting it with the gouge. Turn off the lathe to test the handle's fit in your hand. Remove the tool rest when you're done.

7 Sand the handle and ferrule. Make a smooth transition between them. Start with #120-grit sandpaper; continue with #150-, #180- and #220-grit paper. When you're done, remove the handle and insert a Jacobs chuck in your lathe's headstock.

8 Deepen the handle's hole. Put a 5/8" bit in the chuck and set the lathe at a slow to medium speed. Mount the handle with the bit inserted into the handle's shallow hole. Simulaneously grip the handle and turn the hand wheel to make a 1-5/8"-deep, perfectly centered hole (Fig. A). Next, insert a 7/16" bit and drill a hole 3-¾" deep. Turn off the lathe, remove the handle and use a small handsaw to remove the waste material from the handle's end.

TAILSTOCK
DRILL BIT
DEPTH GAUGE
JACOBS CHUCK

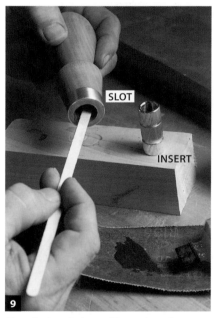

SLOT
INSERT

9 Glue the knurled metal insert into the handle using 30- to 60-minute slow-set epoxy. Spread epoxy inside the hole, but not on the insert. The insert has two slots on one end. Put the opposite end in the hole first.

10 Tap the insert into the hole. To seat the insert, turn the handle over, set it on a wood block and strike the handle. Remove any glue drips from inside the handle. Sand the saw marks on the handle's end.

11 Apply two coats of finish. I like to use an oil or an oil and varnish mixture. Assemble the shaft and bits. Your screwdriver is ready to go to work!

SOURCES Rockler, (800) 279-4441, www.rockler.com 4-in-1 kit, including insert, ferrule, hollow stem, No. 2 Phillips, standard slot and two square drive bits, #37707, $7. ◉ Penn State Industries (800) 377-7297, www.pennstateind.com 4-in-1 screwdriver kit, including two reversible bits, brass ferrule and endcap, and a reversible steel bit holder, #PKSDK4, $6. ◉ Packard Woodworks, (800) 683-8876, www.packardwoodwork.com No. 1 and No. 2 Morse taper arbor key chucks, $37.

CHAPTER THIRTY-THREE

PROJECT 19 Handles for Turning Tools

Customize your own perfect fit

Decades ago, woodturning tools came without handles, and turners would simply fashion their own. This makes perfect sense, because a handle that fits and feels "right" gives a turner confidence. And who better to custom-fit the handle than the person who'll use the tool?

Turning and installing your own handles is a great exercise in designing, turning to fairly tight tolerances, and drilling wood on the lathe. To get started, you can buy tools unhandled (still an option) or remove their commercial handles (really easy).

Use Strong, Dry Wood

Select stock with straight grain, especially for the tool end of the handle (use the strongest grain orientation for this critical area). Traditional hardwoods, many exotic woods, and even local woods that you harvest and dry yourself are all good options. Do not use weak woods such as pine, poplar, butternut, willow, spruce or fir.

Make sure the wood is dry. If you have any doubt about the moisture content, let the handle stabilize for several days (or longer) after rough-turning and drilling the initial hole.

I make each handle unique, by using different woods and finish colors, so that I can immediately identify each tool. I normally start with stock that's 1-¾" to 2" square (**Photo 1**). The length of the blank depends on a number of factors, including personal preference and the

1 Choose straight-grained hardwood for the handle. Use brass, copper or steel fittings to make the ferrule, which reinforces the joint between the tool and the handle. Copper couplings make excellent ferrules.

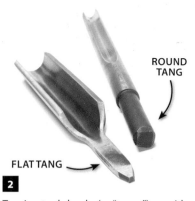

ROUND TANG

FLAT TANG

2 Turning tool shanks (or "tangs") are either round or flat. Both types mount in holes bored in the end of the handle. Flat-tang tools require stepped holes to accommodate their tapered shape.

3 Start by drilling a pilot hole for the tool's tang in one end of the handle blank. Then use a cone-shaped center to mount the blank on the lathe, so the pilot hole will be centered when the blank is turned round.

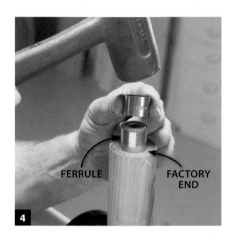

FERRULE FACTORY END

4

Drive on the ferrule after turning a tenon to fit. This ferrule is a copper coupling that's been cut in half. If the tenon is longer than the ferrule, use another ferrule (the other half of the coupling) to drive the first one home.

BULB

SPINDLE ROUGHING GOUGE

5 Turn a bulb directly behind the ferrule, to provide the greatest support for the tool's tang. Most of the handle's shaping can be done with a spindle roughing gouge.

tool itself. Figure A (below) lists handle lengths that work well for me. It's always better to make a handle too long, rather than too short.

FIG. A: Suggested Handle Lengths

Parting tool	12" to 14"
Skew chisel	12" to 16"
Spindle/detail gouge	10" to 14"
Spindle roughing gouge	14" to 18"
Scraper	14" to 16"

Ferrule Stock

Every woodturning tool handle must have a metal ferrule to reinforce the joint between the handle and the tool's shank, or "tang" (**Photo 2**). Hardware stores and salvage yards are good sources for ferrule stock. Copper couplings (used to join copper pipe and tubing) are some of the best. They're available in a variety of diameters and each one can be cut in half to make two ferrules. Choose a diameter that allows plenty of wood between the tool's shank and the ferrule, usually at least ¼"–if there's any question, go with a larger diameter.

Make a Handle

The first step is to drill a ⅜" dia. x ¾" deep pilot hole for the tang in the blank (**Photo 3**). Note: If the tang is smaller than ⅜", match the pilot hole's diameter with the tang. The end you choose for mounting the tang should have straight grain and be free of checks and knots. Clamp the blank in a vise and use a hand-held drill.

Install a live center with a cone in the tailstock (see Sources, page 144). The cone will automatically center the pilot hole when the blank is mounted on the lathe. If you don't have a cone-type live center, turn a tapered piece of wood to fit into the blank's pilot hole and protrude about ½" beyond it. When you mount the blank, center the live center's point on the protruding end.

Turn the ferrule end–or the entire blank–to round, using a spindle roughing gouge.

Turn a tenon on the end to match the ferrule's length and inside diameter–go for a driven-on fit. Slightly taper the tenon's end to help get the ferrule started. Drive on the ferrule, factory end first, all the way to the tenon's shoulder (**Photo 4**). This orients the ferrule's rough-cut end with the end of the tenon. Turn down this rough edge after reinstall-

6 Shape the handle to fit your grip, gradually and selectively reducing the diameter, until it feels just right. Remove the handle often, to check the way it feels in your hand.

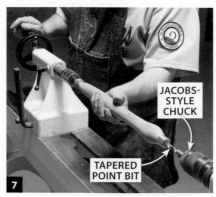

JACOBS-STYLE CHUCK

TAPERED POINT BIT

7 Install a chuck in the headstock to drill the tang hole. With the lathe running at slow sped, simultaneously grip the handle (so it doesn't turn) and crank the tailstock, to carefully drive the handle onto the spinning bit.

8 Drive the handle onto the tang, using a waste block to protect the edge. Check frequently to make sure the tool and handle remain properly aligned.

ing the blank on the lathe. If the edge is very rough, use a mill file, off the lathe.

For safety, turn a bulb over the part of the handle that will house the tang (**Photo 5**). This provides maximum strength in the event of a catch or dig-in.

Turn the blank to a diameter slightly larger than final size. Then use a detail/spindle gouge to round the back end of the handle.

Turn the gripping area of the handle into a shape that you like (**Photo 6**). Be sure to test the grip with the hand that you will use to control the tool. As the gripping area nears perfection, shape the transition to the bulb to create the optimal feel and balance, but beware of making any portion too thin.

Finish-sand the handle and ferrule to #150-grit, with the lathe running. Turn off the lathe and sand with the grain to finish the job.

Remove the tool rest to drill the tang hole (**Photo 7**). For round-tang tools, the hole's depth should be one fourth to one third of the tool's length. For flat-tang tools, the hole should house the entire tang—almost to the tool's shoulder. Mount a Jacobs-type drill chuck in the headstock (see Sources) and install an ordinary tapered-point bit (other types of bits won't enter the pilot hole accurately). Place the handle's pilot hole against the bit, bring up the tailstock, and lock it. Advance the live center to engage the center hole on the waste end of the tool handle. Put on a full-face shield and set the lathe's speed between 400 and 600 rpm.

Turn on the lathe and check to see that the handle runs true. There should be little or no "ghosting" at the ferrule

end. If you see ghosts, stop the lathe and re-center the drill bit in the pilot hole. Once all is running well, take two simultaneous actions to drill the hole: Grasp the spinning handle about halfway back with one hand while cranking the tailstock's handwheel with the other. Go slowly. If you feel too much resistance, slowly back out of the hole, to remove chips.

If the hole must be made larger, to accommodate round tangs that are larger than ⅜" dia., simply repeat the drilling operation, using the appropriate larger tapered-point bit. Drill stepped holes to accommodate tools with flat tangs. Drill the small dia. hole the full length of the shank; drill the larger hole only as far as necessary.

Finish the back end of the handle off the lathe. Simply cut off the waste with a handsaw and then sand.

Set the tool into the handle. This step is critical. I'm a firm believer in using epoxy to anchor the tool, so start by pouring a generous amount into the hole. Drive the handle onto the tang (**Photo 8**). Stop about every quarter of the way to check for alignment—sighting the tool and handle much as you would sight a gun. Look for misalignment left or right and up or down. Tap the tool with the mallet to make corrections.

My favorite tool-handle finish is the one that comes from hard use: sweat, dirt, wear–and maybe even a little blood. A pure oil finish is another option, but any film-forming finish (including wipe-on oil-varnishes) will make the handle too slick.

SOURCES Oneway Manufacturing, www.oneway.ca, (800) 565-7288, Live Center with Cone (#2 Morse taper), #2064, $120.95. Craft Supplies, woodturnerscatalog.com, Keyless Drill Chuck #104-578 $45.50. Alan Lacer, alanlacer.com, alan@alanlacer.com, variety of unhandled lathe tools.

CHAPTER THIRTY-FOUR

Three-Legged Stool

Combine your woodworking and woodturning skills

CUTTING LIST INCHES

REFERENCE	QUANTITY	PART	STOCK	THICKNESS	DIAMETER	LENGTH	COMMENTS
A	1	Seat	White oak	1-5/8	13-½		a
B	3	Leg	White oak	1-7/8		23-5/8	b, c, d
C	1	Long stretcher	White oak	1-¾		15	e, f
D	1	Short stretcher	White oak	1-7/8		11-¾	e
E	1	Domed cap	White oak	3/8	1		

Comments:

a) Drill three 1" dia. x 1-¼" d holes in the bottom, spaced 120°, centered 1-½" from the outside edge, and angled 12°.

b) Length includes a 1-3/8" l tenon on one end. Trim tenon length to fit holes in seat.

c) In two legs, drill a ¾" dia. x ¾" d hole 9-5/8" from the bottom, angled 12°.

d) In one leg, drill a ¾" dia. x ¾" d hole 12-5/8" from the bottom.

e) Length includes 1" l tenons on both ends. Trim tenon length to fit holes.

f) Drill a ¾" dia. x ¾" d hole at the midpoint.

FIG. A EXPLODED VIEW

FIG. B SEAT CROSS-SECTION

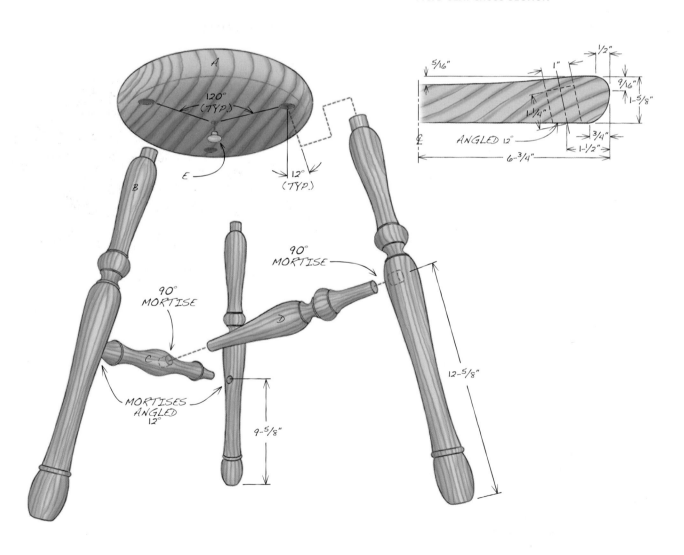

FIG. C SPINDLE DIMENSIONS

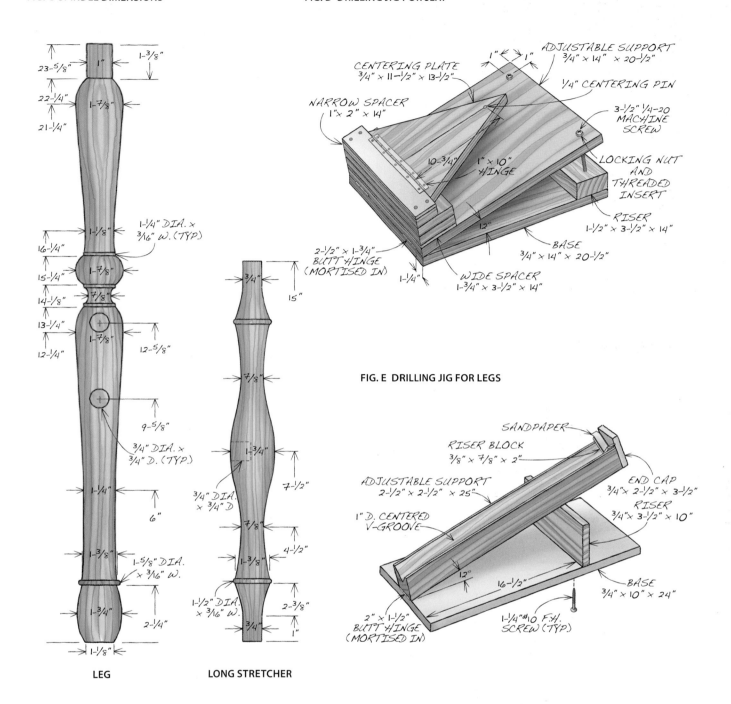

FIG. E DRILLING JIG FOR LEGS

LEG   **LONG STRETCHER**

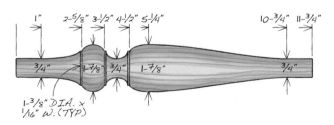

SHORT STRETCHER

1 Mount the seat blank on a screw chuck after rough-sawing the shape, flattening its back face and drilling a centered pilot hole. After threading on the blank, engage the tailstock center for additional support.

2 Shape the outside edge using a bowl gouge and working from smaller to larger diameters, so you cut across the end-grain, rather than into it.

3 Hollow the seat using the bowl gouge, working from large to small diameter.

If you enjoy building furniture and woodturning, but never really combined the two, here's an exciting challenge. Turning this stool requires planning, accuracy and sound joinery. Why only three legs? Beyond simple elegance, a three-legged stool has the distinctive ability to sit securely on almost any surface.

At 23-½" tall, this stool is just right for me—I'm 5'10" and prefer to sit with my knees slightly bent and my feet firmly on the ground. You may want to vary the stool's height based on your own height and sitting preferences. You also have the option to angle one of the stretchers.

Choose any dry, strong wood—you can't go wrong with cherry, maple, walnut, hickory, ash or oak. Use straight-grained stock for the legs and stretchers. The stools shown here are made of quarter-sawn white oak.

Start with the Seat

Everything else flows from this part (A, Fig. A, page 146 and Cutting List, page 146). Glue up the seat blank and mount it on a screw chuck (see Sources, page 151). A screw chuck makes it easy to remove and remount the seat and leaves only one hole.

Flatten the bottom side of the blank and drill a hole for the screw chuck. Note the screw's length and the desired final thickness at the center of the seat, and add plywood spacers behind the blank, if necessary, to limit the screw's penetration. Mount the blank and engage the tailstock center to add extra support and safety (**Photo 1**).

Use a bowl gouge to round the blank and shape the seat's asymmetrical rim (**Photo 2** and Fig. B). Pull away the tailstock to hollow the seat (**Photo 3**). Start at the rim and lightly hollow to the center. Be careful, as hollowing too deep will make the stool uncomfortable. It's a good idea to

remove the seat and test it during this process. I hollow to a depth of ⅜" at most. A large curved scraper can be helpful to blend and level the final shape (see Sources). Make sure the transition from the rim to the seat is smoothly rounded, so it doesn't cut into the back of your legs.

Sand the seat, using a soft pad (see Sources) and a corded, reversing drill. Position the disc low and then raise it to meet the outside edge of the rotating seat. Work around the rim to sand the face (**Photo 4**). You may need to turn off the lathe and sand by hand to remove all of the sanding marks.

Before removing the seat, pencil a circle on the bottom, 1-½" from the rim, to locate the mortises for the legs.

Drill the Leg Mortises

Use geometry or trial-and-error to divide the circle drawn on the seat into three equal parts (**Photo 5**). The legs splay 12°, so the mortises must be drilled at that angle. You can buy a lathe attachment to drill these mortises (see "The Drill Wizard," page 151), or make a jig (Fig. D, page 147). This jig is adjustable—to change the drilling angle you adjust the long machine screws. (If you want to experiment with a larger or taller stool, you may want to change the angle at which the legs splay.) When you build this jig, size its centering pin to fit the hole you drilled in the seat for the screw chuck.

Square up your drill press before drilling the mortises and install a 1" Forstner bit that's marked with tape to drill 1-¼" deep. Use a protractor to set the jig at the 12° angle. Then use the centering pin to install the seat. Clamp the seat to the jig with the jig's pointer aimed directly at the first mortise. Then clamp the jig to the drill press, aligned parallel with the table's front edge and positioned to drill the mortise (**Photo 6**). Drill the first mortise, then rotate the seat to drill the second and third mortises.

4 SOFT PAD

Sand the outside edge, using a disc mounted on a soft pad. Then work around to sand the seat's hollowed face. Keep the disc below the seat's centerline and reverse its rotation as necessary to keep it spinning against the seat's rotation.

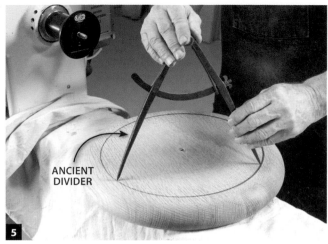

5 ANCIENT DIVIDER

Locate the leg mortises by dividing a circle marked on the seat's back into three equal sections.

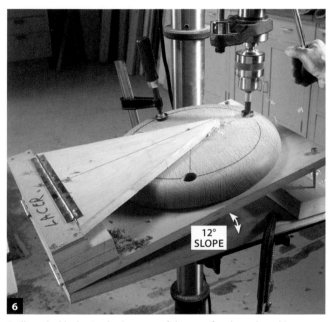

6 12° SLOPE

Drill angled holes in the bottom of the seat for the splayed legs, using a shop-made jig. Before drilling, make sure both the jig and the seat are securely clamped.

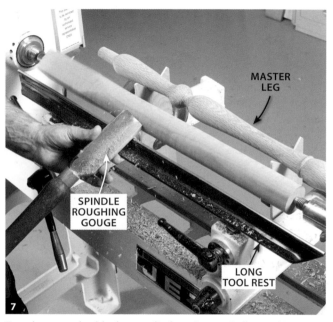

7 MASTER LEG / SPINDLE ROUGHING GOUGE / LONG TOOL REST

Turn the square leg blank to a cylinder using a spindle roughing gouge. A long tool rest allows working the entire blank. A master leg mounted behind the blank makes it easier to turn legs that match.

Turning Duplicates

Turning three legs that look the same is not as difficult as you might think, because they don't have to be absolutely identical—just reasonably close facsimiles. However, turning duplicates does require controlling several variables:

Wood: Use stock that matches (in this case, rift- or quartersawn stock), preferably cut from the same plank or tree.

Profiles: Work with a master turning positioned so you can easily sight over the blank to compare the desired profile with the one you're creating.

Placement: Create a "story stick" that locates key elements (including one or both ends) and identifies key diameters.

Drive small brads into the edge of the stick at transition points between elements and at the center of important diameters. Clip the brads so they extend about ³⁄₁₆". Move the tool rest close to the cylindrical blank. Start the lathe and place the stick on the tool rest, parallel to the blank and aligned at the bottom end. Then gently push the stick into the spinning blank, so the brads score the wood at all the key points.

Diameters: Use outside calipers that firmly hold the setting to accurately size diameters. Fully round the two ends that contact the wood, so they won't catch. It's convenient to use different calipers for each diameter.

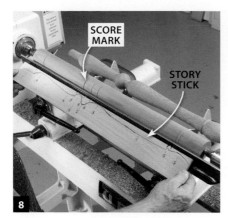

Use a story stick to score the spinning blank. The stick contains precisely located brads that transfer the turned profile's key transition points and diameters.

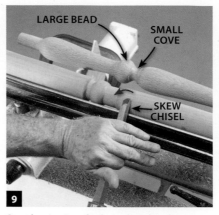

Start by turning the large bead in the middle of the leg and the shoulder below it. Do not cut the cove between them, though. Turning such a small diameter now will cause excessive vibration during the rest of the turning process.

Shape the leg's lower contoured portion. Establish the bead at the bottom; then follow the profile on the pattern leg as you "connect the dots." Shape the foot last.

Turn the Legs

If you decide to turn a different leg profile than the one shown here (Fig. C), plan ahead for the placement of the stretchers and keep the diameters large enough to support an adult's weight. Turn a model leg, or even a model stool, to make sure the profiles look good in three dimensions and work well together.

When turning the legs (and other spindles with similar length and diameters) you're likely to encounter ribbing, an unwanted texturing of the surface that occurs when the wood flexes. When ribbing begins, most turners place a hand on the back side of the spindle to keep it from flexing. Make sure your hand touches only the back of the spindle, direct the force of the tool along the spindle's axis (as much as possible), and work with sharp tools. Also, wait until near the end of the turning process to turn the smaller diameters to final size. Follow the turning procedure described below to minimize ribbing.

Install a small headstock drive on your lathe (see Sources). A long tool rest adds convenience, but requires a second tool rest banjo (see Sources). Mount a square leg blank and turn it to a uniform 1-⅞" cylinder (**Photo 7**). Then use a story stick to mark the leg blank (**Photo 8**). Note that the bottom of the leg is at the tailstock end.

Turn the leg's large bead first (**Photo 9**). Use calipers and a parting tool to cut the fillets on both ends and widen them for clearance. Below the bead, extend the fillet to the shoulder below the cove. Then round the bead and roll the shoulder with a detail/spindle gouge or a skew chisel. Do not cut the cove yet—doing so now will severely weaken the blank.

Size the small bead near the foot and both of its shoulders using the calipers and parting tool. Use the skew chisel to shape the bead. Then switch to the spindle roughing gouge and shape the adjacent concave profile (**Photo 10**). It may be helpful to use the detail/spindle gouge when you work near the small bead. Turn the foot using the detail/spindle gouge or a

skew—use the calipers to size its base.

Return to the middle of the leg and complete the cove (**Photo 11**). Then shape the contoured section above the large bead. Turn the tenon last, leaving it slightly oversize, and finish by rounding the shoulder below it to its final shape. Remove the tool rest and sand everything except the tenon to #220-grit.

Use a go/no-go gauge to turn the tenon to its final diameter (**Photo 12**). The goal is a friction fit in the mortise—one that neither binds nor wobbles. Be careful, as removing a small amount of wood from the tenon makes a big difference. When you've dialed in the perfect fit, trim the tenons so the leg's shoulder rests against the bottom of the seat while leaving the maximum tenon length inside the mortise.

Drill the Stretcher Mortises

Another shop-made jig is used to drill mortises in the legs for the stretchers (**Photo 13**; Fig. E, page 147). On this jig you adjust the slope by moving the riser forward or back and securing it with screws at the desired angle. The two mortises for the horizontal stretcher (C) are drilled at 12°, the same angle as the seat mortises. Set the jig's slope at 12°. Install a ¾" Forstner bit, position the jig on the drill press as before and drill ¾" deep holes 9-⅝" from the bottom of the leg.

To make sure the drill bit is centered on the leg, place a square block of wood in the v-grooved support, so it stands on edge, like a diamond. When the bit is perfectly centered, its point will touch the diamond's point.

The mortise for the angled stretcher (D) is drilled at 90°, 12-⅝" from the bottom of the leg. To drill this mortise, just remove the jig's riser so the v-grooved support lies flat. If you want both stretchers to be horizontal (as on the dark stool pictured on page 145), drill all three leg mortises at 12°. Note: Angled stretchers appear in historical pieces and in stools by contemporary turners such as Alan Leland and David Scotts.

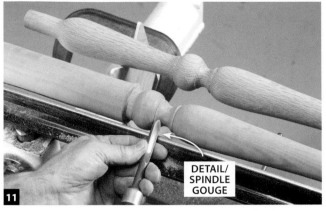

11 DETAIL/SPINDLE GOUGE

Return to the center of the blank and cut the cove. Now that the leg's lower portion and most of its middle details have been completed, it's safe to turn to this small diameter.

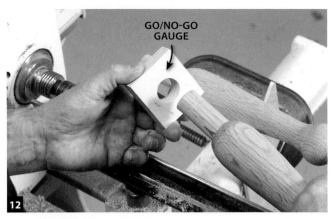

GO/NO-GO GAUGE

12

Use a simple gauge to precisely size the tenon at the top of the leg. The gauge is just a scrap of wood that's been drilled with the same bit used to drill the holes in the seat.

Turn the Stretchers

Install the legs in the seat and verify the length of the horizontal stretcher by measuring between the two 12° mortises and adding 1-½" for the tenons. Then follow the methods used to create the legs to turn this stretcher, size its tenons and drill its 90° mortise.

Reassemble the stool, including the horizontal stretcher, to verify the length of the short stretcher. Then turn it.

Assembly and Finish

Dry-assemble all the parts to make sure everything fits.

Repair a loose mortise-and-tenon joint by wrapping and gluing a wood shaving from a hand plane around the tenon.

After making any necessary adjustments, glue the stool together, using slow-setting glue such as Titebond Extend to allow plenty of working time (**Photo 14**). Apply glue to the mortises only, using a small brush to spread the glue evenly around the sides. Assembling all the parts at once requires finesse and a gentle touch. Use a rag dampened in hot water to remove any glue that squeezes out. Clamping shouldn't be necessary because the joints are under tension, but keep a fabric band clamp handy to pull everything tight, should you feel any looseness.

Have some fun with the hole left by the screw chuck in the bottom of the seat. Turn a small decorative finial or domed cap with a tenon (E) and glue it in.

12° SLOPE

13

Drill holes in the legs for the stretchers. Angle these holes to match the holes in the seat. Drill no deeper than halfway through the leg.

14

Glue the stool together. Assemble the legs and stretchers and then install all three legs at the same time. Tap lightly with a dead blow mallet to gently seat the joints.

Apply your favorite finish. The light-colored stool featured on page 145 has a shop-made oil/varnish blend finish. The dark-colored stool has been ebonized.

Special thanks to Bill Hull of Norman, OK, for his help in designing and making the drilling jigs for this project.

SOURCES Craft Supplies, woodturnerscatalog.com, 800-551-8876, 1 1/4" Radius Scraper #979-710 $82.20; ½" Stebcenter (small drive center), #104-625, $69.50 ⊚ Glaser Hitec, glaserhitec.com, 805-293-1678, Glaser Hitec Screw Chuck, 1-¼ x 8tpi, $155. ⊚ Oneway Manufacturing, oneway.ca, 800-565-7288, Drill Wizard, #3377, $120; #2 MT Safe Driver (small drive center), #2593, $42. ⊚ Robust Tools, turnrobust.com, 866-630-1122, Double Posted Long Tool Rest, $50 + $3 per inch of length. ⊚ Sanding Glove, thesandingglove.com, 800-995-9328, variety of sanding discs, Soft Sanding Disc Holder, 5" dia., #SM-5M, $16. ⊚

CHAPTER THIRTY-FIVE

Table Lamp

PROJECT 21

Whether shaped as a vase, a column or even as an egg, a turned lamp is more than an attractive project. Its flowing convex and concave contours offer excellent skill-building challenges for turners of all levels. Similarly, applying this lamp's eye-catching finish encourages thinking beyond stain and varnish.

You'll need a ½" or ⁹⁄₁₆" detail/spindle gouge to shape the lamp's contours (see Sources, page 155). You'll also need a ¼" parting tool, a ½" or ⅝" skew chisel, a 1-¼" to 1-¾" spindle roughing gouge and a pair of outside calipers to set the diameters. If you turn a finial, you'll need a ¼" detail/spindle gouge to shape its tight coves.

The harp, socket, cord and other hardware can be purchased as a kit at a lamp store, a home center or online (see Sources). And the answer to the inevitable question, "How the heck do I get the hole through the center?" is simpler than you might think.

Initial Choices

You can use just about any wood—just make sure it's adequately dry. Knowing the lamp's height and diameter before you begin turning is important, because these dimensions affect how you prepare the turning blank you start with and the method you use to drill the hole through its center.

This lamp stands just over 16" high without the harp and shade (Fig. A, page 155). The 7-¼" dia. of its body virtually rules out using a blank made from a single piece of wood, so gluing up 8/4 stock is the best option. The 8-¼" dia. of the lamp's base is even larger, but because the base is a separate part, it can be turned from a single piece of 8/4 stock.

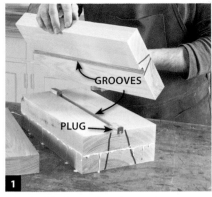

1. Glue the blank together after cutting grooves and installing plugs so the grooves form a channel for the wiring. The plugs also allow mounting the blank on the lathe.

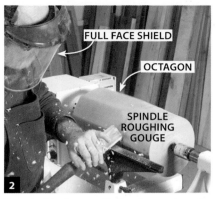

2. Turn the blank to a cylinder after sawing off its square corners to create an octagon. Then define the lamp's convex middle section by reducing the diameters at both ends.

FULL FACE SHIELD
OCTAGON
SPINDLE ROUGHING GOUGE

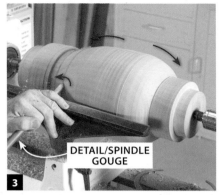

3. Start at the high point to shape the middle section. Roll the gouge in the direction of the curve as you work toward each end.

DETAIL/SPINDLE GOUGE

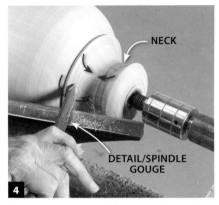

4. Create an asymmetrical cove at the neck by cutting in from each side. Start with the gouge on its side and slowly roll it upright.

NECK
DETAIL/SPINDLE GOUGE

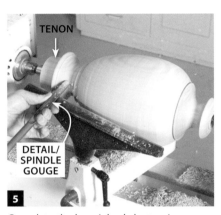

5. Complete the lamp's body by turning another asymmetrical cove at the bottom, just above the tenon that fits into the base.

TENON
DETAIL/ SPINDLE GOUGE

6. Drill through the plugs at both ends of the lamp body. Then use a bell hanger's bit to clear the center channel.

BELL HANGER BIT

The Center Hole

Drilling through the wood to create the center hole is a viable option when the lamp's body is relatively short or consists of a single piece of wood. However, starting with a glued-up blank almost always makes the job easier. You simply saw or rout centered grooves in the two inside faces of the lamination to create a 7⁄16" square channel to house the threaded lamp pipe (**Photo 1**). This method works regardless of the lamp's diameter or height.

TIP The large diameter of a lamp's base is not a minor detail—it's an important safety feature designed to keep the lamp from tipping over. In order to meet UL (Underwriters Laboratories) standards, a lamp must withstand an 8° tip without falling over.

Glue up the Blank

Make sure the boards you plan to laminate are flat. Cut the centered grooves 7⁄16" wide and slightly more than 7⁄32" deep. Then size a pair of 1-1⁄2" long plugs to fit. The boards must close tightly together when the plugs are installed.

Spread an even coat of glue on both surfaces of each lamination and glue the plugs flush with the ends of the boards. In addition to aligning the grooves, the plugs are used to mount the blank on the lathe. Standard white or yellow glues work well, although glues such as Titebond III and plastic resin glues have less creep. Clamp the blank properly, allow the glue to dry for 24 hours and wait at least another 24 hours before turning. Cut the blank into an octagon before mounting it on the lathe; it's too massive to mount as a square.

Turn the Lamp's Body

Use a spur center in the headstock and a high quality live center in the tailstock to securely mount the blank on the lathe. Spin the blank by hand to make sure it doesn't contact the tool rest before turning on the lathe. Then rough the blank into a cylinder using the spindle roughing gouge (**Photo 2**).

7

Use a parting tool to accurately size the mortise in the lamp's base after roughly hollowing it with the detail/spindle gouge. Shape the base's shallow ogee profile using the same gouge.

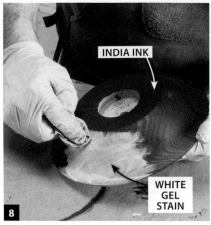

8

Apply the distinctive "salt and pepper" finish in two steps. First, brush on a coat of India ink. Then wipe white gel stain into the wood's pores. This lamp is made of ash, which has large pores.

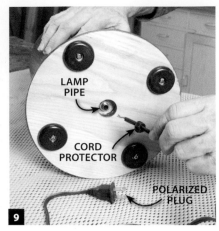

9

Insert the cord in the lamp pipe and push through a sufficient length to make connections at the socket. Install a cord protector to keep the cord from rubbing against the metal lamp rod.

Size the diameters at both ends, using a parting tool and outside calipers. Then locate and size the critical diameters for each detail. However, do not size the coves to their final depth, as this will prematurely weaken the blank.

Shape the large, convex middle section first, using the detail/spindle gouge (**Photo 3**). Make multiple cuts to complete this egg-shaped form, gradually deepening and refining its overall shape. The goal is to create a flowing, continuous curve that fully realizes the form.

To cut with the grain when the blank is oriented as it is here—with its grain running parallel to the lathe's bed—you must work from larger to smaller diameters. In this case—shaping a convex form—that means working from the high point to both ends of the curve.

Next, move to the tailstock end to work the top section of the body, called the neck (**Photo 4**). Use the parting tool to establish the final diameters, then switch to the detail/spindle gouge to complete the details. Save the deep asymmetrical cove for last. Cut in toward the center from both sides. Start with the gouge on its side and gradually roll it face-up as you cut in to the center. Strive to create graceful, flowing curves.

Finish the body by completing its bottom section (**Photo 5**). Establish the final diameters and rough out the tenon that will be used to mount the body on the base. Then, as before, complete the details and turn the deep, asymmetrical cove. Lastly, use the parting tool and calipers to turn the tenon to its final diameter.

Sand the lamp's body to remove any torn grain; then work through the grits until the sanding marks are gone.

Take the body off the lathe to drill through the plugs (**Photo 6**). Then make sure the center channel is clear of debris from end to end by running a 7/16" bell hanger bit all the way through (see Sources).

Turn the Lamp's Base

Band saw a disc of 8/4 stock for the base and mount it on the lathe using a 3" dia. faceplate with screws that penetrate about 1/2" into the underside. Use the detail/spindle gouge to round the disc, level its top surface and roughly hollow to size the mortise for the lamp body's tenon. Then cut straight in with the parting tool to finish sizing the mortise (**Photo 7**).

Cut the mortise slightly deeper than the tenon's length and about 1/16" larger in diameter. The goal is to allow for the difference in wood movement over time due to the cross-grain orientation of the lamp's body and base. The threaded lamp pipe will be used to securely connect these two parts.

Measure the body above the tenon and mark this diameter on the disc. Then use the detail/spindle gouge to create an ogee curve on the face of the disc, from just outside the diameter line to a point about 1/4" up from the bottom at the edge.

To cut with the grain when the blank is oriented as it is here—with its grain running perpendicular to the lathe's bed—you must work from a smaller to a larger diameter. So, start the cut from just outside the diameter line and work toward the outside edge. Shaping this reverse curve requires finesse, so take it in stages, refining the look until you're satisfied.

Complete the turning by cutting a small chamfer on the underside of the base that rises to meet the end of the ogee curve. Finish-sand the base. Then drill a 7/16" dia. hole through the center, with a 3/4" deep x 1" dia. counterbore on the underside. Fasten feet (see Sources) to raise the base just high enough for the lamp cord to exit.

"X" IS THE AREA THAT REMAINS SQUARE (POMMEL)

1 Lay out the pommel (area to remain square) with a square and pencil. Only one line is necessary at the shoulder of the pommel because the spinning wood will show the line clearly.

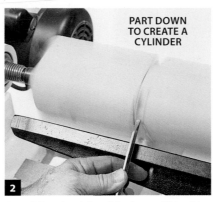

PART DOWN TO CREATE A CYLINDER

2 Cut 1/8" to the right of the layout line with a parting tool. Make sure the edge is keen; the handle is low; take only light cuts; and widen the cut as you go deeper to prevent binding. Cut to the left until you reach the layout line.

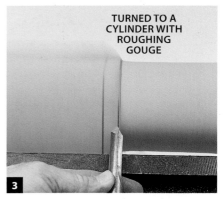

TURNED TO A CYLINDER WITH ROUGHING GOUGE

3 Turn the area to the right of the pommel to a cylinder. If you're making rounded shoulders, turn the corners of the pommel with a ½" detail gouge. The line to the left of the shoulder indicates the top of the rounded portion.

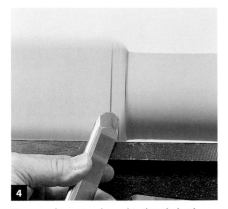

4 You can also use a skew chisel to do both square-shouldered or rounded pommels. The long point (toe) of the skew is down and leading the cut. Skews leave the best surface, but require more skill and practice to use.

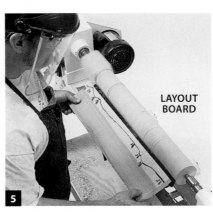

LAYOUT BOARD

5 Use a layout board with cut pins to accurately lay out the placement of elements below the pommel. Securely place the board on the tool rest and push it into the cylinder below the pommel.

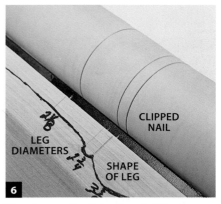

LEG DIAMETERS

CLIPPED NAIL

SHAPE OF LEG

6 The pins are simply brads or finish nails driven into the edge of a ¾"-thick board at the critical points and clipped off about ¼" from the surface. On longer work it's often easier to manipulate the layout board by making it in two or three sections

- Make at least one prototype before you commit to four legs. Even if you have an accurate drawing to scale, the transition from two dimensions to three will surprise you.
- As you make the prototype leg, remove it often from the lathe and view it in an upright position, as it will be viewed mounted on the table. The transition from horizontal viewing to vertical is also astonishing, and may lead you to changes in design.

Wood to Turn

You'll need four pieces of 3-½" by 3-½" by 30" squared stock cut exactly to the same length. (Note: I used two pieces of 8/4 ash, glued and squared on the jointer.) Having squared stock is critical when leaving pommels on the finished piece. Cutting all the blanks the same length greatly simplifies leveling the table.

Tools and Supplies

- A spur or modified dead center (highly recommended

if you are a novice turner) for the headstock side, and a live center for the tailstock side.
- An outside calipers, at least 4" capacity. (I keep a number of pairs sized and labeled for the different diameters. For a project of this kind even three pairs would suffice to speed the process along.)
- Double-posted 24" tool rest. (This is optional, but very convenient if you plan to do longer spindle work on a regular basis. This rest also requires an additional tool rest base or banjo.)
- Turning tools: a roughing gouge (any size); a ½" detailing gouge ground to a fingernail shape (see page 12); a ½" or larger skew chisel; and a parting tool (any size).
- A square and a pencil.
- Layout board materials: 6" wide by 28" long ¾" poplar, 1" brads or finish nails, a hammer and a nippers.
- Sandpaper; four sheets each of the following grits: #100, #120, #150, #180 and #220.

DRIVING WITH A DEAD CENTER

Although normally used in the tailstock, the dead center is a good alternative to a spur center for driving the work at the headstock. By controlling the pressure on the tailstock handwheel, you can determine the amount of slippage in driving the work—a real benefit in case of a catch or if you are intimidated by a large spinning square. You also can remove and accurately remount the leg several times, which is important for viewing the leg vertically during the design process.

To use the dead center for driving, file the shoulder of the dead center to a sharp edge. You can cut several shallow scallops along this edge to increase its grip on the wood. This shaping is easily done with a rotary tool and a small stone or a chainsaw file. Prior to mounting turning stock on the lathe, drive the center into the headstock side of the blank with a deadblow mallet to make an indentation.

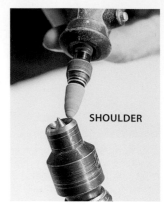

SHOULDER

SCALLOP

7

Use a calipers and parting tool to size critical diameters. The calipers must have rounded edges and make contact only on the side opposite the cutting tool. There must be no gap between the wood and tool rest. Hold the parting tool handle low, tucked under your forearm.

8

Round the ends of the outside calipers with a fine mill file or rotary tool before using on the spinning wood. I finish off the process with #220-grit sandpaper. The goal is to eliminate any sharp edges or corners that might catch on the wood.

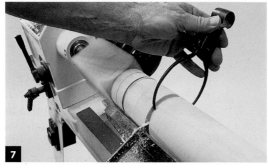

9

Cut details with the detailing gouge. For long, gradual curves, cylinders or straight tapers, use the roughing gouge. After turning the pommel, work from the headstock toward the tailstock until the leg is finished. Control the shape by watching the upper horizon of the piece rather than the tool tip.

10

Use the skew chisel (long-point down) to add shadow lines, crispness and emphasis to beads, shoulders, fillets and other details. Be sure to check the leg by removing it from the lathe and examining it in a vertical position. Complete the leg with final sanding.

SHADOW LINE

SOURCES Oneway Manufacturing, www.oneway.ca, (800) 565-7288, Safety Center (dead cup) #2MT #2593 $42. Oneway also makes tool rest bases (banjo) for other lathes or contact the maker of you lathe for a second banjo. Robust Tool (866) 630 1122 www.turnrobust.com Double-posted, long tool rests of up to 36" long, $50 flat fee + $3/inch.

CHAPTER THIRTY-SEVEN

23 Door Knob

Get a grip on unique interior door openers

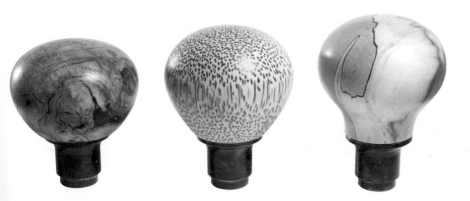

W hen's the last time you noticed a doorknob? They're so ordinary these days, they're virtually invisible. Here's a chance to return to those exciting days of yesteryear when wooden doorknobs were the rule rather than a rarity. Make matching sets for every door if you like. But why not mix things up? Using different woods and shaping each knob to fit the style of its room is a creative way to add a distinctive, personal touch to the decor.

Turning a wooden doorknob requires only basic turning tools and skills, and the idea is as old as the hills. The difficulty lies in obtaining decent hardware—that's why turned wooden doorknobs are so uncommon. Until recently, the only options were to purchase a new or antique porcelain knob set and break off the porcelain (and melt out the lead inside the antique set). These options work quite well, but a new interior door hardware kit promises to change the game (**Photo 1** and Sources, page 162).

Tools and Materials

To turn the knobs and escutcheons, you'll need a spindle roughing gouge, a ⅜" or ½" spindle/detail gouge and a parting tool. A ½" or larger skew chisel is optional. For the lathe, you'll need a four-jaw scroll chuck, a 3" dia. faceplate, a Jacobs style chuck to fit the tailstock and a ¾" high-speed steel or carbide Forstner drill bit (see Sources).

The sky is the limit when it comes to wood species—and even the knob's length—as both are issues of design and personal preference. I prefer to work with solid wood rather than laminated stock.

Each knob set requires a hardware kit or the metal parts stripped from an

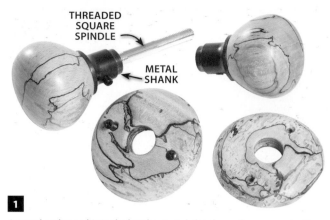

1

A new hardware kit includes the metal shanks and square spindle needed to make wooden doorknob sets for interior doors (see Sources).

2

Make the doorknob first. Turn the blank to a cylinder. Then cut a tenon on the front end with a parting tool or a skew chisel, so you can mount the blank in a scroll chuck.

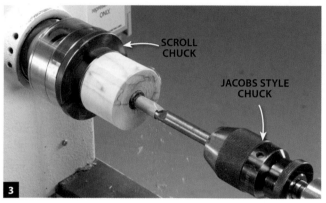

3

Turn the blank end-for-end and mount it in the scroll chuck. Then use a Jacobs style chuck to bore a hole for the doorknob's metal shank.

4

Use the spindle/detail gouge to shape the back of the knob. Make a rolling cut toward the hole in the end of the blank.

existing doorknob set. You'll also need woodturner's double-faced tape and glue, such as E6000 or slow-set epoxy (see Sources).

Turn the Knobs

For each knob, use dried wood ranging from 2-½" to 3" square and approximately 3" long. Mount the blank between centers and turn it into a cylinder with the roughing gouge. Turn a ¼" long tenon on the tailstock end—this will be the outside (front) face of the knob (**Photo 2**). Size the tenon's diameter to fit the scroll chuck's jaws.

Remove the blank, turn it around and mount it in the scroll chuck. Then use the Jacobs style chuck to drill a ¾" dia. x 1" deep hole in the end (**Photo 3**). Use the spindle/detail gouge to roughly shape the back of the knob (**Photo 4**). At its base, leave a flat or slightly concave area around the hole for the metal shank to seat against. This seating area should be no smaller than 1-¼" in diameter. Check the shank's fit to make sure it slides in without binding and seats flat against the wood. Then remove the knob from the lathe.

Create a jam chuck by mounting a 3" x 3" x 2" long waste block in the scroll chuck and turning a ¾" dia. x ¾" long

tenon on the end (**Photo 5**). The roughed knob will mount onto this tenon, so true it slowly with a parting tool or skew chisel. The goal is to create a fit that's tight enough to hold the knob securely, but loose enough to allow removing it when the time comes—not a very large window!

Mount the partially turned knob on the jam chuck and make sure it runs true. It's helpful for initial shaping to bring up the tailstock for extra support. Be sure to cover the point of the center with a small piece of wood or other material so it won't mar the knob's front face (**Photo 6**).

Use the spindle/detail gouge to refine the shape of the knob (**Photo 7**). At this point, you can shorten its overall length, detail its face, add a bead—whatever you desire. A ball shape or an asymmetrical form both function well as a shape for the hand. Finalize the shape and then pull away the tailstock to complete the turning on the very end. On the headstock end, turn the back of the knob to its final shape (**Photo 8**). Finish-sand the knob to #220- or #320-grit. If you plan to apply a finish such as melamine on the lathe, now is the time to do it. Melamine is a pre-catalyzed lacquer that's easily applied while the lathe is running (see Sources).

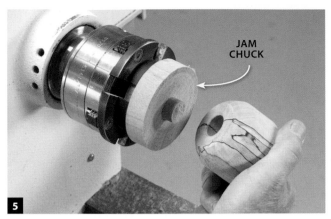

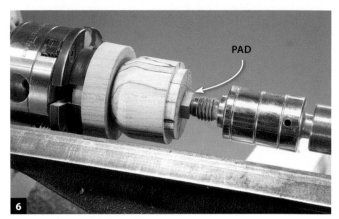

Make a jam chuck to remount the knob for final turning. It's a disc with a flat face and a tenon. The fit between the tenon and the knob's hole must be snug, so the knob stays put.

Bring up the tailstock to support the blank. Install a pad so the point of the tailstock's center doesn't mar the end of the blank.

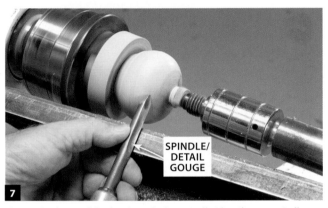

Shape the front of the knob with the spindle/detail gouge. Pull back the tailstock when you near the final shape, so you can finish turning the front end.

Refine the shape at the base of the knob, turning away the jam chuck as required for access. The final diameter at the base must be the same size or larger than the metal shank.

Turn the Escutcheons

Make the escutcheons from a dry face-grain blank that's between ¼" and ½" thick and has one flat face. Cut the blank into 3" dia. discs, one for each escutcheon. Mount a 3-½" dia. x ¾" thick disc of MDF, plywood or scrap solid stock onto a 3" faceplate. This disc provides a cushion of waste material that can be cut into when you turn the escutcheon. True this "waste disc" round and flatten its outside face (check with a ruler).

Use woodturner's double-faced tape to fasten the escutcheon blank to the waste disc (**Photo 9**). Align the tape with the grain and place it on the blank's flat face. Usually two 3" long strips of 1" wide tape is sufficient. Center the blank and press it onto the disc. Bring up the tailstock to serve as a clamp. Install a 2" square pad or disc to evenly distribute the pressure. Wait about 20 minutes before turning.

Turn the escutcheon to the desired diameter. As the blank is face-grain material, you must cut across its edge to reduce the diameter, rather than into its edge. Using the spindle/detail gouge, work from the face of the blank toward (and into) the waste disc. Do not use a parting tool or a skew chisel for this step.

Drill a ¾" dia. hole through the center of the blank

(**Photo 10**). Then shape the face of the escutcheon with the spindle/detail gouge, working from small to large diameter (**Photo 11**). Finish-sand the escutcheon and apply the finish while it's still on the lathe, if desired.

To remove the escutcheon from the waste disc, carefully slide a chisel under an end-grain edge. Then gently apply slow, steady pressure to break the tape's bond and pry off the escutcheon.

Assemble and Mount the Doorknobs

Glue the metal shank into the turned knob, using flexible epoxy or glue such as E6000 (**Photo 12** and Sources). Allow plenty of curing time (two to three days) before you mount the knobs on the door.

You'll need some screws and a latch assembly to mount the doorknobs. Usually the door's existing latch assembly works fine. For new installations, you can purchase the latch assembly alone at almost any hardware store or home center for $10 or less.

The screw lengths depend on the thickness of the door and the thickness of the escutcheon. I typically use black or brass oval-head sheet metal screws to contrast or

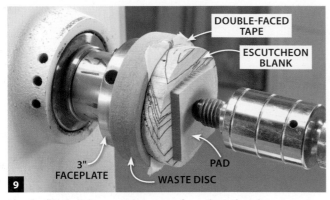

Use double-faced tape and pressure from the tailstock to mount the rough-sawn escutcheon blank on a waste disc that's mounted to a faceplate.

Drill a hole for the doorknob's metal shank after turning the escutcheon blank to its final diameter.

Turn the escutcheon's face with the spindle/detail gouge. Avoid tearout by working from the center to the outside edge.

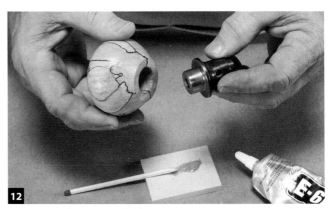

Glue the shank into the knob, using E6000 adhesive—it's flexible, so it's excellent for adhering wood to metal, because it allows for the wood's seasonal movement.

complement the wood. The doorknob hardware kit has two nylon barrels that the screws thread into from each side to hold the escutcheons in place. If you use the existing latch assembly, you may be able to use its screws and metal spacers instead of new screws and the nylon barrels from the kit.

Drill a pair of matching countersunk mounting holes in each escutcheon. Align the holes with the grain to allow seasonal movement and drill the holes slightly larger than the screw shanks. Sometimes the screw size and spacing are determined by holes in the latch assembly.

Install the latch assembly and mount the escutcheons. Don't over-tighten the screws. Mount one knob on the spindle and secure it with the setscrew. Slide the spindle through the door and latch assembly. Then thread the remaining knob onto the spindle until it fits softly against the escutcheon—neither so tight that the knobs won't turn nor so loose that the knobs wobble. When the fit is satisfactory, fasten the loose knob to the spindle with the setscrew.

Finish Options

For a natural appearance that will patinate over time, use a drying-type oil (such as pure tung oil or boiled linseed oil), or an oil/varnish blend. For a more durable finish, use brushing varnish that's been reduced 50 percent with mineral spirits so you can wipe it on, or melamine, as mentioned earlier.

SOURCES Alan Lacer Woodturning, alanlacer.com, 715-426-9451, Doorknob Kit (includes 2 shanks, 1 spindle and 2 nylon barrels for mounting the escutcheons), $21.95 each. ☺ Craft Supplies USA, woodturnerscatalogue.com, 800-551-8876, Vicmarc Four-Jaw Scroll Chuck, #100-327, $241.50; Keyless Chuck #104-578, $45.50; 1" Double-Sided tape #104-982, $27.50; Melamine Lacquer, 16.2 oz #102-584, $18.90. ☺ E6000 Adhesive can be purchased at Walmart, Amazon, many hardware stores and home centers.

CHAPTER THIRTY-EIGHT

PROJECT 24 Door Stop

Perfect for the house that has everything

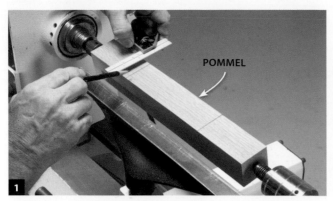

1

Divide the blank into three parts. Only the end portions will be turned, as each blank contains two doorstops. The pommel will be cut diagonally to create the wedge-shaped stops.

POMMEL

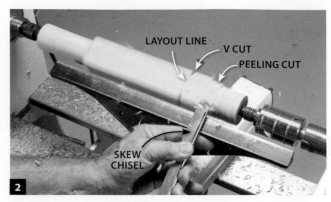

LAYOUT LINE   V CUT
               PEELING CUT

SKEW
CHISEL

2

Rough out the pommel with the skew chisel, alternating between shallow V cuts made slightly outside the layout lines and peeling cuts used to round the ends.

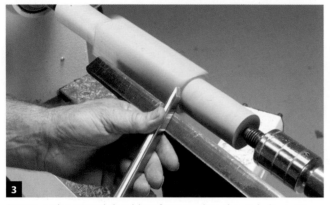

3

Square each pommel shoulder after rounding the ends, by cutting in at the layout line, using the skew with its long point down.

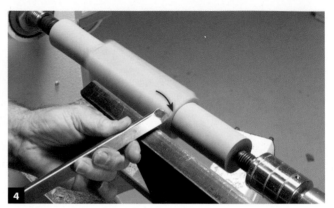

4

Round the pommel shoulders in stages by making successive rolling cuts with the skew (long point down) or the detail/spindle gouge.

Take the humble rubber doorstop—please! Then head to your lathe and create something that you can't buy in a store—a doorstop that looks as great as it works. In addition to creating a functional item and a unique gift, this simple project provides an excellent opportunity to practice the art of creating pommels (a pommel is any part of a spindle turning that's left square). Disaster lurks at the end of a pommel, where the turning changes from round to square, because one wrong move can cause ruinous splintering. That's why artfully making the transition is an important technique to master. As each blank produces two doorstops, you'll be able to practice creating pommels in both directions with every blank. Doorstops take a real beating, so use tough wood; oak, maple, cherry and walnut all work well. A 12" long by 1-½" to 1-¾" square blank is a good size to start with, although the pitch of the stop's wedge and its overall length will often be dictated by the gap under the door.

A parting tool, a skew chisel and a detail gouge are the only turning tools you'll need. A band saw and a stationary belt sander are desirable, but not absolutely necessary—a handsaw and a sanding disc mounted on the lathe also work quite well. Add a straightedge, a square, an awl and a pencil

and you're ready to go.

Square the blank using a table saw or planer and remove any milling marks by sanding.

Create centered mounting holes on both ends of the blanks. Carefully scribe from corner to corner using the straightedge and the awl. Push in with the awl where the two lines intersect to make the holes.

Mount the blank, making sure that both lathe centers are in the mounting holes.

Both ends will be turned into knobs, so measure about 2-½" in from the ends and mark a line at both points (**Photo 1**). The area between the lines (the pommel) will be left square. Marking all four faces makes the lines easier to see when the workpiece is spinning. Use a white or yellow pencil if the blank is a dark-colored wood.

Start the turning process by creating square shoulders on the ends of the pommel. Creating a clean square shoulder is one of the hardest parts of the entire process, so practicing on waste material is good preparation. Using the skew chisel long point down, make a series of V cuts slightly away from the lines, in the areas that will turned into knobs. Because of the skew's bevel, the initial V cuts cannot go very deep.

DETAIL/
SPINDLE
GOUGE

5

Shape the knobs with the detail/spindle gouge and the skew. The knobs don't have to match, because you're creating two separate doorstops. Ball or bulb shapes are easiest to grip.

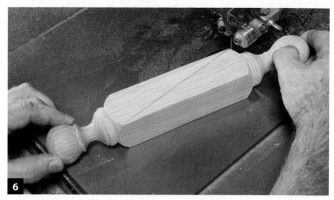

6

Cut diagonally across the pommel to create two wedge-shaped doorstops. The sawn edges are the bottoms. Flatten them by sanding.

7

Round the end of each doorstop to reduce chipping and create a more graceful look.

SELF-ADHESIVE
CORK DRAWER
LINER

8

Keep the doorstops from slipping on hardwood or tile floors by attaching a piece of foam or cork to the bottom. Trim the waste with a utility knife.

Instead, alternate between shallow V cuts and peeling down the turned end portions to create clearance (**Photo 2**). Go easy, as a peeling cut that goes deeper than the preceding V cut can splinter the pommel. When the end sections are nearly rounded, cut in a clean square shoulder right at the layout line (**Photo 3**). Square shoulders can also be created with a parting tool, but it's risky: Delicate cuts are necessary to avoid splintering the shoulders. Finish by truing the two rounded sections with the skew—make planing cuts moving from the outside end right up to the shoulder.

Use either the long point of the skew or a detail/spindle gouge to round over the pommels' shoulders (**Photo 4**). Rounded shoulders are much more durable than square ones, which are prone to splintering.

Shape the knobs (**Photo 5**). Turn the knob at the tailstock end first, to avoid working with a weak spot (the narrow neck) near the drive center. The knobs' concave and convex shapes can both be cut with the detail/spindle gouge, but a skew will leave a cleaner surface on the convex shapes.

(Using the skew, though, requires more skill and practice.) Leave at least ¼" of waste at both ends for removing the mounting holes.

When you're happy with the knobs you've created, reduce the diameters at both ends. Then finish-sand to #220-grit.

Take the blank off the lathe and remove the waste at both ends with a small saw. Then finish-sand the ends by hand.

Mark one of the blank's flat pommel faces from corner to corner. Then saw this line to create two wedge-shaped doorstops (**Photo 6**). Sand their sawn faces flat.

Shape the end of each doorstop (**Photo 7**).

Use any finish you like—or none at all. Leave the bottom face unfinished in order to apply a cork face or some other anti-slip material (**Photo 8**). This is especially important when using the stops on wooden or tile floors. Check out drawer or toolbox liners sold at home centers and hardware stores. The self-adhesive cork liner shown in the photo costs about $8 for a 4' roll—that means you'll have plenty left over to upgrade your tool drawers.

CHAPTER THIRTY-NINE

PROJECT 25 Christmas Ornaments

Develop a delicate touch by creating graceful shapes

TURN THE SPINDLE

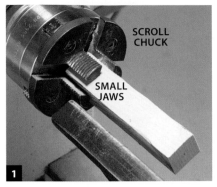

1 Each ornament contains a bulb, a cap and a long spindle. Mount a blank for the spindle in the chuck. Engage the tailstock center and round the blank.

SCROLL CHUCK
SMALL JAWS

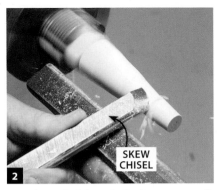

2 Turn the end of the spindle down to a small diameter, after removing the tailstock. The goal is to create a spindle that's thin and delicate, like an icicle.

SKEW CHISEL

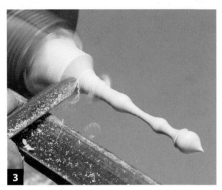

3 Create tiny details, working from the end of the spindle toward the headstock, to avoid a break. Flare the shoulder near the chuck, leaving sufficient room for a tenon.

As an alternative to mass-produced items, Christmas ornaments rank high on the list. They easily become treasured keepsakes and the delicate spindle work and hollow turning involved will certainly test your skills.

Each ornament contains three parts. I suggest making the long, slender spindle first, then the top cap and last, the hollow bulb. This approach allows careful fitting of the spindle and cap to the bulb as well as working out the proportions to enhance the overall look.

Part of designing wooden ornaments is selecting and mixing materials. For the spindle work, almost anything goes, but dense woods such as hard maple, cherry, cocobolo and goncalo alves are well-suited for turning the thin diameters and fine details that characterize the best ornaments. The hollow bulb shaped body can be turned from virtually any interesting-looking wood or other material, including dyed, bleached or colored wood, spalted wood, plywood, plastic—even Banksia pods (see Sources, page 169).

To hollow the bulb, you'll need a small straight scraper and at least one offset or bent scraper (see Sources). The rest of the turning can be done with basic spindle-turning tools: a roughing gouge, a detail gouge, a thin-kerf parting tool and skew chisel.

Turn the Spindle

Install a ¾" to 1" square blank in a scroll chuck, using the small jaws (**Photo 1**). This blank can be as long as you want, but 4" is a good length to start with. Use the tailstock to center the blank in the chuck: Loosely mount the blank in the chuck, after marking the center of its tailstock end. Bring up the tailstock and engage its live center in the blank's center mark. Then tighten the chuck.

Round the blank with your roughing gouge, being careful to not get too close to the chuck's jaws.

Pull away the tailstock and taper that end of the blank down to about ⅜" dia. (**Photo 2**). Then turn tiny details of

4 Cut a short tenon with a thin-kerf parting tool. Undercut the back of the flared shoulder, so it will fit snugly against the rounded bulb. Then part off the spindle

THIN-KERF PARTING TOOL

your own design, starting from the tapered end. Move one step toward the headstock after finishing each detail (**Photo 3**). It's quite difficult to go back, due to the small diameters.

As you near the chuck jaws, leave room for three elements: a flared shoulder, a ¼" long tenon and sufficient waste material for parting off (**Photo 4**).

The tenon is based on the size of the bulb, so a diameter just over ½" is a good starter for the ornaments shown here.

Undercut the inside of the flared shoulder with the long point of the skew or a thin kerf parting tool. This is tricky, because you're working so close to the chuck jaws, so go at it carefully. The goal is to create a concave area that the bulb will nest into in order to create a clean-looking joint.

Complete the spindle by blending the shoulder into the detailed part of the turning. Finish-sand and then part off the spindle from the chuck.

Turn the Cap

You can make the cap from wood left in the chuck from turning the spindle, a contrasting wood, or material of a larger diameter than the icicle. Whichever you choose, mount the blank in the scroll chuck.

TURN THE CAP

5

Mount a short, square blank for the top. As before, work from the tailstock end of the blank towards the chuck. On a short cap like this one, the tenon can go on either end.

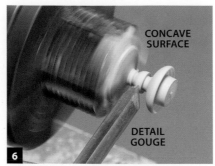

CONCAVE SURFACE

DETAIL GOUGE

6

Finish the cap by creating delicate details above a flared or rounded shoulder. Once again, undercut the shoulder to create a concave mounting surface.

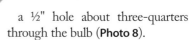

Establish and turn the tenon for mounting the cap to the bulb (**Photo 5**). If you intend to turn a cap with long and delicate shaping, it's best to turn the tenon on the headstock end, as shown while turning the spindle. If the cap is short, the tenon can go on either end of the blank. I normally turn this tenon to the same diameter that I used for the spindle's tenon.

Turn tiny details and a concave shoulder, as on the spindle (**Photo 6**). Again, the concave shoulder will create a clean, flush fit when you attach the cap to the bulb.

Decide how the ornament will hang, either from a hole drilled through the cap or from a metal eyelet threaded into top of the cap. For an eyelet, just provide a small flat area for mounting. For a through hole, turn a ¼" to ⅜" diameter round or elliptical shape at the top of the cap. Finish sand and part off the cap from the chuck.

If you decided on through-hole hanging, flatten the shape you turned at the top of the cap by sanding both sides. One easy way to do this is to mount a small sanding disc in the headstock, using a Jacob's style chuck. Finish up by drilling a ⅛" hole through the flattened area. If you're going to thread in an eyelet, simply drill a small pilot hole on the top of the cap.

Turn the Bulb

Decide on the bulb's shape and dimensions. Shaping options include a ball, an ellipse and an egg, to name a few. The bulb's size can be quite varied, but I suggest starting with something around 1-½" to 1-¾" in diameter and about 2" in length. Allow extra length for mounting the blank in the chuck as well as the additional material that you'll need for turning the bulb from both ends.

Start the square blank between centers to create a tenon for the scroll chuck's small jaws or install the chuck's regular jaws and directly mount the blank.

Create the bulb's basic shape, but do not reduce the diameter completely at the headstock end (**Photo 7**).

Using a Jacob's style chuck mounted in the tailstock, drill

a ½" hole about three-quarters through the bulb (**Photo 8**).

Fit the spindle to the bulb. You may need to slightly enlarge the hole to fit the tenon. You may also need to lightly shape the end of the bulb, so it fits into the spindle's concave shoulder. When the spindle fits perfectly, finish-sand the outside of the bulb.

Hollowing through a small opening is a form of blind turning. Using a small straight scraper, open up the inside of the bulb. Stop to clear chips often and be careful to work the shape to roughly match the outside. Keep the walls at least ¼" thick at this time.

To create a lightweight bulb, you'll need to further reduce the wall thickness. Use a bent-shaped scraper to reach the inside areas from the bulb's midpoint to just below the rim (**Photo 9**). Start from the rim, measure often, and follow the bulb's outside shape until you reach the end of the drilled hole. Strive for a finished wall thickness between ⅛" to 3/16".

This process requires making frequent, careful measurements of the wall. Sometimes it's possible to use small double-ended calipers for measuring, but I use nothing more than a section of stiff, but springy wire (**Photo 10**). Bend the wire like a safety pin, closed down to about ¼" at its opening. With the lathe off, insert the tool and simply move it from the rim along the wall. When the wall thickness is ¼" the tool will just pass through. Thinner areas will show as a gap above the outside; thicker areas push the wire open.

TURN THE BULB

Shape the bulb blank into an egg or ball form, using the roughing gouge and the skew chisel. Leave the headstock end a bit oversize.

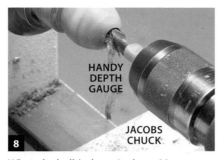

HANDY DEPTH GAUGE

JACOBS CHUCK

When the bulb's shape is about 80 percent complete, install a Jacob's chuck in the tailstock and drill a hole approximately three quarters of the way through the bulb.

BENT SHAPED SCRAPER

Hollow the bulb. First, use a straight scraper to expand the drilled hole. Then switch to a bent-shaped scraper to work the inside walls.

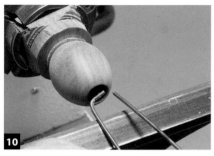

Use a piece of bent springy wire to gauge the wall thickness. Strive for a finished thickness between 1/8" and 3/16"—the thinner the walls, the lighter the bulb.

SKEW CHISEL

Part off the bulb after you've finished turning the headstock end and sanded to #220-grit, so no tool or scratch marks remain.

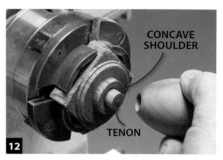

CONCAVE SHOULDER

TENON

Remount the bulb on a tenon and concave shoulder you've turned on the remaining waste material. Then complete the unfinished end: Drill through, shape the inside and sand the outside.

In order to hollow the other end of the bulb and complete the turning, the bulb has to be removed, rotated end-for-end and remounted, using a technique called "reverse chucking."

Part off the bulb from the chuck, a tiny bit longer than its finished length (**Photo 11**). Using the waste that remains in the chuck, turn a tenon to mount the finished end of the bulb and a concave shoulder to secure it (**Photo 12**). This step is tricky, because the tenon and shoulder have to hold the bulb firmly enough to drill and lightly turn the unfinished end, but loosely enough to allow pulling the bulb off when it's finished. If the tenon ends up slightly undersize, shim it with tissue paper so you can complete the bulb.

Mount the bulb on the tenon. Then drill all the way through, using the Jacobs chuck, as before. With the bent-shaped scraper, lightly, hollow the inside walls to blend into the walls previously hollowed from the opposite direction.

Fit the cap to the bulb the same way you fit the spindle. This involves fitting the tenon and lightly shaping the area around the bulb's opening to create a clean fit. Finish-sand the entire outside of the bulb, then remove it from the chuck.

Glue the cap and spindle to the bulb. You can use just about any glue; I use quick-set epoxy. Hang your completed ornament with fishing line or thread.

Finishing

I usually apply finish while the pieces are still on the lathe. You have numerous choices, including shellac, wiping varnish or oil finish. Wax is also an option, to adjust the sheen. If you wait until the ornament is assembled, you could suspend it before applying the finish—then you could even use a spray-on finish.

SOURCES Keyless chuck#111022 $37.95; Oneway Talon Scroll Chuck #112670 $206.95 + insert adapter for your lathe #11206 $24.95; Small Hollowing Tools Set (one straight, two bent-shaped) #10338 $109.26. Crafts Supplies, woodturnerscatalog.com, 800 551 8876, Banksia Pods #104-349, $8.35 each for standard size, $11.25 for jumbo. Springy wire can be found at most hardware stores. ◇

CHAPTER FORTY

PROJECT 26 Christmas Trees

Create controlled curled shavings with a modified skew chisel

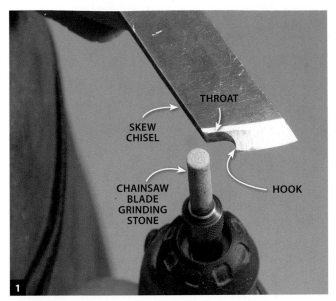

Modify the short point of a skew chisel to create a hook, so you can roll shavings into curls. Round over all the sharp edges on the hook's throat.

Use the modified skew to practice rolling shavings on a scrap block of green wood turned to a cylinder. Start by positioning the point of the hook at a low entry level.

These trees come all the way from the Erzgebirge ('erts-ge-bir-ge). Actually, I made them in Wisconsin, but the unique curl-turning technique I used evolved in that mountainous region of eastern Germany, which borders on the Czech Republic. With an understanding of this technique and a bit of practice, you can have some real fun making trees in a variety of shapes and sizes as stand-alone decorations, parts of a scene or hanging ornaments. You can also make flowers.

What may look simple, however, is actually a bit tricky. Skills with a skew chisel—and a modified one at that, the right amount of pressure and depth of cut, the right feed rate and just the right wood are all factors in this style of turning. The key to success—being able to consistently turn attractive, lifelike trees—is practice.

Use Wet Basswood

Basswood is one of the most desirable woods for this method, due to its "stringy" quality. The best stock has straight grain (riven stock is preferred as a rule) and on the wet side—15 to 18 percent moisture content. Green basswood is an excellent choice. Pine, spruce and fir tend to give a coarser look than basswood, but are certainly worth experimenting with.

Plan to use 5" long blanks that are either 1-¾" square or 1" square. If only air- or kiln-dried wood is available, soak the blanks in a bucket of water for a day or two, using rocks to keep them submerged.

The completed trees don't require finishing, but they can be colored with spray paints or by dipping in water-based dye. Their exposed trunks and bases can then be hand-painted, for a more realistic appearance.

Modify an Old Skew

You'll need to grind a hook on a ¾" or 1" skew chisel to facilitate the process (**Photo 1**). While a "normal" skew will work to some extent, this modification definitely helps to roll the curls into position with more control and less breakage of the fibers. With a normal skew, even when leading with the short point in the wood, it's far too easy to unintentionally cut off the curl.

Of course, this modification dedicates the tool to rolling curls, unless you want to grind away a lot of metal. So, plan to modify an inexpensive skew (or even a woodturning scraper) rather than your pride and joy (see Sources, page 173).

Starting at the bottom of the skew, grind the area behind and below the short point into a slight concave shape (the "hook"). Then soften all of the hook's sharp edges. In German this type of turning is referred to as "sharp and soft turning," because the hook's sharp point and softened edges are both used to form and control the curl. So make sure that all of the hook's edges are beveled back and the shape is as smooth and polished as you can make it. After grinding with the round stone, work the hook's edges with a slipstone or round abrasive rod.

Sharpen the skew's remaining edge in the normal fashion—angled approximately 70° from long point to short point, with the bevel's width about 1-½ times the thickness of the steel. Be absolutely certain that the short point is razor-sharp.

Outfit your lathe with a scroll chuck with standard jaws for the 1-¾" blanks or spigot jaws for the 1" blanks (see Sources). You'll also need a few regular spindle turning

Make a planing cut using only the point, after hooking it into the wood. The hook's curved throat helps to bend the shaving into a curl.

Practice extending the curl by continuing the cut for approximately 1". Experiment with shorter and deeper cuts as well as varying the angle of approach.

Pull another curl. The finished tree consists of multiple curls, so practice controlling the length of each curl while leaving even spacing in between.

Apply your newly learned skills to practice creating long curls on a tapered, cone-shaped blank. Now, you must work from smaller to larger diameter while drawing the tool toward you.

tools: a roughing gouge, a ¼" or ⅜" detail/spindle gouge, a ½" or larger "normal" skew and a parting tool.

Practice, Practice, Practice

Start by practicing on 1" diameter round stock, held in the scroll chuck with small jaws. Understanding how to handle a skew chisel—and especially how to make the planing cut—will be essential for learning this process.

Hook the short point into the wood at a low entry level (**Photo 2**). Then make a planing cut to lightly raise or fluff up the wood into a curl (**Photo 3**). Experiment with the entry angle, depth of cut, feed rate and speed of the lathe. (I run the lathe between 1,500 and 2,000 rpm for this style of turning.) See how far you can roll the curl without breaking it or cutting it off (**Photo 4**). Roll some curls tight against the preceding ones; roll others leaving a gap of about ⅛" or so between curls (**Photo 5**). Periodically plane off the curls so you can roll new ones.

When you're able to roll curls consistently, move on to the next step. Taper the blank down to a point at the tailstock end, using a roughing gouge or a regular skew chisel. Then, starting about 3" from the tapered point, roll a curl for approximately 1" (**Photo 6**).

During this exercise you'll be doing the opposite of normal practice, which is to "follow the grain" by turning downhill, from a larger to a smaller diameter. In this case, you cut uphill, from a smaller to a larger diameter. Roll a second curl, stopping about ⅛" from the previous curl. Then roll additional progressively shorter curls until you have nothing but a small point.

Showtime

Begin by making a small tree. Plan ahead for the overall height and the base section—either the curls will go all the way to the bottom, so the trunk doesn't show, or the section below the bottom curl will be turned to form a trunk and

7

Create a series of evenly spaced curls to perfect your technique. Make each curl slightly shorter than the previous one to mimic a Christmas tree's form and the shape of its branches.

8

Finish shaping the tree by using successively shorter curls to taper its top end to a point. This is tricky, because you have to leave enough material at the tip to create the last few curls.

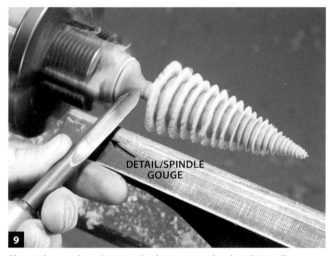

9

DETAIL/SPINDLE GOUGE

Shape the trunk and create the base using the detail/spindle gouge. Then use a parting tool to separate the completed tree from the waste.

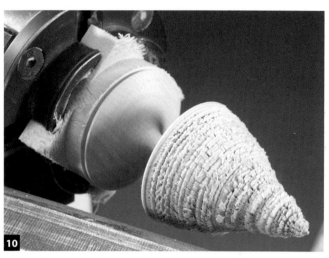

10

Turning dry wood creates a different look, because the curls roll under rather than flaring out. You can stack these tight curls right on top of each other or leave spaces between them.

base. Much of this will be a repeat of the practice sections, with tight curls that touch each other or looser curls that stand slightly apart. One subtle move is to vary how much you roll over the shape of an individual curl: more for the lower branches and steadily decreasing as you reach the top (**Photo 7**). As you approach the top of the tree you may need to re-turn the taper to maintain the desired shape (**Photo 8**).

If you've decided on an exposed trunk and base, turn it now, using a ¼" or ⅜" detail/spindle gouge (**Photo 9**). Then use a regular or thin-kerf parting tool to cut the finished tree from the blank.

Curling Dry Wood

Using dry stock creates an equally attractive but significantly different look because the curls lack the flared, open shape that you can achieve with wet stock (**Photo 10**). Generally speaking, dry stock produces tighter curls, so they must be shorter and more closely spaced.

SOURCES Oneway Manufacturing, oneway.ca, 800-565-7288, Talon Scroll Chuck with standard jaws, #2985, $232; Spigot Jaws, #3016, $40.95. ☺ Penn State Industries, pennstateind.com, 800-377-7297, Skew chisel, 1" wide, #LX020, $18.50. ☜

Alan Lacer's Woodturning Projects & Techniques. Copyright © 2015 by Alan Lacer. Printed and bound in China. All rights reserved. No part of this book may be reproduced in any form or by any electronic or mechanical means including information storage and retrieval systems without permission in writing from the publisher, except by a reviewer, who may quote brief passages in a review. Published by Popular Woodworking Books, an imprint of F+W, A Content + eCommerce Company, 10151 Carver Rd. Blue Ash, Ohio, 45236. First edition.

Distributed in Canada by Fraser Direct
100 Armstrong Avenue
Georgetown, Ontario L7G 5S4
Canada

Distributed in the U.K. and Europe by
F+W Media International, LTD
Brunel House, Ford Close
Newton Abbot
Devon TQ12 4PU, UK
Tel: (+44) 1626 323200
Fax: (+44) 1626 323319

Distributed in Australia by Capricorn Link
P.O. Box 704
Windsor, NSW 2756
Australia

Visit our website at popularwoodworking.com or our consumer website at shopwoodworking.com for more woodworking information.

Other fine Popular Woodworking Books are available from your local bookstore or direct from the publisher.

ISBN-13: 978-1-4403-4095-6

18   17   16   15   14   5   4   3   2   1

Editor: *Scott Francis*
Designer: *Angela Wilcox*
Production Coordinator: *Debbie Thomas*

a content + ecommerce company

METRIC CONVERSION CHART

To convert	to	multiply by
Inches	Centimeters	2.54
Centimeters	Inches	0.4
Feet	Centimeters	30.5
Centimeters	Feet	0.03
Yards	Meters	0.9
Meters	Yards	1.1

Dedication

This book is dedicated to my late father, Ray Lacer, a wounded warrior of WWII. He was never quite sure what I did for a living, but was always a huge supporter.

Acknowledgments

As these articles represent my tenure with *American Woodworker* magazine, I would like to acknowledge the professional contributions of editors Dave Munkitterick, Tim Johnson and Tom Casper. Photographers Bill Zuehlke and Jason Zentner always did an outstanding job and were a pleasure to work with, as well as were art and design directors Vern Johnson and Joe Gohman.

About the Author

Alan Lacer has been involved in the turning field for more than 38 years as a turner, teacher, writer, exhibition coordinator, expert witness, demonstrator and past president of the American Association of Woodturners. His work has appeared in a number of regional and national exhibitions. Alan has been a regular instructor and demonstrator of the craft—having worked in all 50 states as well as five foreign countries. He has published more than 150 articles, columns and tips, covering technical aspects of woodturning, many specific projects, stories related to both contemporary and historical woodturning and the turning traditions of Japan and Germany. He has also produced five videos on his own, with three of them winning a total of five national awards. In 1999 the American Association of Woodturners awarded him their Lifetime Honorary Member Award for his contributions to the field. He has also appeared on national TV woodturning programs on PBS and DIY.

IDEAS • INSTRUCTION • INSPIRATION

These are other great Popular Woodworking products are available
at your local bookstore, woodworking store or online supplier.

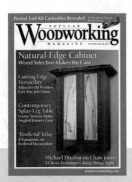

Popular Woodworking Magazine

Get must-build projects, information on tools (both hand and power) and their use and technique instruction in every issue of *Popular Woodworking Magazine*. Each issue (7 per year) includes articles and expert information from some of the best-known names in woodworking. Subscribe today at popularwoodworking.com.

Subscription • 7 issues/year

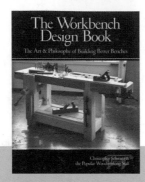

The Workbench Design Book
By Christopher Schwarz

How many times have you heard this: "The workbench is the most important tool in your shop." While the statement is absolutely true, it doesn't help you answer the more important question: Which workbench should you build? This book explores that problem with a depth and detail you won't find in any other source in print or online.

Hardcover • 256 pages

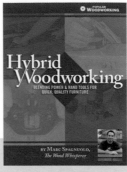

Hybrid Woodworking
By Marc Spagnuolo

Known online as The Wood Whisperer, Marc Spaguolo presents a fresh approach to woodworking and furniture making by showing the most efficient ways to utilize both power tools and hand tools in the furniture building process. Not only will you learn which tools are best for which tasks, but you will also find tips for how to use, maintain, and fine tune them.

Paperback • 192 pages

Ultimate Workshop Solutions
By Popular Woodworking Editors

From better clamp storage, to the perfect miter saw stand to benches and beyond, you'll find 35 projects specifically designed to improve and organize your favorite space. These projects have been created by the editors of *Popular Woodworking Magazine* for your shop, and now we're pleased to share them with you.

Paperback • 192 pages

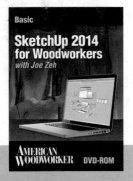

Basic Sketch-Up For Woodworkers
By Joe Zeh

SketchUp has helped thousands of woodworkers create, correct and perfect their furniture designs before the first piece of expensive wood is cut. Now Joe Zeh, an expert in Sketchup and Computer-Aided Design (CAD) will show you the brand-new 2014 edition and how much easier and more versatile it is to use.

Available at Shopwoodworking.com DVD

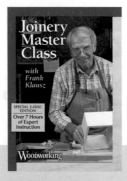

Joinery Master Class With Frank Klausz
By Frank Klausz

Frank Klausz, expert craftsmen and experienced woodworking teacher, shares with you on this 2-DVD set the joinery skills he's learned in a lifetime (edge-joint options, bridle joints, dovetails, mortise-and-tenon variations and more!). Plus five projects to help you put your joinery knowledge into practice.

Available at Shopwoodworking.com DVD & download

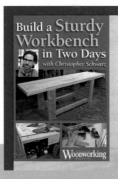

Build A Sturdy Workbench In Two Days
By Christopher Schwarz

With a base built from standard 4x4 lumber, a base with half-lap construction, and a top made from two IKEA countertops, this two-day workbench is a seriously sturdy shop workhorse that no one will question for quality. With this solid workbench, you'll have no shortage of working surface or dog holes.

Available at Shopwoodworking.com DVD & download

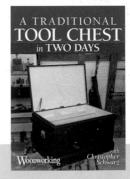

A Traditional Tool Chest In Two Days
By Christopher Schwarz

Woodworkers who use traditional tool chests swear they're the most convenient way to organize tools. Now, you can make one in just two days using modern materials and contemporary joinery techniques. Whether your focus is hand tool or power tool woodworking, you'll find this tool chest indispensable (a quick to build!).

Available at Shopwoodworking.com DVD & download

Visit **popularwoodworking.com** to see more woodworking information by the experts, learn about our digital subscription and sign up to receive our free newsletter or blog posts.